THE LOGIC OF S

M000114104

In American history and throughout the Western world, the sub-jugation perpetuated by slavery has created a unique 'culture of slavery'. That culture exists as a metaphorical, artistic, and literary tradition attached to the enslaved – human beings whose lives are 'owed' to another, who are used as instruments by another, and who must endure suffering in silence. Tim Armstrong explores the meta-phorical legacy of slavery in American culture by investigating debt, technology, and pain in African-American literature and a range of other writings and artworks. Armstrong's careful analysis reveals how notions of the slave as a debtor lie hidden in our accounts of the commodified self and how writers like Nathaniel Hawthorne, Rebecca Harding Davis, Booker T. Washington, W. E. B. Du Bois, Ralph Ellison, and Toni Morrison grapple with the pervasive view that slaves are akin to machines. Finally, Armstrong examines how conceptions of the slave as a container of suppressed pain are reflected in disciplines as diverse as art, sculpture, music, and psychology.

TIM ARMSTRONG is Professor of Modern English and American Literature at Royal Holloway, University of London. He previously taught at University College London, University College Cork, and the University of Sheffield. He is the author of *Modernism, Technology and the Body: A Cultural Study* (1998), *Haunted Hardy: Poetry, History, Memory* (2000), and *Modernism: A Cultural History* (2005). He is the editor of *American Bodies* (1996) and *Thomas Hardy: Selected Poems* (1993, 2009) and the co-editor of *Beyond the Pleasure Dome: Writing and Addiction from the Romantics* (1994).

CAMBRIDGE STUDIES IN AMERICAN
LITERATURE AND CULTURE

Editor
Ross Posnock, *Columbia University*

Founding Editor
Albert Gelpi, *Stanford University*

Advisory Board
Alfred Bendixen, *Texas A&M University*
Sacvan Bercovitch, *Harvard University*
Ronald Bush, *St. John's College, University of Oxford*
Wai Chee Dimock, *Yale University*
Albert Gelpi, *Stanford University*
Gordon Hutner, *University of Illinois, Urbana-Champaign*
Walter Benn Michaels, *University of Illinois, Chicago*
Kenneth Warren, *University of Chicago*

Recent books in this series

(continued after index)

This book is dedicated to my three brothers, Rick, Bill, and Roger Armstrong, and to the memory of Harry Bruhns, 1951–2011

THE LOGIC OF SLAVERY

Debt, Technology, and Pain in American Literature

TIM ARMSTRONG

Royal Holloway, University of London

CAMBRIDGE
UNIVERSITY PRESS

CAMBRIDGE UNIVERSITY PRESS
Cambridge, New York, Melbourne, Madrid, Cape Town,
Singapore, São Paulo, Delhi, Mexico City

Cambridge University Press
32 Avenue of the Americas, New York, NY 10013-2473, USA

www.cambridge.org
Information on this title: www.cambridge.org/9781107607811

© Tim Armstrong 2012

This publication is in copyright. Subject to statutory exception
and to the provisions of relevant collective licencing agreements,
no reproduction of any part may take place without the written
permission of Cambridge University Press.

First published 2012

Printed in the United States of America

A catalog record for this publication is available from the British Library.

Library of Congress Cataloging in Publication data
Armstrong, Tim, 1956–
The logic of slavery : debt, technology, and pain in American literature / Tim Armstrong, Royal
Holloway, University of London.
pages cm. – (Cambridge studies in American literature and culture)
Includes bibliographical references and index.
ISBN 978-1-107-02507-3 (hardback) – ISBN 978-1-107-60781-1 (paperback)
1. Slavery in literature.   2. American literature – 19th century – History and
criticism.   3. American literature – 20th century – History and criticism.   4. American
literature – African American authors – History and criticism   5. Slavery in art.   6. Slavery
– United States – History.   7. Slavery – Psychological aspects.   8. Slavery – Economic
aspects.   9. Commodification.   10. Reification.   I. Title.
PS217.S55A76   2012
810.9'355–dc23   2012012609

ISBN 978-1-107-02507-3 Hardback
ISBN 978-1-107-60781-1 Paperback

Cambridge University Press has no responsibility for the persistence or
accuracy of URLs for external or third-party Internet Web sites referred to in
this publication and does not guarantee that any content on such Web sites is,
or will remain, accurate or appropriate.

Contents

Figures

Acknowledgements

Any work in this field is indebted to a range of recent research on the cultural ramifications and inheritance of slavery and race, and alongside historians of slavery like Ira Berlin, Eric Foner, Eugene G. Genovese, Thomas D. Morris, and Judith Kelleher Schafer, I would like to acknowledge a community of critics, among them Ian Baucomb, Stephen Best, Malcolm Bull, Hazel Carby, Henry Louis Gates, Paul Gilroy, Saidiya Hartman, Sharon Patricia Holland, Walter Benn Michaels, Toni Morrison, Orlando Patterson, Ross Posnock, Eric Sundquist, and Marcus Wood. In different ways these scholars ask how the category of 'race' has been constructed historically, and trace its legacy of violence and troubling residue within the Atlantic world.

Portions of the work published here have appeared in other contexts. An early draft of Chapter 1 appeared as 'Slavery, Insurance and Sacrifice in the Black Atlantic', in *Sea Changes: Historicizing the Ocean*, ed. Bernhard Klein and Gesa Mackenthun (New York: Routledge, 2004); and a small section of the same chapter appeared as 'Catastrophe and Trauma: A Response to Anita Rupprecht', *Journal of Legal History*, special issue on the *Zong* case, 28:3 (2007). An early version of some of the material in Chapter 3 appeared as 'The Delay of the Machine Age', in *Homo Orthopedicus: Le corps et ses prosthèses à l'époque (post)moderniste*, ed. Nathalie Roelens and Wanda Strauven (Paris: L'Harmattan, 2001). My thanks to the editors and publishers involved for permissions. For permissions to reproduce pictures, I am grateful to the institutions and rights holders listed in the legends.

I would like to thank respondents to this work at the various seminars where I have delivered papers over more than a decade: at the 'Homo Orthopedicus' conference, University of Antwerp, 1999; the Collegium for African-American Research conference, Winchester, 2003; the 'Legitimacy and Illegitimacy' symposium on law and literature at the Huntington Library, Los Angeles, 2005; the 'Bodily Extensions' conference, University of Nottingham, 2005; the 'Zong Case and the Law' conference, London Metropolitan University, 2006; the 'Pathologies' conference, University of Glamorgan, 2007; the 'Sculpture and Literature in the Nineteenth Century' conference, Royal Holloway, 2009; and research seminars at the Universities of Sussex, Durham, Cambridge, Oxford, and Exeter, as well as Kings, Royal Holloway, and Birkbeck Colleges and SOAS, University of London. A draft of Chapter 4 was delivered as the 2009 Kate Fullbrook Memorial Lecture at the University of the West of England.

Work on the first chapter was begun during a period of leave funded by the Leverhulme Foundation in 2000, and I am extremely grateful for the Foundation's support and its patience as the shape of this work changed and other projects displaced it for considerable periods. I am also grateful to Royal Holloway for research leave.

I would also like to express gratitude to the students in my African-American literature class over the past two decades at Sheffield and Royal Holloway for their enthusiasm and insight. It was the challenge of that teaching which drew me to this book. Finally, my thanks to Cambridge University Press's two readers for their responsive and helpful reports; and to friends and colleagues who have discussed work over the years and offered comments and encouragement: among many others Oli Belas, Bob Eaglestone, Sophie Gilmartin, John Gomez, Vicky Greenaway, Sam Halliday, Laura Marcus, Erica Sheen, Mike Wainwright, and, as always, Sue and Nicholas Wiseman.

Introduction

This book began with work on two quite distinct topics: the theory of technology and the history of shipwreck and risk in the Atlantic world. Reading separately in both these areas, I realized that the slave was a figure around which various questions clustered – in writings about technology a point of reference for talking about bodies and machines; in the maritime world an object of insurance claims, a body in need of ransom, and also a figure of pathos in shipwreck narratives. It was this set of observations which impelled me to seek figurations relating to slavery in other areas – a search that eventually took in sculpture, recorded music, the psychology of trauma, and debt, among other possible topics. The questions that arose were, of course, intertwined with the history of slavery and involved both African-American and a wider Atlantic culture.

What follows is a report on findings. While the study of slavery has understandably been focused on its history and experience, it became clear to me that there is more to be said about the figural implications of slavery's presence in Western tradition, the way it subtly infiltrates the fabric of other modes of thoughts and shapes what is thinkable, informing what could be called a culture of slavery. What is involved in this book is in part the investigation of the hidden consequences of slavery; in part a tropology, a study of metaphor.

In *Seeing Things Hidden*, Malcolm Bull has characterized the modernity produced by slavery as what he calls a 'coming into hiding', not simply in the sense of repression, but in a sense that the hidden becomes a category of analysis, so that the dark contradictions of an inherited world become more sharply apparent.[1] And indeed, forms of occlusion are central to slavery: the effacement of the self-possession, work, and voice of the slave. These denials enter African-American tradition, as so many writers have noted, in notions of a veiled and secret identity. But they also inform a wider tradition in less self-conscious and more oblique ways. I will argue that a splinter of the cultural legacy of slavery enters our thinking when

I

we insure ourselves, emote at the pain of others or the past; when we admire a commodity's surface without considering its making, think of the power of our machines, or perhaps even simply feel imposed on by the assumptions of others. The history of slavery, that is, is knitted into the way in which we see ourselves as having an assignable value; the way we understand technology and making; the way we understand our relation to history and memory. It is this distribution of slavery as a shadowy presence across other fields that allows us to talk of a wider 'culture of slavery' which is both historical and discursive.

Toni Morrison wrote in 1992, 'Race has become metaphorical – a way of referring to and disguising forces, events, classes and expressions of social decay and economic division far more threatening to the body politic than biological "race" ever was'.[2] This implies a linguistic entanglement that is longstanding in the history of Atlantic slavery, a transportation of material suggested by the root meaning of 'metaphor', a conceptual passage binding slavery to the way we see a range of economic, social, and legal relations. But to say slavery provides (or involves) metaphor may seem like a weak claim, given the harsh actuality of slavery's experience. Why not write on slavery itself? One answer to that question is that slavery itself is *necessarily* metaphorical: no human being is in any direct or literal sense an instrument of another or a commodity; no collective memory is in fact a wound. The violence with which terms are imposed on human subjects and human bodies makes such metaphors necessary objects of study: not simply in Foucault's sense that discourse involves power relations, but also in the sense that subjects are required to contain, internalize, and meditate on those meanings.

As Morrison's sensitivity to these issues suggests, it is in the African-American tradition that the tropes generated within slavery and its aftermath have received their most considered and self-conscious treatment. In particular, they are written into the topics and styles of African-American discourse, whether the legends of the tar baby or John Henry or the philosophical notion of the 'veil'; or vernacular modes and expressions which register the operations of power like the toast or 'reckless eyeballing'. From Wheatley in the eighteenth century to Du Bois to Morrison, black writers have found ways to understand the history of race in America which are not simply descriptive; which register its conceptual underpinnings, language, and psychic consequences. Wheatley's translation of Ovid deals with pain sealed within the self by using the story of Niobe, a woman turned to stone. In the figure of Du Bois, American literature sees one of its titanic self-originators, in that the multi-generic work which is *The*

Souls of Black Folk codifies the analysis of the logic of slavery from the point of view of its inheritors, assimilating all that has gone before but rendering it a unique fusion of performance and analysis in Du Bois's discussions of debt, hope, sacrifice, doubling, and music.

In such writings, figuration, cognition, and power are shown to be carried across time in ways that present both dangers and opportunities, which may be bound into the self and which may also be subject to revision and analysis and unbound. In focusing so often on African-American writing, my argument on the cultural presence of slavery mirrors that which one could make about 'race' as a concept: it cannot be seen in any essentialist fashion (as biological, as 'blood' or 'spirit'), but neither can it be dissolved into culture (making it performative, sociological), because it has been forcibly imposed on groups of identifiable people as a historical experience.[3] Du Bois is perhaps the best example of a writer who, as Ross Posnock has suggested, managed to sustain both a romantic notion of racial soul and a pragmatism which declared that race would eventually be transcended.[4] But it is interesting that when Du Bois wrote his essay 'The Concept of Race' in 1940, he provided a detailed *narrative* of his family history, both white and black, not a coherent formal definition.[5] The same narrative account (of encounters with race, of its presentations) is characteristic of a great deal of African-American writing, and it suggests that cultural metaphors should be seen in terms of something like a *typology* (in the biblical sense used by so many African-American texts): as modes of expression which work through a series of re-presentations which carry historical memory with them; which have a point of origin in the actualities of the past (here slavery) but are also sites of further work.[6] Thus Du Bois's sense of Africanness is conveyed under the sign of Freud's *nachtraglich*: he remembers his grandmother's song as an emblem of a lost Africa; but it is his encounters with racism in the South that energize the identification with Africa which gives that song meaning:

[S]ince the fifteenth century these ancestors of mine and their other descendants have had a common history; have suffered a common disaster and have one long memory.... But the physical bond is least and the badge of color relatively unimportant save as a badge; the real essence of this kinship is its social heritage of slavery; the discrimination and insult; and this heritage binds together not simply the children of Africa, but extends through yellow Asia and into the South Seas.[7]

While this is less than adequate as a global analysis of race, it brilliantly captures the way in which the understanding of slavery is historically perpetuated, carried from context to context and reinterpreted; here as disaster, badge, and bond.

One important issue in this study is thus the legacy of slavery. That legacy could be conceived in two ways: firstly, as the question of the actual long-term effects of slavery (economic, political, institutional); and secondly, as the question of the resonance of slavery in collective memory and the way slavery has been imagined or even deployed as a conceptual resource, an available way of thinking. Clearly the first set of issues is important, involving histories of segregation, disenfranchisement, economic and educational deprivation, and legal inequality which begin in slavery and still have a major impact on American society. But a study of this kind, with its focus on slavery and culture, is necessarily drawn towards the latter set of issues. Two things might be added to that: firstly, the culture I examine centres on but is necessarily wider than that of African-American writing, because slavery was knitted into American society as a whole; and secondly, the question of actual inheritance, on the one hand, and that of memory or representation, on the other, are once again bound together: because ideas have a psychological and social legacy; because cultural memory has a politics; because we think in a language marked by history and agency.

The most obvious example of the situation in which historical inheritance and memory are mixed is the debate on reparations for slavery, which involves quite specific legal arguments (so far largely unsuccessful in the courts) about the historical liability of institutions and the state, and much more compelling arguments about moral debt, a stolen inheritance, and ultimately about American national identity and the shape of history. The relation between actual damage carried across generations and its perception is also central to Toni Morrison's project in *Beloved* and in her comments on the sources of the novel in an interview. Morrison asks, implicitly, what the status of African Americans would be if there were no memory of slavery, if all they knew was their people's situation *now*. Her answers, encapsulated in syntactic modulations of the phrase 'This is not a story to pass on', are too complex to easily summarize, involving the suggestion both that forgetting is impossible and that remembering has dangers, and involving also the insistence that this is a matter of possible disavowal for white as well as black Americans. What examples such as Morrison's suggest, then, is that slavery's 'residue' is not an easy issue to address in a way that separates history from its representations, or politics from rhetoric.

If its central materials are literary, this study also touches on law and economics, art and aesthetics, philosophy and psychology, history and ethics.

Eric Sundquist suggests in relation to African-American tradition that 'justice and value must … be recognized to be aesthetic as well as philosophical terms, to have literary as well as legal application' – a plea which leads one towards an analysis embracing all these terms.[8] The finer structure and linkages of the book are provided by a few commonplaces derived from the long history of slavery: commonplaces in the sense that they both mark and mask a place where power works on the subject. These formulas derive from the status and condition of the slave: the slave as a captive; the machine with a human voice; the hands of others; the master–slave relation; manpower versus horsepower; the climate of slavery; the wound; the veil. In examining the topics which these commonplaces generate, my aim is once again to move from the familiar ground of the actuality of slavery to its legacy and culture: as the work of scholars like Saidya Hartman and Stephen Best implies, the ideas applied to slavery have mutable locations and applications.[9] And because what I examine includes both African-American writing and anglophone culture generally, because it can be traced across different contexts and authors in ways which occasionally estrange it from those contexts (i.e., from the immediate conscious control of authors), because we can trace slavery's presence across different intellectual and artistic domains – for all these reasons we can, as I suggested earlier, refer to a 'culture of slavery' which is more than simply an available rhetoric; which is linked firmly to the oppressive presence of race in Western history. The figures which are linked here by a logic of juxtaposition – a net of meanings which is at times admittedly stretched by my desire to encompass a diversity of examples – are ultimately referable to the violence with which values are imposed on bodies and persons.

The argument in this study is organized around three related topics – debt (or economics), technology (the tool and the use of others), and pain – each with two main chapters assigned to them. Chapters 1 and 2, and to an extent Chapter 4, deal with the forced *abstraction* of the body of the slave to an object of value: its reification and negation; its consumption; and the figuration of the slave in terms of debt, as well as the narrative consequences of that figuration. Chapters 3 and 4, and in part Chapter 5, deal with the *instrumentalization* of the body of the slave into notions of technology and intellectual labour. The slave provides a way of thinking about the scale of technology and its relation to the human body; about what it means to use others; about what might humanize a machine. Chapters 5 and 6 deal with the way that history is *reproduced* and unbound in the aftermath of slavery. How is its pain released, and what work can it do?

In all these paired cases we move, sometimes between chapters and sometimes within chapters, from a metaphor which is articulated or indeed enforced more or less consciously as simile – a slave is 'like' a machine or a machine is 'like' a slave; a slave 'owes' his or her labour to another – to a more hidden understanding of the same equation in which it informs a buried metaphor: the mechanical as a 'ghost'; the narrative consequences of foreclosure; sacrifice as the operation of power; the 'curing' of the self. Thus slavery as captivity is linked to the history of life insurance in the opening chapter, which includes a discussion of the metaphor of sacrifice as founding a group identity, and maritime cannibalism as an emblem of sacrificial inequality. Slavery considered as debt is explored in terms of narratives of self-purchase in the second chapter, but also in terms of its formal legacy in effects of narrative closure in the African-American tradition and in Faulkner. Slavery's presence in debates about technology is considered in Chapter 3, which explores the Aristotelian understanding of the slave as a tool and the tradition of reading slavery as inhibiting technological development in both Greece and the American South, but also the way in which the slave returns as metaphor registering the presence of the human body in twentieth-century discussions of machine culture. Technology is explored further in a discussion of the making of sculpture in the nineteenth century (Chapter 4), where the focus is what happens when the same metaphor of the human instrument is written into the aesthetic as a hidden presence, central to its status. Both Chapters 4 and 5 deal with the issue of a stored pain. If the statue contains a hidden message of pain, spirituals and other music considered in Chapter 5 also figure that storage and its release, as if the statue could speak its feelings and history. Here, in recorded music, the slave's close alignment with technology eventually comes to signify from within the technological itself: as a guarantor of technology's humanity but also, because of the enduring trauma and pain associated with slavery, as an index of technology's ability to contain and transmit feeling, to sound the depths of the past.

Trauma is central to the story of slavery: when the abolitionist movement applies a moral sympathy derived from Adam Smith to the slave, stories of pain enter Western consciousness, opening up (as Marcus Wood has argued) a narrative of wounding and identification which is still with us.[10] It is perhaps an exaggeration to say that the story of slavery founds what we think of as 'trauma studies'; but certainly the story of slavery and its historical consequences is bound up with the notion that trauma might inform a collective identity. For this reason, my last chapter (Chapter 6) attempts to unpick some of the metaphors of occlusion – of enduring debt and pain – which were discussed earlier in the book, providing a counter to the traumatic understanding of slavery's legacy in its analysis of an alternative figure, that of the weather and weather's more localized states of mind.

The temporal focus is that of the *longue durée*. *The Logic of Slavery* ranges over the history of slavery from the eighteenth century to its present memory, though there is a rough structure in the discussions which moves us from the external to the internal; from captivity to the work of the slave and the former slave; from resistance in the nineteenth century to rebuilding and memory in the twentieth. The materials are various – popular narratives, legal writings, musicology, histories of technology, art, sculpture, and writing on sculpture. But as I have suggested, the central resource is the African-American tradition and related American literature, to which I return often as I explore the self-understanding of those who have experienced slavery and its inheritance.

One background issue requires further commentary in this introduction, because it is implicit in a great deal of what follows. That is the Aristotelian description of slavery and the questions it generates: a description in which the slave is a 'natural' slave, inferior to the master, and whose deficiency of will is compensated for by the master (though Aristotle also admits that some slaves are simply captives of war, not at all inferior). The slave becomes, for Aristotle, an instrument of living, an extension of the master. Aristotle's account of slavery is contradictory and ultimately unsustainable. Nevertheless, it is the only systematic defence of the practice in antiquity and has been of huge influence in subsequent analyses, including those of Hegel and Du Bois.[11] Much of what I discuss here has its origins in three governing metaphors which structure Aristotle's thinking in the *Politics*: body/soul, craftsman/tool, and whole/part.[12] These can be set against Aristotle's more shameful suspicion, implicit in the *Nicomachean Ethics*, that slavery is merely a legal convention and an effect of power, a debt imposed on others (a topic I take up in Chapter 2).

In a recent study of the 'black Frankenstein', Elizabeth Young points out that the romantic reanimation story is thematically linked to accounts of metaphor which stress its power to give life to objects; to notions of synecdoche which stress part-for-whole relations at a bodily level; and to notions of 'dead metaphor' which can only awkwardly be brought to life.[13] Slavery works in a similar manner, though with a much longer history. Aristotle's account of the slave as instrument makes the human take on qualities of the thing, embodying a set of ideas about control, worth, and action. The 'vehicle' for the various metaphors implicit within slavery – the metaphor of value, the metaphor of control – is the body of the slave. Moreover, for the Greeks the control of language in rhetoric is in a general sense the public equivalent of the management of slaves in the household. The control of plot, diction, and language in Aristotle's *Poetics*, as well as the elevated level at which the action of epic and tragedy are addressed, involve a social and linguistic order in which the slave – conceived as a barbarian or linguistic outsider – is subordinated to his or her superior.[14]

The most fundamental element of the Aristotelian account of slavery is the ascription of a superiority of soul to the master. The slave lacks *thymos*, or 'spirit'; indeed, he or she is likely to come from a non-Greek people who lack that capacity as a whole. The master supplies that spirit, inaugurating a separation of the power to direct instruments and that which enacts his decisions, the body of another. Georges Canguilhem argues that the closely related distinction between knowledge and being, set up by the Aristotelian definition of man as 'reasoning animal' (*zwonlogikou*), means that 'the Aristotelian theory of the active intellect, a pure form without organic basis, has the effect of separating intelligence from life', or the final cause from its embodiment.[15] The Cartesian understanding of knowledge or rationality is divorced from the body, and formative action (or work) is related to the Aristotelian distinction: it is the theorist who unifies knowledge, overcoming the partial and local knowledge of the artisan; physics subsumes mechanics. Canguilhem invokes Descartes's contempt for 'technique without understanding' (*VR*, 221); but elsewhere he cites a well-known countervailing passage from Kant's *Critique of Judgement*, in which the issue is reversed:

Art, regarded as human skill, differs from science (as ability differs from knowledge) in the same way that a practical aptitude differs from a theoretical faculty, as technique differs from theory. What one is capable of doing, as soon as we merely know what ought to be done and therefore are sufficiently cognizant of the desired effect, is not called art. Only that which a man, even if he knows it completely, may not therefore have the skill to accomplish belongs to art. [Petrus] Camper [the morphologist] describes very carefully how the best shoes are made, but he certainly could not make one.[16]

It is the *slave* who establishes a point of difference here: the person in whom art and technique are invested, but from whom (in theory) a directing rationality is removed; who enables thought to be dissociated from making, while at the same time grounding the production of the object in the mechanism and habits of the body. Notably, the actual agency and self-direction of the slave are over-written in these formulas.

Tools thus found the Aristotelian conception of slavery: if there were no need for tools, he says, there would be no need for slavery (though this comment is in conflict with the idea that the slave has a deficiency in self-direction that requires another's will). Aristotle's tangled arguments about 'natural slaves' seem in that respect a justification of what has already been established as necessity in the Greek world. (This a topic taken up in Chapter 3, which explores slavery and technology.) The slave as tool is related in turn to the distinction between soul and body, whole and part. Reflecting on the history of human evolution and Leroi-Gourham's declaration that 'it is the tool, that is *tekhne*, that invents the human, not the human who invents the technical', Bernard Stiegler comments that 'here the human is the interior: there is no exteriorization that does not point to a movement from interior to exterior'.[17] The tool inaugurates a difference which both defines the human and produces an 'illusion of succession' (of the human hand coming before the tool). The prosthetic view of technology is thus intimately linked to the existence of the slave as extension of the master's body in Aristotle's account, and the slave as figure represents a putting-outside of the human, allowing its putative 'inside' status (the mind as the director of instruments) to be sustained; it both disguises and represents the fact that *the tool is us*. The paradoxes here are drawn out in the mocking opening arguments in Hegel's introduction to the *Phenomenology of Spirit*, where he stresses that if the 'tool' (*Werkzeug*) of cognition is used to comprehend the Absolute, then that entails a forming of the thing and a change in the thing, so the Absolute is no longer absolute.[18] For Hegel, that which acts and that which acts upon it cannot be so clearly separated, and as a consequence the master is stranded, as it were, in his own sense of the personal absolute.

The notion of whole versus part governs Aristotle's thinking on the incomplete soul of the slave. Canguilhem points out that Aristotle uses the term *organon* to designate 'a functional part (*morion*) of an animal or vegetal body such as a hand, beak, wing, root or what have you' (*VR*, 206). *Organon*, 'tool', is a term derived from 'the lexicon of artists and musicians'. A famous passage of the *Politics* imagines a world of tools:

[A] slave is a sort of living piece of property; and like any other servant is a tool in charge of other tools. For suppose that every tool we had could perform its task, either at our bidding or itself perceiving the need, and if – like the statues made by Daedalus or the tripods of Hephaestus, or which the poet says that 'self-moved they enter the assembly of the gods' – shuttles in a loom could fly to and fro and a plucker play a lyre of their own accord, then master-craftsmen would have no need of servants nor masters of slaves. (1253b23, p. 65)[19]

This finds an echo in earlier and later Greek and Roman writers (Crates and others), though always in a comic mode: automaticity is hilarious as things fly about in a self-animated fashion. Aristotle himself seems to regard the possibility of such automaticity with suspicion: all human activities which tend towards the automatic and focus on one part of the body alone – such as the display of skill in the playing of musical instruments – are suspect, because they reduce the human to the status of the instrument (1341a5–1341b8, pp. 469–71). Such tasks and skills are more suitable to slaves than citizens. The master, on the other hand, is the person who can judge the whole – whether it is the musical piece and its performance, the functioning of the household, or the thing which the slave makes, the best shoes or what have you. (This is a topic I take up in relation to slavery and music-making in Chapter 5.)

However, in making music a central example, Aristotle links the slave to action (*praktikon*) rather than to making (*poesis*). While this is usually explained by referring to his assumption that he was talking about domestic slaves (as opposed to those in the mines, fields, or factories, say), it also indicates the way that the conception of the slave as tool or extension of the master's body refuses to see the slave's work in terms of an agency which is expressed in the object (the foundation of Chapter 4). This has a number of consequences. One is an aristocratic distain for labour, even if skilled. But another countervailing consequence, taken up by Hegel, is the possibility of a different account of the slave's relation to work and of the master's narcissistic self-regard. Hegel says that the master depends on the slave for validation of his status, and indeed for his relation with material reality (*Dingheit*), since all he does is consume the slave's products. For the slave, the struggle with subordination produces self-knowledge. Initially – having founded his identity in the debt which is his existence, when he is defeated and chooses captivity over death – he is an extension of the master's will. But by his labour and by making things, the slave becomes aware of autonomy and freedom, conceived as an internal renunciation and the projection of a self outwards. This allows us to throw in relief the danger implicit in the slave–machine equation: the danger of a narcissistic solipsism in the master, as well as the fantasy of reversal, whether that reversal appears as comic dependency (Bertie Wooster and Jeeves) or the revolt of the machines. A much-cited passage from Pliny's *Natural History* comments on the loss of selfhood implied by the detachment of actual work from the master: 'We walk with another's feet; we see with another's eyes, we greet by another's memory; we live by another's work ... only pleasures do we keep for ourselves'.[20] Here the *alien* is taken into the self; the logic of extension proposed by Aristotle is replaced by a dangerous substitution in which our organs become those of another, the part taking over the whole.

Both Paul Gilroy and Malcolm Bull have argued that Hegel's master–slave relation and the idea of 'double consciousness' which descends to Du Bois via William James and others are foundational descriptors of power relations in the modern world, especially as those relations are taken up into the historical existence of the self. Bull writes of 'the essential Aristotelian trinity of relationships in which master–slave and tyrant–subject relations are both analogous to one another, and simultaneously analogous to and sustained by a third type of relationship, internal to the person'.[21] That is for Bull a relationship of hiding: the metaphor of veiling which Du Bois develops suggests that a portion of the self is sequestered, invisible from without because denied adequate existence in the public realm (this is implicit in the discussion of trauma and its alternatives in Chapter 6). That sequestering also applies to the inheritance of the past, since Du Bois formulates an alternative version of double consciousness in chapter 10 of *The Souls of Black Folk* ('Of the Faith of the Fathers'), one determined by a split historicity, involving a latency founded on the 'not yet' of historical promise:

> From the double life every American Negro must live, as a Negro and an American, as swept on by the current of the nineteenth while yet struggling in the eddies of the fifteenth century, – from this must arise a painful self-consciousness.... The worlds within and without the Veil of Color are changing, and changing rapidly, but not at the same rate, not in the same way; and this must produce a peculiar wrenching of the soul, a peculiar sense of doubt and bewilderment. Such a double life, with double thoughts, double duties, and double social classes, must give rise to double words and double ideal, and tempt the mind to pretence or to revolt, to hypocrisy or to radicalism.[22]

These formulas address the mainstays of Western thought since the French Revolution: the extremes of a desire to refigure and unify the self in a violent act, on the one hand, and, on the other, an accommodation which allows for the notion of local improvement, but risks a sense of fundamental inauthenticity in the face of forms of inherited determination. For this reason, slavery is bound up with notions of a traumatic public sphere – a social order informed by historical violence – which we inherit from the abolitionist movements of the end of the eighteenth century and later. In the stories of mass subjection, sadism, and cruelty, loss of self-control, and alienation from work bequeathed to us by slavery, a melodramatic version of the self is proposed in which it is scarred by historical experience. But since that self as proposed by slavery is also bounded by instrumentality and, at the limits, a technological imagination, the traumas of slavery are also tied into our accounts of technicity and reproduction.

Slavery, Insurance, and Sacrifice: The Embodiment of Capital

In March 2000 the American insurance company Aetna apologized for participating, more than 150 years earlier, in the insurance of slaves. Later the same year in California, the Slaverholder Insurance Policy Bill was passed, requiring insurance companies in the state to disclose slave policies in their archives.[1] Both these actions are part of the ongoing debate on 'reparations' for slavery, a debate which participates, at the historiographic level, in a culture of catastrophe and compensation in which, ironically enough, insurance is itself central. In this opening chapter, I will investigate that culture in relation to a specific issue, slavery and marine insurance, using the notorious 1781 *Zong* case and others. As we will see, the topic demands that in looking at risk and the realizable value of a human life, we also attend to a number of other issues which bind together slavery and insurance, including, perhaps surprisingly, that of maritime cannibalism.

Most policies produced to support the recent accusations relate to a trade which developed in the American South in the last two decades of slavery. Insurance was most commonly taken out on slaves hired out for manufacturing, construction, railroad work, or forestry, or even as servants – that is, on an investment to be safeguarded over a fixed term.[2] In many ways, this represented the inevitable logic of slavery as a patriarchal, agricultural system increasingly penetrated by capitalist modes of production. At the same time, life insurance, and thus the situating of the individual within a logic of exchange, was becoming increasingly common in the nineteenth century.[3] But are these two equivalent? Were the slaves insured as property or as persons?[4] As we will see, the unstable status of the insured slave, given the mixture of personhood and property intrinsic to slavery, was an important issue in the development of life insurance.

IN TRANSIT: INSURING SLAVES

The history of insurance begins with the sea. Three developments are central to the conceptual framework established by marine insurance. First
is the 'bottomry' agreement, or 'sea loan', in which money is loaned at
a steep rate for a voyage, the risk falling to the lender. This is the first
instance of the doctrine of *substitution* which underlies insurance: for a
fee, the insurer stands in the place of the insured. Second is the notion
of 'Perils of the Sea' – the earliest form of the concept of *insurable risk*, of
the accident to which no blame is attached. And third is the concept of
general average, that is, the idea that losses undertaken voluntarily to save
a boat (jettison, cutting down masts in a storm, ransom) represent a risk
shared among those investing in a voyage. This is the origin of the notion
of a *distributed risk*.[5]

General average works this way. When a cost is incurred to save the
ship, then whoever incurs the cost – the owner whose mast is cut or the
merchant whose goods are jettisoned – is compensated by the others. As
John Weskett, the writer of the first English textbook on insurance, noted
in 1781, the term 'general average' represents the *system* of compensation
and is used 'to signify a contribution to a *general* loss, and ... to signify
a *particular* loss'.[6] The more specific term that has always been used in
maritime insurance for the original jettison is 'sacrifice'. 'Sacrifice' requires
that the ship be under immediate threat and what a Lloyds expert in 1824
called 'the agency of man'.[7] We will come back to sacrifice, which is, as
Susan Mizruchi points out, central to nineteenth-century thinking about
the social contract.

Life insurance is a late development, requiring among other things a
statistical view of life expectancy. Throughout most of Europe in the early
modern period, insurance on the lives of persons was banned because it
was associated with blasphemy (death is God's prerogative), with conspir-
acy (killing the insured), and with gambling (betting on the lives of kings,
etc.). The United Kingdom was the exception, partly, Geoffrey Clark suggests, because of the absence of Roman law tradition and its dictum that
the free man cannot be valued: *hominis liberi nulla estimatio*.[8] But even in
the anglophone world constraints were placed on life insurance during
the eighteenth century, reflecting a suspicion of the practice after the collapse of dubious schemes in the period of the South Sea Bubble. The legal
concept of *insurable interest* was developed to overcome these problems,
suggesting that one could insure the life of another only to the extent that
one could demonstrate financial dependency.[9] This is part of the evolving

conception of the commoditization of human relations implicit within modernity. What is less obvious is that the notion of insurable interest may have a relation to slavery.

In Europe, a loophole existed in the prohibition of life insurance: the ransom insurance that travellers could take out against capture by Barbary pirates or others. This was the *Ordonnance de la Marine*, the source of much modern maritime law, drafted by Louis's minister Colbert in 1681:

Article 9
All seafarers, passengers and others, may take insurance upon the liberty of their persons, and in that case the policy shall set out the name, the nationality, residence, age and quality of the person thus insuring himself; the name of the ship, that of the port of departure and that of her final destination, the sum to be paid in the event of capture to cover the ransom and the expenses of returning home, the person to whom the money is to be paid by the insurers, and the penalty for delay in the payment.

Article 10
Insurance upon the life of persons other than slaves is forbidden. [*Défendons de faire assurance sur la vie des personnes.*]

Article 11
Nonetheless, one may take insurance upon a person whom one ransoms from captivity [*esclavage*], for the amount of the ransom, which the insurers must pay if on the journey home the person is captured anew, killed, or drowned, or perishes by other cause, natural death excepted.[10]

Douglas Barlow, in the modern translation from which this is taken, adds the clause 'other than slaves' to Article 10, arguing that 'slave-cargo insurance escaped the prohibition in Article 10 [because] in law slaves were not persons' – that is, slaves were, by common usage, articles of trade. Yet this seems a retrospective construction of the collocation of these articles. As John Weskett noted as early as 1781, it is *by analogy with* ransom provisions that the French began to insure the lives of 'black captives (slaves)' from Guinea to the Colonies.[11] Clark spells out the reasoning:

[T]he legal variance granted by the Sun King had had important practical consequences since French merchants involved in the slave trade wanted to insure their human cargoes on the Middle Passage and needed a legal basis to remove the insurance of slaves from the *Ordonnance*'s ban. Ransom insurance provided the loophole. Because a ransom could be seen as a price on freedom, the law could treat insurance against captivity as something different in kind from the money valuation of human life itself, payable whatever the circumstance of death. According to this legal fiction, then, slaves acquired on the Guinea coast could be regarded as held in ransom ... thereby allowing slave traders to insure for the market price of their goods.[12]

In what seems akin to a legal version of Gödel's Principle, the enslaved European has a 'market' price set from outside the system of humane law; his or her entry into the market in persons is prompted by an external hazard – though one which has an afterlife.[13] As Article 11 states, the insurance of the person does not necessarily stop the moment he or she is ransomed, but instead lasts through the voyage home, until the person's return or the termination of the policy. So while ransom insurance nominally serves to protect 'liberty' rather than a life, it is perforce the *life* that is valued on the return: 'the insurers must pay if on the journey home the person is captured anew, killed, or drowned, or perishes by other cause, natural death excepted.' It is this liminal, in-transit condition that is assigned to the slave at sea, with a value which is now explicitly negotiable. Those who can insure a person against capture, the *Ordonnance* states, include family members who have a financial interest in the insured – an early version, surely, of 'insurable interest'. But at the same time the doctrine of assignability meant that 'insurable interest was required only at the inception of the policy, [which] meant that subsequent lack of interest could not annul the contract'[14] – a negotiability of the valued life which again parallels that of the slave.

Slavery thus occupies a middle position in the progress from insurance on goods to insurance on persons, providing a way of thinking about the value of a life. The ransom as an externally imposed 'market' value, in a situation of 'emergency', serves as a historically contingent measure for what was to become a more general equation of the person and economic value.[15] Historically, when we insure our lives, we are imagining the possibility of capture, or 'buying ourselves back'. But from what? Not from death, surely. What we can buy back is only that part of our lives which is economically quantifiable and for-others – which is that sense alienated from us in any case. This quantification has its origins in the life of the slave, and one might underpin this with an investigation of the way in which the Hegelian account of the self emerges from the master–slave relation. To insure ourselves is thus to confront the fact that in one sense the social contract is a form of captivity.

We have seen that the notion of *general average sacrifice* signals a distribution of risk among investors; they are all – literally – in the same boat. In the case of life insurance the notion of sacrifice becomes embodied: the object jettisoned from the system, whose 'owners' (i.e., dependants) are compensated, is a human body. The subject of insurance is expelled, as it were, from the system; to cash yourself in you have to die. This means, I would argue, that life insurance has a sacrificial logic inscribed within

it and, moreover, that it contains what could be described as a fundamental instability centred on the objectival status of the human body
and the embodiment of capital. One might explain this as a case of what
Adorno and Horkheimer call 'the introversion of sacrifice' in 'Excursis I'
of *Dialectic of Enlightenment*: 'Renunciation, the principle of bourgeois
disillusionment, the outward schema for the intensification of sacrifice,
is already present *in nuce* in that estimation of the ration of forces which
anticipates survival as so to speak dependent on the concession of one's
defeat, and – virtually – on death.'[16]

The more historically specific question of whether slaves are people
or cargo is raised starkly in a series of legal cases relating to the insuring
of slaves. Most took place under the administration of William Murray,
Lord Mansfield – the Lord Chief Justice credited with establishing and
regularizing the corpus of English commercial law needed by an expand-
ing trade; his maritime law was codified in James Park's *A System of the
Law of Marine Insurances* (1787). According to the legal thinking which
evolved in this period, slave ships could be insured against shipwreck, pir-
acy, arrest, and shipboard rebellion – unpredictable forces constituting
'Perils of the Sea'.[17] The deaths of slaves owing to sickness or want of water
and provisions ('natural death') were not insurable; the same eventually
applied to death on voyages prolonged by poor winds (which could theoretically have been anticipated as a hazard) or by miscalculation.[18] What is
the purpose of these distinctions? They cannot clearly be explained by the
assumption that 'natural death' was entirely predictable, since death rates
on the Middle Passage could rise catastrophically for reasons beyond the
master's control.[19] Rather, the implication is that it is not the human life
of a slave which is insured, but rather his or her status as goods in transit;
and as in insurance generally, what cannot be insured in goods is their
own internal constitution, their inherent weaknesses.

The problems generated by considering humans as goods are also
reflected in the law's treatment of slave insurrections. Slaves were part
of general average, so that jettison of goods could be offset against the
value of slaves.[20] Slaves killed in rebellions were treated as general average, destroyed in order to preserve the ship. As John Weskett explained in
1781: 'The average arising from insurrection is understood to mean *general
average*, and to be borne by the value of ship and cargo, &c. not by that of
the slaves only, as a particular average thereon; because the loss or damage
(whether to ship, or cargo, or both) which happens by means of an insurrection, and the endeavours used in quelling the same, arises from the
whole interests, together with the lives of the crew, being in danger.' But

insurrection implies agency, making slaves something more than goods. Weskett notes that a clause is normally inserted in insurance contracts to specify that slave ships are 'free from loss or average, by trading in boats; and also from *average* occasioned by *insurrection* of slaves, if under 10 *per cent*'.²¹ This seems to imply that insurrection up to a certain level is *expected*, both on the coast of Africa and on board ship; again it attributes an agency to the slave. In another case, involving a Bristol slaver in 1785, *Jones v. Schmoll*, there was a question of how losses of slaves following an attempted rebellion were to be decided. The policy had, as usual, indemnified such losses above '10*l. per cent* to be computed on the first cost of the ship, outfit and cargo' – that is, they were part of general average. But what losses were to be allowed, given that the owners claimed for a range of damage from those killed to subsequent deaths, and even market losses caused by a reputation of rebelliousness? The jury, under Mansfield's direction, decided that those who were lost by wounding or bruising were covered; but those who 'swallowed salt water, and died in consequence thereof, or who leaped into the sea, and hung upon the sides of the ship, without being otherwise bruised, or who died of chagrin, were not to be paid for'. Mansfield himself ruled out market losses as 'too distant'. This is a strict general average interpretation: only immediate 'sacrifices' of goods are allowed; the consequent damages, which relate to the status of the slaves as persons and personalities, are ignored, except insofar as they constituted an external peril threatening the ship.²² The law was, again, struggling with the paradoxical status of slaves, as goods which might threaten themselves.

These issues were drawn out in a remarkable set of cases brought in appeal in the Louisiana Supreme Court in 1842 after a famous mutiny the previous year on the slave ship *Creole*. The *Creole* looms large in African-American memory, with fictional versions of the events written by Frederick Douglass ('The Heroic Slave'), William Wells Brown, Lydia Maria Child, and Pauline Hopkins, though the subsequent insurance cases have received little or no attention.²³ The ship was travelling from Richmond to New Orleans. The legal issues included deviation (loading at ports not specified in the policy); overcrowding and negligence, which prompted a rebellion in which one of the owner's agents was killed; and 'arrest' of foreign powers (the slaves sailed to the Bahamas, where the British released those not directly involved in the murder, causing a major diplomatic incident; American demands that the owners be indemnified for their lost 'cargo' were not settled until 1855). An incisive set of briefs was prepared by Slidell, Benjamin, and Conrad for the Merchants' Insurance

Company, which was contesting liability – written (it is hard not to notice the irony) by the young Judah P. Benjamin, later Confederate Attorney-General and then, in exile, a famed barrister in England.[24]

Benjamin's successful argument covered a variety of issues, but one central plank was the assertion that slaves are inherently prone to rebellion. He invokes a distinction, 'as old as the contract of insurance', between the 'inherent vices of the subject insured' and 'external accidents'.[25] In a passage which surely invokes Shylock's plea in *The Merchant of Venice*, the Jewish lawyer asks: 'Now, what in the present case was the "vice propre de la chose"? What is a slave? He is a human being. He has feelings and passions and intellect. His heart, like the white man's, swells with love, burns with jealousy, aches with sorrow, pines under restraint and discomfort, boils with revenge, and ever cherishes the desire of liberty' (27). The slave experiences the same feelings as others, and some things more passionately. He 'is prone to revolt in the very nature of things. . . . Will any one deny that the bloody and disastrous insurrection of the Creole was the result of the inherent qualities of the slaves themselves, roused, not only by their condition of servitude, but stimulated by the removal from their friends and homes ... and encouraged by the lax discipline of the vessel, the numerical weakness of the whites, and the proximity of a British province?' (28). According to the French legal tradition Benjamin draws on, death from despair and death from rebellion are part of the situation and state of soul of the captive: 'L'une et l'autre ont pour motif les même causes, qui prennent naissance dans la caractère de la chose' (both have their grounds in the same causes, born of the nature of the thing).[26] Because 'intrinsic' risks are not insured, slave rebellion is, Benjamin insists, covered only where it is specifically inserted as a risk in the policy (33–34). Adding that the 10 per cent clause normally limits the risk to catastrophic rebellion, Benjamin draws out the logic of earlier cases under Mansfield. Rebellion is intrinsic to slavery. Moreover, slavery is, he argues in a brief for one of the other cases, an institution which has since Justinian been described as *contra naturam* and a result of local conditions rather than of universal application; the British thus had no obligation to return slaves. The more general implication is that the slave's situation is temporary and reversible.[27] The slave can never definitively be treated as an owned thing.

THE *ZONG* CASE: *GREGSON V. GILBERT*

We can now turn to the most famous of all cases relating to slavery and insurance, *Gregson v. Gilbert*, or the case of the slave ship *Zong*. It was an action on the value of 'certain slaves', that is, 132 (or 134, according to different counts) out of around 470 embarked, who were thrown overboard over a period of days from 29 November 1781 after the boat missed Jamaica, with sickness endemic and water supplies low. Captain Luke Collingwood thus brutally converted an uninsurable loss (general mortality) into general average loss, a sacrifice of parts of a cargo for the benefit of the whole. The result was two sets of proceedings, one before the King's Bench and another parallel case (only recently investigated in detail) in the Court of Exchequer.[28] In the former case, the owners were awarded damages in which the losses were allowed; but in an appeal hearing before Mansfield (who had also presided in the first hearing) and two other judges, this judgement was overturned, since the Captain's mistake could not be called a 'Peril of the Sea', and there were a number of factors suggesting that water supplies were not seriously depleted.[29]

Murder was not the formal issue: despite commenting on the shocking nature of the case, Mansfield insisted repeatedly that in law it was as if horses had been jettisoned. But as the records of the arguments around the case made by the abolitionist Granville Sharp suggest, murder, and specifically murder at sea, was central to the way the case was in fact argued.[30] As Ian Baucom has suggested, Sharp's intervention was designed to interrupt the time of slavery with a Badiouian 'event' which would render its logic visible.[31] Similarly, Anita Rupprecht, in her discussion of the role of the *Zong* massacre in abolitionist writings, suggests that the *Zong* served, in its above-decks visibility, as a stand-in for the below-decks invisibility of an experience of which there are almost no eyewitness accounts left by those who experienced it: the Middle Passage itself. In Rupprecht's account it circulates in the writings of Thomas Clarkson and others as an emblem both of the horrors of slavery and, in descriptions of the court case, of the cold-blooded equation of persons and property.[32]

If Rupprecht is right that the story of the *Zong* tends to stand in the place of accounts of the Middle Passage in such narratives, Sharp's records mark the beginning of a chain of memory which has secreted within it an unacknowledged freight, one in which a single instance acts as the vehicle of a multiple horror. The ship is overloaded, as it were; it carries symbolic matter below the waterline in the form of legions of victims of slavery. In this respect the story has the shape of trauma; it demands, in Freudian terms, a 'working-through' which might deal with what is repressed and lost to understanding – though here we must understand 'working-through' in a way that Freud only occasionally countenanced, as dealing with historical experience.[33] There are, as I will suggest in the final chapter of this book, some problems associated with seeing history under the heading of trauma – for example, in the scene of black passivity and melodramatic spectatorship produced by the *Zong* story. But equally, there are good reasons for attending to the emblematic status of the case and asking why the *Zong* resonates in historical consciousness to the extent it does.

One context for that resonance is abolition's place in a broader stream of humanitarian activity in the late eighteenth century: the philanthropic concern with orphans, foundlings, and prostitutes, and perhaps particularly the campaigns for the revival and rescue of the drowned and drowning associated with the Humane Society. The institution now called the Royal Humane Society was founded in 1774 as 'the Institute for affording immediate relief for persons dead from drowning' and slightly later known as 'the Society for the recovery of persons apparently drowned'; it became the Humane Society in 1776 and 'Royal' in 1787.[34] With its motto, *Lateat scintillula forsan* (a little spark may remain concealed), it encouraged efforts at resuscitation, publicized new techniques, awarded prizes, and endowed an annual sermon in which rescuers were praised and the rescued gave thanks. In 1799 one of its stalwarts, the Quaker surgeon Anthony Fothergill, published *An Essay on the Preservation of Shipwrecked Mariners*, including a survey of lifesaving devices, lifeboats, the loading of vessels, and other factors. Subsequently, the Society moved its emphasis from resuscitation and apparent death (an obsession of its founder, William Hawes) to rescue, promoting lifeboats, lifebelts, and other lifesaving apparatus.

Such humanitarian activity can be linked to the central place of the shipwreck in accounts of the perils and individual costs of maritime enterprise in the period. The shipwreck, in hundreds of popular pamphlets, collections, ballads, and other writings, and in a wide range of maritime painting, serves as a sublime scene of sympathetic identification in which questions of stoic distance, ethical involvement, and the 'shocks' of modern life circulate. In a related philosophical *topos*, explored by Hans Blumenberg, it provides a place for meditation on such issues in Kant, Hegel, and others: Who can look on these terrible scenes with detachment? Does morality involve empathy?[35]

One of the most famous British shipwrecks of the eighteenth century occurred just three years after the *Zong* case came to the courts: the wreck of the *Halsewell* East Indiaman off the Isle of Purbeck on 2–6 January 1786, in which 170 people died, including the captain's young family. The *Halsewell* generated numerous narratives, poems, and even an appearance in Philippe Jacques de Loutherbourg's *Eidophusikon*, a pioneering *son*

et lumière show in London which had as its centrepiece a storm and shipwreck (hastily remodelled to suggest the *Halsewell*).³⁶ The following verse
from a pamphlet captures the mood of such narratives:

> Behold, alas! the awful Moment's come
> Big with the *Halsewell*'s final Fate and Doom,
> Inwrap'd by *Erebus*, in horrid Gloom!
> She's drive with Fury on the much-fear'd Rock,
> Splits in the Centre – Ah! I feel the Shock!
> About the Captain's Neck, his Daughters cling,
> As if (*poor Souls*) he could them Succour bring!
> But all's in vain! – Those Shrieks and bitter Cries,
> Move no Compassion in the angry Skies.³⁷

In the introduction to his six-volume collection of shipwreck narratives,
The Mariner's Chronicle (1810), Archibald Duncan writes in terms which
underscore the identification involved: 'Man never beholds with indifference his fellow-creatures struggling with adverse fortune, or exposed to
great and imminent danger, even in the empire of fiction; his imaginary
sufferings extort tears of commiseration, and excite the most anxious concern for his fate.'³⁸ For Duncan this aesthetic takes on a political edge:
given the centrality of the sailor to trade and national security, his fate
'cannot be indifferent to those who remain at home, enjoying that security, and those conveniences, which his exertions so materially contribute to
procure'. Such pleas received an answering discourse in the development
of new lifesaving techniques around 1800: mortars and rockets carrying
lines, buoys, and other devices were used, often watched from the shore
by crowds. In the accounts of the lives of the inventors of these devices,
the witnessing of a shipwreck off the British coast is often described as the
terrifying moment which inspired their efforts.³⁹

Unsurprisingly, then, slavery and shipwreck come together in abolitionist writings. Perhaps the best example is provided by Mary Robinson
('Perdita'), who wrote a number of poems on the shipwreck as a moral
scene ('Lines Written on the Sea-Coast', 'The Alien Boy') and on the overturning of despotic powers. In two poems, 'The Wreck' and 'The Negro
Girl', this subject is directly applied to the plight of the slave. In the latter, the heroine Zelma sees her lover Draco captured, shipped out, and
shipwrecked:

> The topmast falls – three shackled slaves
>   Cling to the vessel's side!
> Now lost amid the madd'ning waves –
>   Now on the mast they ride –

See! on the forecastle my DRACO stands
And he now waves his chain, now clasps his bleeding hands.[40]

Another example is provided by *The Slave Trade*, an anonymous poem published in 1793 which inspired a well-known set of abolitionist images by George Morland. The poem was, according to its title page, written in 1788, when the *Zong* was a recent memory. It posits a shipwreck on the coast of Africa:

Suppose by tempest's rage, on *Afric's* shore,
　Your ship is driv'n, with all her pallid crew,
What help from Blacks! – dare you their aid implore?
　Will they forget their foes, and save them too?

Unspotted Truth, triumphant, answers yes!
　The sympathetic spark of heav'nly fire
Pervades a Negro's breast, he feels the bliss
　Which human kindness ever must inspire.

Dauntless they plunge amidst the vengeful waves,
　And snatch from death the lovely sinking fair;
Their friendly efforts, lo! Each Briton saves!
　Perhaps their future tyrants now they spare.

Hence vain distinctions, prejudice to sight!
　The social union knows no diff'rent hue,
And Nature's pencil paints him purest white,
　Who feels for others, and most good will do.[41]

Here, as in Morland's painting *African Hospitality* (Figure 1, inspired by the wreck of the *Grosvenor* off the Pondoland coast of South Africa in 1782), the sympathy of Africans is explicitly contrasted with the rapacious attitudes of slavers, and implicitly with the British wreckers against whom so much legislative energy was directed in the eighteenth century: these spectators do not remain indifferent or strip the ship of goods, ignoring the victims.[42]

To refuse to bear witness to what is involved in disaster – and in the spectacle of slavery as well – was to be blind to the costs of both human commerce and the commerce in humans. Abolitionists described the case of the French slaver *La Rodeur* in 1819, whose captain threw overboard thirty-nine slaves because of blindness caused by the eye disease ophthalmia (prevalent on slave ships); the eventual result was, as in the *Zong* case, a fraudulent insurance claim. All but one man became blind, then all:

Then there came a storm. No hand was upon the helm, not a reef upon the sails. On we flew like a phantom ship of old, that cared not for wind or weather, our

Figure 1. John Raphael Smith, after George Morland, *African Hospitality* [1791].
Mezzotint (1814). © National Maritime Museum, Greenwich, London, E9126.

masts straining and cracking; our sails bursting from their bonds … the furious
sea one moment devouring us up, stem and stern, the next casting us forth again,
as if with loathing and disgust. Even so did the whale cast forth the fated Jonah.
The wind, at last, died moaningly away, and we found ourselves rocking, without
progressive motion, on the sullen deep.[43]

The crew hear the sound of another ship, which passes by; they then meet
another ship, the *Saint Leon*, which astonishingly is in the same plight.
The resonant story of two ships passing each other, the blind calling to
the blind, was quickly used as an emblem of the slave trade by Samuel
Webber (physician and son of a president of Harvard) in his poem *The
Slave Ship* (1821).[44] My suggestion is that readers of abolitionist accounts
would have been primed to read the *Zong* in this way: as a melodramatic
scene of shipwreck in which spectators are impelled into political action;
in which the failure to see or 'count' the Africans involved as part of the
ship's company is underscored.

We must introduce another concept. As noted earlier, the traditional
term for the loss of goods under duress at sea is 'sacrifice'. As one authority
explained in 1824, '[A] *sacrifice* made for the *preservation* of the ship and
cargo is general average.'[45] Sacrifice can thus be seen as one of the earliest
concepts informing notions of collective enterprise and shared risk, well

before the earliest example the *Oxford English Dictionary* gives of 'sacrifice' in the secularized sense of giving up something for a larger good, in *Romeo and Juliet*. The slaves killed by Collingwood were claimed by the Solicitor General John Lee, acting for the owners, as a general average sacrifice made to avert an insurrection and further deaths (*Sharp Transcript*, 52–53). The discourse of sacrifice permeates every aspect of the *Zong* case. The petition to the Court of Exchequer prepared for the insurers of the ship demanded an inquiry into 'whether the said Luke Collingwood did not make a wanton of wicked sacrifice of the Lives of the Said Slaves so thrown into the sea'.[46] During the trial Mr. Heywood, counsel for the insurers, applied the term to the case itself: 'if your Lordship was to determine in favour of these owners I don't know but Millions of our fellow Creatures may hereafter fall sacrifice to this very Decision' (*Sharp Transcript*, 41–42). We can see this as an attempt to draw out the ambiguous logic of commercial sacrifice in relation to human cargo. But another topic also intrudes: the comparison between this case and those of maritime peril in which crew members are sacrificed by lot – a form of sacrifice which we might see as offering a parallel with general average.

Two issues were important here. The most telling legally was the nature of the emergency which caused the slaves to be jettisoned. General average sacrifice applies only to situations of immediate peril. The situation was not, counsel for the insurers suggested, catastrophic: no one was on short rations; water was available within sailing distance; more slaves were killed after the 'providential shower' of 1 December. The second issue was the non-random nature of the selection of slaves. Another of the counsels for the insurers, Mr. Davenport, argued that '[t]here never was a Moment of short Allowance for that is the only thing that I call actual necessity – then one easily sees why the slaves are to go first & why the sick ones are to go or those that would sell for the least Money are to go before the more Healthy and Valuable[,] one easily sees when this Captain had missed Jamaica' (*Sharp Transcript*, 8–9). It was awareness that he had 'lost his Market' that determined and structured Collingwood's actions. This was an argument that Mansfield seems to have supported at the retrial hearing, since he too noted the fact that there seemed to be no immediate peril.

Why is randomizing the selection of slaves so important to the argument? General average acts are deemed to take place in 'the agony of the moment' and are not to be subject to unwarranted scrutiny 'in the comfort of the Admiralty Court'.[47] One seizes the goods nearest to hand for jettison rather than (say) carefully sorting out the cheapest cargo. Random selection thus might be seen as way of mimicking a state of emergency, disguising human agency as Nature. But there is more to it than this, since slaves are, of course, human beings who exist as part of a collectivity on a ship. Mr. Pigot, also acting for the insurers, raised the issue of randomizing selection via a case that had recently been in the news: that of Captain J. N. Inglefield and the Royal Navy ship *Centaur*. The *Centaur* sailed from Jamaica in September 1782, and after a gale it became leaky and lost its mast and rudders; as it was sinking, Inglefield and some others got off in a pinnacle, which drifted for weeks without food and water.[48] For Pigot – ignoring Inglefield's self-selection for the boat and rumours of cannibalism on the pinnacle – this provides a model of action in which collective suffering is morally superior, and the casting of lots a secondary expedient in cases of necessity: 'Captain Inglefield distributed that Water as long it lasted equally – Did they even upon the footing of equality cast lots for their Lives? No, they trusted ... [in Providence]' (*Sharp Transcript*, 29). The Court of Exchequer petition made a similar argument: 'And your Orators [the formal term for a petitioner] charge that if there had been an absolute & immediate necessity that any lives should be lost in order to preserve the rest (which your Orators charge was not the case) Lot ought to have been first cast that it might have been known on whom the Lot fell to become sacrificed' (*Sharp Transcript*, 124). Here, the sacrificial logic of lots serves as a possible amelioration of murder. In the absence of lots, commercial sacrifice becomes a targeting of spoiled goods rather than a distribution of risk. And in rendering that logic explicit, the insurers' case was won.

We will return to the issue of drawing lots. But to draw the argument thus far together, it is clear that the legal position of the slave is unstable: goods and yet not goods; an external threat, but also internal to the ship in terms of general average; an unpredictable risk whose resistance is predictable. The aim of abolitionist discourse is often to draw out these contradictions and to insist on a confusion of goods and persons. Granville Sharp threatened an indictment for murder over the *Zong* case, and after much protest the recovery of slave losses through insurance was legislated against in a series of statues from 1788. Sharp's own protest to the Admiralty insisted on collapsing the distinction between life and property:

The *property* of these poor injured Negroes *in their own lives*, notwithstanding their unhappy state of slavery, was infinitely superior, *and more to be favoured, in law*, than the slave-holders' or slave-dealers' iniquitous claim of property in their *persons*: and therefore the casting them alive into the sea, though *insured* as property, and valued at thirty pounds per head, is not to be deemed the case of throwing over *goods*, &c.[49]

A note by Sharp in the record of the case, responding to the Solicitor-General's claims that the slaves are 'real Property', elaborates:

But at the same time it is also the Case of throwing over living Men, and tho' in one sense they may be considered as goods, yet this does not alter their existence & actual Rights as living Men; so that the property in their Persons is only a limited property, limited I say by the necessary consideration of their human Nature. (*Sharp Transcript*, 48)

'Existence' is a key term here, suggesting an actuality that has been destroyed. Indeed, a related distinction had been drawn by Mansfield in his well-known judgment on James Somerset (the 1772 case which declared that slavery was such an evil that it could not be legally sustained on English soil in the absence of any 'positive law' justifying it). Mansfield distinguished between the contract for sale, which remained a valid commercial document about an abstract person, and 'the person of the slave himself', the body which is before the court and over which the owner is exerting 'so high an act of dominion' in taking the slave against his or her will to the West Indies. In earlier cases, settled out of court, slaves were produced under a writ of habeas corpus, and Mansfield referred to this point of origin in his judgment.[50] For this reason producing the human body, refusing its liminal, contractual, and in-transit status, is central to abolitionist writings and iconography.

MARITIME CANNIBALISM, OR WHY EATING
PEOPLE IS WRONG

What are we to make of the rather strange comparison between the *Zong* and instances of shipwreck and the drawing of lots? What ties them together is an understanding of the logic of sacrifice in which the pressures of maritime life produce particular sets of decisions. Shipwrecks have regularly produced boatloads of starving passengers and crew members, or groups of castaways, who have resorted to cannibalism. Many of those eaten were, of course, already dead, but in numerous cases documented in the huge corpus of shipwreck narratives, it is the living who are killed and eaten, usually after the drawing of lots. This is the 'Custom of the Sea', for centuries regarded as a horrific but unavoidable part of maritime life. It was only with the prosecution of the crew of the *Mignonette* in London in 1884, for killing and eating Richard Parker, the ship's boy, that the practice was judicially condemned. (Bizarrely, Parker shared his name with the victim in Poe's *Narrative of Arthur Gorgon Pym of Nantucket*, published some fifty year earlier; in Yann Martel's more recent *Life of Pi* it becomes the name of the Bengal tiger with which the young hero shares a lifeboat for 227 days).

In his magisterial book on the *Mignonette* case, Brian Simpson argues that one motive for the prosecution was an attempt to discredit the harsher implications of Social Darwinism and its utilitarian calculus (a calculus of sacrifice which is, we have seen, part of the logic of insurance).[51] The sailors selected Parker because he was closest to death and had no dependants. But the final judges, in a highly moralistic argument, demanded that the starving resist eating others, even if it meant their own death. This is akin to Granville Sharp's argument against the jettisoning of slaves: evil cannot be justified by necessity. A case of human jettison, involving the male passengers in an overcrowded longboat being thrown into icy seas by the sailors manning it, had already been prosecuted in America.[52] But I want to avoid rushing to the conclusion that abolition and cannibalism simply intersect on a humanitarian trajectory in which both are increasingly unacceptable. We need to investigate the history and theory of eating people.

Simpson reports that popular legend had it that the *Mignonette* survivors were prosecuted because they failed to observe the Custom of the Sea, not drawing lots. This is not true, but it involves an understandable assumption. Casting lots is an ancient practice, described as early as the story of Jonah – a precedent raised in defence of the crew by their counsel, Sir George Baker.[53] Central to the story of Jonah is the way in which the lots enact a providential and sacrificial logic. The mariners respond to the storm which the Lord sends by throwing 'the wares that were in the ship into the sea, to lighten it of them' (sacrifice). They then cast lots in order to ascertain which of them is being punished. When Jonah admits that he is the cause of the tempest and suggests that he be thrown overboard, the sailors at first refuse – this delay is important in later narratives – before crying, 'We beseech thee O Lord, we beseech thee, let us not perish for this man's life', adding – and again, this disavowal is surely significant – 'and lay not upon us innocent blood: for thou, O Lord, has done as it pleased thee.' Jonah is finally tossed overboard, the seas calm, and a further religious sacrifice is offered.

This providential pattern is reflected in early English sea narratives. *Mr James Janeway's Legacy to His Friends* (1674) includes a series of stories involving the possibilities of cannibalism. In one, after near starvation, '[t]he Motion is, that which the Marriners, in *Jonahs* Vessel, put in execution, *Come let us cast Lots*, &c. only with this difference, they cast Lots to find out the delinquent; and these, which of them, should dye first, to be a Sacrifice for ravenous Hunger to feed upon: Concluding, as he in that case, *It is expedient for us that one man should dye for the People, and that the whole Ships Company perish not'*. As the marginal reference notes, this echoes the words of the high priest Caiaphas in John 11:50, declaring that Jesus should die so that the people might be protected. The sailors cast lots and one is chosen; but the next question is, who is to execute him? Prayers are offered, and the Lord answers, casting 'a mighty Fish into the boat'. They starve again, cast lots again (excusing the one 'that God hath acquitted'), and this time the Lord sends 'a great Bird'. After a final set of lots is cast, the third victim is saved when a sail appears. In another narrative in the collection, a comparable story is told: when a ship is stuck in ice, lots are cast but none of the crew members wishes to be the executioner; providentially the loser dies as he prays, and taking this as a 'good *Omen*' they eat him.[54] Sacrifice is made possible without murder – a logic of substitution which persists in providential narratives up to the nineteenth century.[55]

In the eighteenth century, however, drawing lots became progressively secularized, and doubt as to divination by lot increased. Later commentaries and sermons on Jonah stress that lots are not recommended; they dwell on the humanity of the heathen sailors rather than the violence of their act, their reluctance to abandon Jonah and to resort to lots. The story of Jonah was the subject of the Seatonian Prize (awarded at Cambridge for the best poem on a sacred subject) in 1815. The runner-up, Edward Smedley, writes in his *Jonah: A Poem*, 'him unwillingly they threw / A willing victim to the gulph'. The winning poem, by James Bellamy, managed not to mention the lots and Jonah's ejection at all.[56] George Abbot, Archbishop of Canterbury, in his *Exposition upon the Prophet Jonah* (1600) had already stressed their refusal to single him out and the fact that they probably cast lots many times to confirm the verdict.[57] In *Man by Nature and by Grace: or, Lessons from the Book of Jonah* (1850), W. K. Tweedie comments that the Hebrew word translated 'they took up' (in 'they took up Jonah, and cast him into the sea') means 'to exalt with respect' – the very opposite of jettison.[58] The limits of the redemptive and sacrificial principle which underlies these actions are thus carefully established: these sailors do not *wish* to kill Jonah; when they do throw him overboard they do so in the name of a higher power rather than individual survival. The scheme which makes Jonah a type of Christ (and his three days in the fish's belly a type of Christ's descent to hell, Matt. 12:39–40) reinforces the sense that this is a symbolic action.

René Girard has argued that this story of sacrifice and substitution underlies much Western myth-making, at least until its logic is rendered explicit in Christianity. For Girard, Caiaphas's words are those of a political calculus, the 'transcendent qualities' of the scapegoat 'replaced by the justification of social utility'[59] – precisely that which was condemned on the *Mignonette*. And indeed, if one looks at the operation of lots in a range of shipwreck narratives, one comes to see that it conceals a harsh scapegoating in which the expendable are made to carry the burden. As Neil Hanson urbanely remarks, '[C]ertain features recur in almost every instance'. He points out that despite the ritual of drawing lots (i.e., a supposedly random distribution of victims) an almost inevitable order interposes itself: black people are eaten first; then cabin boys and women; steerage passengers are eaten before crew members; then unpopular seamen and ancillary crew members (cooks, etc.); with ordinary seamen and officers last.[60] The ritual of drawing lots, that is, conceals the operations of power as chance even as it reveals itself within the individuals whose bodies are consumed. This analysis, somewhat bizarrely, finds a confirmation in the pro-slavery polemic of the Southern ideologue George Fitzhugh: his *Cannibals All, or, Slaves without Masters* (1857) depicts all power relations as cannibalism, consuming others, with slavery in his view a benevolent form of that process.[61]

Perhaps the most notorious example of racialized cannibalism of the kind suggested by the preceding list is the wreck of the *Peggy* in 1765–76, a major source of Poe's *Pym*. On board the drifting wreck, the first and as it turned out only person to be killed was the slave Whitshire. The comments on the captain and his owner, David Harrison, nicely demonstrate the logic of sacrifice disguised as chance, co-existing uneasily (as in the *Zong* case with the logic of the slave as goods):

[T]hey had taken a chance for their lives, and the lot had fallen on a Negro, who was part of my cargo. – The little time taken to cast the lot, and their private manner of conducting the decision, gave me some strong suspicions that the poor Ethiopian was not altogether treated fairly; – but, on recollection, I almost wondered that they had given him even the appearance of an equal chance with themselves.[62]

At the end of Harrison's printed narrative is, nevertheless, a legalistic 'Protest for their indemnity' on behalf of the owners, including an insistence that the death of Whitshire *is* general average sacrifice, a loss to be distributed in shares as his body was. Here the two examples I have been using, cannibalism and insurance, recognizably coalesce:

I, the said Notary, at his request do hereby solemnly protest, that all damage, loss, detriment, and prejudice, that shall, or may have happened, for, or by reason or means of the total loss of his before-mentioned sloop Peggy and her cargo; or the killing of the before-mentioned Negro slave, or black man, is, and ought to be, borne by the merchants, freighters, and others interested therein; the same having accrued in manner herein before particularly set forth, and not by or through neglect, default, coincurrence, direction, or mismanagement of him, the appearer. (54–55)

'The appearer' as opposed to the disappearer, the sardonic might say. Interestingly, Poe uses a comparable commercial discourse in *Pym*. As captain, the reluctant Pym is forced to prepare the lot:

But now that the silent, definite and stern nature of the business in which I was engaged … allowed me to reflect on the few chances I had of escaping the most appalling of deaths – a death for the most appalling of purposes – … My mind ran over rapidly a thousand absurd projects by which to avoid becoming a partner in the awful speculation.

The language is that of business; the inescapability of projects, partnerships, and partition. This is a doubled language, at once commercial and savage in the calculus it applies to human bodies. As Parker proposes the lots, we are told that '[t]here was about him an air of self-possession which I had not noticed in him until now.'[63] To possess oneself at the point of sacrifice is to dispose of oneself statistically, as if taking out a life insurance policy. A few hours later the head, hands, and feet of the slaughtered Parker are thrown into the sea, and the rest of his corpse is distributed and consumed.

As Equiano famously suggested, white cannibalism serves as a figure for the rapaciousness of slavery; but more specifically in these cases it enacts a sacrificial logic in which risk is not shared equally, where it is redistributed towards the bodies of the socially and commercially dispensable – bodies which disappear. Another example is provided by William Boys's account of the loss of the *Luxborough Galley*, destroyed by fire in 1727. The ship was a slaver for the South Sea Company, carrying six hundred slaves, many of whom died early in the voyage from smallpox. After offloading in Jamaica the *Luxborough* was taken into naval service. 'Two black boys' (as they are described) spilt some rum in the stores and decided to see if the liquid was water by burning some, creating a fire and explosion. One small boat got off, with twenty-two on board. On the fifth day it was stormy, and the survivors proposed that they 'throw overboard the two black boys … in order to lighten the boat' – on the

Figure 2. John Cleveley, *Escape from the* Luxborough *Galley* (1760). © National
Maritime Museum, Greenwich, London, BHC2387.

model of Jonah.[64] The boys naturally opposed this; the survivors cast lots,
though the captain refused to sanction the act. In any event, before anyone was killed, one of the boys and another man died; they and the subsequent dead were eaten before six survivors landed in Newfoundland.
John Cleveley's painting *Escape from the* Luxborough *Galley* (Figure 2),
one of a series on the wreck and its aftermath which he was commissioned to paint in 1760, depicts a tight and indeed almost monochrome
collectivity, mirrored by the patch-working of the sail – bodies huddled
together on the ship's boat so that they cannot be separated. As in many
other cases this collectivity is *predicated on* the paradoxes of sacrifice:
because it was fragmented violently, because the dead are consumed, this
boat becomes one body.

The case of the *Mary*, reported in the *Gentleman's Magazine* in 1737, is
an equally routine scapegoating. The slaver foundered off the Canaries;
its cargo of slaves, who had been manning the pumps, were left to sink.[65]
Eight crew members escaped in a boat and after some weeks began to eat
each other: 'Our Hunger then being intolerable, we were forc'd to kill one
of our Companions to eat, and it was agreed together to begin with one
of the Portuguese.'[66] Even in texts in which the pathos of shipwreck is
the subject, eating black people is acceptable. In a popular narrative, at

least partly factual, *The Surprising yet Real and True Voyages and Adventures of Monsieur Pierre Viaud, A French Sea-Captain* (1771), it is the black servant who is bludgeoned to death by the hero and the female survivor for food – after the narrator has thought of the maritime custom of casting lots.[67] The 1774 American edition of this text binds it with William Falconer's much-reprinted 1762 poem, *The Shipwreck*, under the heading 'To the Sentimentalist in America', and indeed the narrative has many appeals to fellow-feeling. But while Viaud calls himself a 'barbarian' for killing his servant, the necessity (and legality) of doing so is never an issue.

Elsewhere, a rather different but closely related version of scapegoating operates, in which the person chosen by lot escapes because of the supposed willing intervention of another, usually a dispensable outsider (this is a system repeatedly described by Frazer in *The Golden Bough*). The popular maritime ballad known in English as 'The Ship in Distress' (and under many different titles in versions in other European languages)[68] is described by Brian Simpson:

In most ... versions, the intended victim escapes at the last minute, or his escape is assumed, but the details differ. In some the lot falls on the captain; the cabin boy offers himself as a substitute, climbs the mast for a last look around, sees the Towers of Babylon and the captain's daughter, and marries her. In others, the boy is offered the daughter and money as reward for acting as a substitute but asks for the ship instead.... A Scandinavian version has the king of Babylon in command; lots are drawn, and the unfortunate seaman who draws the fatal lot cannot decently be eaten, since he is closely related to the other sailors; one who is not related offers to die in his place and is sacrificed.[69]

This ballad has, it seems to me, a very close relation to the 'Titanic Toast', the well-known oral recitation which circulated (alongside commercial ballads on the *Titanic*) in African-American communities soon after the *Titanic* went down in 1912. Its many versions describe Shine, a black stoker on this ship with no black crew. When the ship strikes the iceberg he starts swimming, ignoring pleas for help from the captain – who offers him his daughter and money – and from other passengers. He outswims the sharks and when the news breaks is drunk in a bar in New York. As Steve Beil and others have shown, the toast relates to a widespread sense that the *Titanic* was the ship of Anglo-Saxon supremacy, buttressed by reports that Jack Johnson, the famous black boxer, had been refused passage.[70] One might also link it to the decline, since the 1850s, in black participation in the merchant marine. But seeing it as 'signifying' on 'The Ship in Distress' also enables us to read it as a refusal of substitution and sacrifice: this black underling is not going to offer his place to *anyone*.

In the cases described here, the lack of comment on the collective decisions made is, perhaps, simply what one would expect – a version of the rapaciousness of slavery which in Equiano's *Interesting Narrative* is figured as a vision of white cannibalism. What is covered up is a sacrificial logic in which risk is not shared equally, where it is redistributed towards the bodies of the socially and commercially dispensable, bodies which disappear. Where the presence of the victimized body can be forcibly reinserted into this story is in relation to a *topos* which I would christen 'fresh meat' (or perhaps habeas corpus). An example is provided by the wreck of *Nottingham Galley* in 1710, which left a group of sailors on Boon Island off New England.[71] When a rescuer arrives on the rock, 'as they were passing on towards the tent, the man casting his eye on the remains of the flesh, exposed to the frost on the summit of the rock, expressed his satisfaction at their not being destitute of provisions; and the master acquiesced in the justice of his sentiments, without unravelling the mystery.' This wreck combined, interestingly enough, cannibalism and suggestions of insurance fraud. The master, John Deane, stressed that he was persuaded to divide the corpse of the carpenter only after entreaties from the crew and after 'Abundance of mature Thought and Consultation'. He portrays himself as the hero of the hour, presiding over an unruly crew and spotting rescuers.[72] Three of the crew members, including the mate and boatswain, published a dissenting account, stressing the master's cowardliness and negligence, and claiming that the ship was over-insured, and could therefore be wrecked at a profit, and that Deane had attempted to lose the ship earlier.[73] They also, implicitly, linked the alleged fraud to meat hunger and a pleasure in cannibalism which is the scandalous subtext of a number of narratives: in their account the master initiates the flesh-eating, telling them it is no sin, and it is reported that 'he barbarously told the Children in his Lodging, that he would have made a Frigassy of them if he had 'em in Boon Island' (18, 24). The narrative written by Deane and his brother Jasper (the main owner of the ship) has a rebuttal, probably added after the type was set up, claiming that the ship was not over-insured and that no one would deliberately wreck a ship on a remote spot 'where 'twas more than Ten Thousand to one, but every Man had perish'd' (22).

In a later example, the *Narrative of the Shipwreck and Suffering of Miss Ann Saunders* (1827), the frisson of cannibalism is tinged with what can only be described as a healthy pleasure in feminine fortitude. As the title page states, Saunders

was a passenger on board the ship *Francis Mary*, which foundered at sea on the 5th Feb. 1826, on her passage from New Brunswick to Liverpool. Miss Saunders was one of the six survivors who were driven to the awful extremity of subsisting 22 days on the dead bodies of such of the unfortunate crew as fell victims to starvation – one of whom was a young man to whom she was soon to be joined in marriage.[74]

The cannibalism began on the seventeenth day; Saunders – like Jonah's crew – resists for a day, but then takes not only to the eating of the dead but also to their preparation. In what seems like a bizarre parody of the 'one flesh' of marriage, Miss Saunders pleads her claim to 'the greater portion of his [her fiancé's] precious blood, as it oozed, half congealed, from the wound inflicted upon his lifeless body!!' Later, as the only person left on her feet, the 'office' of cutting up the flesh falls to her. Her friend, Mrs. Kendall, also shows more pluck than most, eating the brains of a seaman and 'declaring ... that it was the most delicious thing she had ever tasted!' Rescue comes in the form of H.M.S. *Blonde*. Here again is 'fresh meat':

When relieved, but a small part of the body of the last person deceased remained, and this I had cut as usual into slices and spread on the quarter deck; which being noticed by the Lieutenant of the Blonde ... and before we had time to state to him what extremities we had been driven, he observed 'you have got, I perceive, fresh meat!' but his horror can be better conceived than described when he was told what he saw, were the remains of the dead body of one of our unfortunate companions.[75]

The Lieutenant may have been shocked; his captain may have been more familiar with the scene, as he was Lord Byron, inheritor of the title of the poet who had written of maritime cannibalism so graphically in *Don Juan*.

The visibility of the flesh of the dead has a counterpoint in the stress on the actuality of violent sacrifice in the *Zong* case, most memorably depicted in Turner's painting *Slavers Throwing Overboard the Dead and Dying*, said to have its origins in the case and in the many descriptions of sharks savaging bodies in abolitionist poetry.[76] In both the cannibal feast and the dead body of the slave, what is involved is a materialization of social metaphor, and perhaps also a vision of that which resists exchange – the abject body which cannot be adequately symbolized within society's vision of what bodies are for.

We can draw some tentative conclusions from the collocation of sacrifice in insurance, lot drawing, and cannibalism which I have attempted to sketch. Sacrifice at sea is the original model for all risk in insurance; it corresponds to the sacrificial premium we all make so that others (or ourselves) are compensated in the event of disaster, so that, as well, a system of contractual kinship may be maintained. Susan Mizruchi characterizes life insurance as 'an act of sacrificial protection', at once a symbolic warding off of evil and a way of conceiving community and welfare within a humanitarian calculus.[77] This seems right; the stated legal principle underlying insurance is, after all, 'the insurer's standing exactly in the place of the assured', a form of legally enforceable sympathetic identification. But in the case of life insurance the question of compensation is more troubling: others may be compensated, but that demands a victim whose losses are total, except to the extent that insurance reflects familial and social connectedness (we die happy at least that others are secure). One name for the negative component of this victimage is slavery: the fate of the actual slave whose value and self-investment is abstracted and assigned to another; who is described as goods of livestock. But in a more metaphorical and derivative sense, slavery also acts as a metaphor for the subordination of a person to another person, job, or social role, and this is signalled by its trace within the story of life insurance. This is the sacrifice made by what Hegel calls the unhappy consciousness, the element of the self which wishes to deny an enforced social valuation, a value not defined by self-identity.

Another form of sacrifice at sea, the drawing of lots before the person is killed and ingested, provides a dark model for the operations of power – a model in which the supposedly random operation of fate, and the natural order itself, is mimicked by the lot but which is in fact susceptible to human manipulation and scapegoating, making the social appear natural. And while scapegoats may be portrayed as willing, as in 'The Ship in Distress' and indeed in many shipwreck narratives, this is always a point at issue; the story often seems to conceal a violent subordination. When human beings secularize the distribution of risk and compensation, insurance becomes a reflection of social reality rather than a transcendent principle. In the case of the *Zong* both of the definitions referred to earlier – commercial sacrifice and the sacrifice of bodies – were at work, as the lawyers involved seemed to know. The problem of distributing burdens is always predicated on the question of who is inside and who outside the circle of the assured (as Mizruchi makes clear when she points out that the Nazis forbade insurance on Jews). This is the case for slaves, but as we have seen, simply to ask, 'Is a slave insurable? Under what circumstances?' is also to begin to engage in an identification of human agency which means that the famous slave insurance cases also form part of a history of recuperative action. In a culture of compensation, all losses might ultimately be covered – which is why the issue of reparation is still with us.

CHAPTER 2

Debt, Self-Redemption, and Foreclosure

The last time I was sold, I sold for $2,300, – more than I'm worth
now.

Henry Banner, Works Progress Administration interview, 1930s

The commodification of the person, considered in the preceding chapter
in relation to the topic of insurance, has more general consequences in
African-American culture – consequences I will now consider in relation
to debt. The classical theory of slavery suggested that the slave was the
person who, defeated in battle and often lacking in what Aristotle calls
thymos (spirit, the power of resistance), forfeited his life and chose slavery over death. This is the so-called cowardly contract in which debt is
attached to the slave, conceptualized as one who owes his life to another
or as a captive in need of ransom. As Saidiya V. Hartman, Stephen Best,
and others have suggested, in various ways African Americans continued
to be seen in terms of debt, metaphorically and to some extent legally,
even in the period after Emancipation.[1]

That debt is, of course, a fiction for the racial slave, for whom there can
be no contractual basis for debt and, indeed, to whom making a contract
is notionally denied. As Best comments, '[T]here is no slave in advance
of liability who can will a debt.'[2] A state of debt is sustained only by the
violent imposition of power, which is the position Judge Ruffin, like other
legal realists, came to in the nineteenth century, with his declaration in
State v. Mann not of the fundamental nature of property rights in slaves,
but rather of a political realism: 'the power of the master must be absolute,
in order to render the submission of the slave perfect.'[3] Debt is, then, a fictional inheritance, part of a metaphorical selfhood violently imposed on
the slave and gaining its reality from the shifting history which underlies
that imposition.

A central question addressed by this chapter is, what is the narrative
correlative of debt? One answer is provided by what I will call 'foreclosure'.

37

The *Oxford English Dictionary* suggests that the word's prefix derives from the French, meaning 'outside' or 'out', but also gains some of its weight from other meanings of 'for-' and 'fore-', including those relating to exclusion and abstaining (like 'forbid' or 'forbear') and anticipating ('forecast'). The principal meanings of 'foreclosure' include barring or excluding; precluding an action; closing an issue beforehand or settling it in advance; or establishing an exclusive claim to something. The meaning in law – the act of depriving a mortgager of the power to redeem a mortgaged estate – is, of course, central: a lender forecloses or takes possession of a property when the debtor fails to pay or service a debt. All these meanings come into play in relation to the African-American experience: a forbidding or exclusion; the denial of consideration; the calling in of a debt. The psychoanalytic use of the term is also of some interest: for Jacques Lacan that which is foreclosed is expelled from the psyche and returns in the 'Real', typically as hallucination.[4] What I wish to examine in particular is the temporality evoked by the term and the idea that foreclosure imposes a particular experience of *time* on the subject – the sense of an issue always already settled or an opening towards a future which is cut off.

PERSONS, PROPERTY, AND SELF-REDEMPTION

The legal position of the slave in North America was always complex. As early as 1690, slaves were legally described as chattels. As Gavin Wright shows, the Colonial Debts Act of 1732 played an important role in providing an 'effective legal (and therefore negotiable) status to the bonds given by planters buying slaves on credit', allowing slaves to become part of a credit economy. Wright adds, 'The clear legal trend in the nineteenth century was towards a full alienability of slave property in the market', with slaves treated as chattels or personal property rather than as real property attached to an estate – though at some moments, with typical incoherence, the latter understanding of their status was applied.[5] At the same time, Southern law admitted the humanity of slaves and treated them as agents in relation to some crimes. The Constitution inaugurated a legal tradition in which the slave was regarded as a contracted person whose labour was due to others, and some legal thinkers – for example, Judge Tansey in the *Dred Scott* case – continued that line of thought, seeing the slave as metaphorically a debtor.

The fact that a slave had the 'double character' of person and property (as the Southern jurist T. R. Cobb put it in 1858) was thus fundamental to slavery – and indeed, Cobb claimed it was the allowance of 'various rights as a person' which distinguished modern slavery from despotism.[6] Southern law struggled to negotiate these opposed poles, as well as an important third element, which was the public interest implicit in the power relations involved in controlling a large body of slaves. That element had barely been present in the slave law inherited from the ancients, for whom the treatment of slaves was largely a private matter.[7] The result was an often contradictory body of law and practice which juggled competing demands negotiated among the three poles of human status, property, and the essentially political demands of discipline; between the humanity towards the slave dictated by paternalistic ideology and the 'interest' generated by the slave economy.[8] In the South, the state intervened to limit the master's right to educate and free slaves and allow them to move about; it dictated the punishments he should apply, and in some cases even specified the amount of labour an owner could reasonably extract from them.

The uncertain status of the slave is most clearly signalled by those aspects of his or her legal status which relate to those who may be considered in a liminal or transitional state, or as conduits between slavery and freedom. In Louisiana this was especially marked, because there the slave's status was inflected by the legacy of Spanish (and thus Roman) law. Consider the following articles of the Louisiana Code:

ART. 176 – They can transmit nothing by succession or otherwise; but the succession of free persons related to them which they would otherwise have inherited had they been free, may pass through them to such of their descendants as may have acquired their liberty before the succession is opened.

ART. 193 – The slave who has acquired the right of being free at a future time, is from that time, capable of receiving by testament or donation.

ART. 196 – The child born of a woman after she has acquired the right of being free at a future time, follows the condition of its mother, and becomes free at the time fixed for her enfranchisement, even if the mother should die before that time.[9]

The slave here is in a liminal state: the promise of a deferred freedom may be vested in the unfree body, or freedom may pass through the slave. A mixed status could exist in the North: the 1799 Act for the Gradual Abolition of Slavery passed in the New York state legislature, for example, produced states of limited slavery (apprenticeships, indentured servitude) in which slaves effectively worked off their own value. The 1812 Alabama slave code provides a typical set of examples in which the slave's human status is both acknowledged and negated: slaves could be sold only to settle debts greater than one hundred dollars after other property had been levied, with various provisions limiting the sale of children under the age of 10; slaves guilty of capital offences were tried by jury in the same way as whites, but the same jury had to assign a value to the slave and the slave's owners could claim half of that value from the state treasury after the slave's execution – except in cases of insurrection.[10] In such legislation, the slave's status is hybrid: determined partly by human status, partly by commercial value, and partly by the disciplinary power in which one was imposed forcibly on the other. As Thomas D. Morris shows, this latter consideration resulted in a series of progressively harsher legal judgments in cases of manumission or partial manumission in which issues of public policy clashed with the dicta of possessive individualism, and owners were denied the right to liberate slaves or even to establish them as an independent economic unit under the oversight of a nominal owner.[11] Ideologically, slaves could not be freed from their obligation to labour for others.

The template provided by the law is, of course, only part of the picture of slave relations. Reading accounts of slavery, one comes across accounts of arbitrary violence, sadism, and murder on the part of slaveholders, but also of extra-legal punishment of the perpetrators of such violence. One reads of anti-manumission laws circumvented in the name of feeling, of slaves who fought and even killed overseers without substantial punishment (because they were too valuable to lose, and the overseer was seen as akin to a man who could not control a horse). The intensity of the struggles involved was marked: as Mark V. Tushnet comments, '[S]lave social relations are total, engaging the master and the slave in exchanges where each must take account of the entire range of belief, feeling, and interest embodied in the other', whereas 'bourgeois social relations are partial'.[12] This may overestimate the recognition of slaves, but nicely suggests the intimacy of struggle we see in many accounts of domestic slavery. Slaves in their everyday working lives had to be seen in more complex ways and in relation to particular tasks: as needing discipline or reward; as potentially escaping or potentially free; as forming relationships with employers, neighbours, and each other; as dependants as well as assets and instruments.

Within the slave system, the value assigned to the slave is realizable only at certain points at which the totality of relations previously described is stripped away: the point of purchase or sale, the point of an insurance claim. In *Uncle Tom's Cabin* and other abolitionist texts, episodes which move brutally from relationship to the realization of value are central to an understanding of slavery as system: it is the slave on the block or in transit who exposes its abstraction of human value; and it is the dying slave who finally removes ownership and assigns it to what is for Stowe a higher order. Conversely, the fugitive represents property in a state in which value is rendered virtual, a debt which must be reclaimed. The dicta from Roman law is 'The slave who absconds ... steals himself'.[13] At one level this is the joke which the runaway Jim makes in *Huckleberry Finn* when he declares that – his slave savings scheme having failed – he is nevertheless rich, having an item worth eight hundred dollars in his possession. Even 'stealing away' in the sense of absence without permission embodies this logic, making freedom the refusal of a debt vested in the self.[14] The epigraph of this chapter is taken from a former slave interviewed in the 1930s who could remember a value he now ironically claims as his own: 'The last time I was sold, I sold for $2,300, – more than I'm worth now.'[15]

In a parallel way, the author of the slave narrative must, W. J. T. Mitchell argues, move from slavery to freedom in order to *have* a narrative.[16] The threshold must be crossed, and value transferred or removed from the person, in order for the self-authoring subject to emerge. But the property rights invested in the slave remain central to the narrative. That is why so many slave narratives have a double trajectory: that of the subject (various 'awakenings' and turning points, learning to read, the awareness of abolitionist) and that of the object (various owners, contracts, commercial properties) – a duality overcome only at the point of escape or redemption. In what follows, I will consider the way in which the black subject must deal with assigned value and the meanings, simultaneously economic and personal, of such terms as 'negotiate', 'redeem', and 'realize'. The slave narratives most studied and celebrated are, understandably, tales of escape north, in which the subjects heroically endure, struggle, and finally place themselves outside the system of slavery. But in contrast to the narrative of escape, I want to discuss narratives of self-redemption, in which slaves work to *buy* their freedom rather than steal it (the term 'redemption' comes from the Latin *redemptio*, 'ransoming or buying the freedom of a slave or someone who has taken a military oath'). In such accounts, the theoretically immutable boundary between chattel and personhood is traversed by the narrative itself; the paradox of self-redemption lies in what is nominally an object having agency over his or her own chattel status.

Self-purchase is a possibility within many slave systems in the Latin world. It was on the basis of a universal right to self-redemption at a fixed price that Charles Chesnutt stressed the superiority of Portuguese slave regimes in the Americas over Spanish and anglophone regimes.[17] The right known as *coartación* existed in Louisiana under Spanish jurisdiction and contributed to the distinctive character of slavery there, creating the beginnings of an urban Creole society in which, according to Ira Berlin, 'the line between slavery and freedom became increasingly permeable'.[18] As Berlin reports, 'Some 1,500 black people purchased their liberty or that of others in New Orleans between 1769 and 1803' – though self-purchases were probably a small proportion of these cases.[19] While rights of self-purchase and manumission were restricted after its integration into the United States in 1803, Louisiana remained the most liberal of slave states, allowing slaves to sue for freedom in cases where it had been promised to them or was otherwise in dispute.[20] Complex cases involving promises of emancipation *in futuro* continued until the right was definitively ended in 1857.[21] Elsewhere in the South, self-purchase was discouraged and pro-scribed after 1800 (as, increasingly, was manumission). Slaves were not, in theory, permitted personal capital. But in practice, an increasingly com-plex and potentially self-contradictory tangle of commercial arrangements surrounded slavery in general. As the nineteenth century advanced, slaves in many areas formalized certain tightly circumscribed (and often local) rights, quasi-legal or customary – and the latter included the right to earn money from work done outside allotted hours on their own plots. Often slaves were permitted to grow crops or raise chickens and hogs and market them to their owner or others; many white communities were reliant on such 'truck'.

Perhaps the most important and destabilizing such development in the decades leading to the Civil War was the hiring out of slaves and a radical extension of that practice, self-hire arrangements. Slave owners hired out slaves to neighbours; to railroads, mines, and ironworks; or to those farm-ing the new territories in the West. In self-hire arrangements, slaves with skills were sent to the city to seek work and return a set tariff, using the balance to support themselves. Despite official disapproval and a Southern fear of urbanization in general, the system was essential to the economic flexibility of many states, shifting slaves from areas where there was a sur-plus to areas of need.[22] Sharon Ann Murphy notes that in the upper South 'on the eve of the Civil War, approximately six percent of rural and thirty-one percent of urban slaves were hired out'.[23] The most general result, as Jonathan Martin shows, was an undermining of the paternalistic ideology which supported slavery: slaves became individual 'units of investment' rather than part of the extended family.[24] Many smallholders had to think carefully about whether they could afford to use their slaves rather than hire them out.

As the preceding chapter has already suggested, the risk involved in such hire was increasingly managed by insurance. The Baltimore Life Insurance Company underwrote its first policy on a slave in 1831, and while it initially disliked such policies, by 1850 they amounted to more than half of the company's business, and in the 1850s Baltimore Life began to aggressively promote the practice. Murphy notes that '[l]ife insurance was fast becoming a key component of industrialization in the Upper South'.[25] Todd Savitt reports that in Virginia and North Carolina 'about 3% of all industrial slaves and a substantially smaller number of plantation bondsmen employed during any year in the 1850s were covered by life insurance'.[26] The law of bailments was developed from property law to deal with the duty of care involved, overlaid with more traditional patriarchal assumptions.[27]

One outcome of hiring out slaves was an increasing specificity applied to slavery (the local as the place of resistance will be taken up in the final chapter). Slavery varied with different employment needs; different arrangements had different risks: river trades were notorious for producing escape attempts and attracted high premiums, for example. It was often thought – and courts supported this idea – that a slave who had been allowed to travel to free states and live as free had little defendable value. In New York prior to the War of Independence, the act of hiring out a slave could itself allow a claim for freedom. Escape attempts lowered value; so did a slave mother's harbouring her daughter as a fugitive.[28] Rather than slave status being absolute, that is, it was influenced by acts and environments. The slaves themselves were changed by their experience of hire: they acquired independence and negotiating skills, and exploited the situation to create pockets of relative freedom. The urban environment with its flows of information and aid was itself a stimulus to escape, as was the fact that (as the story of the self-hiring caulker Frederick Douglass shows) slaves were confronted concretely with their own alienation, forced to remit most of the fruits of their skilled labour to an owner. Some self-hirers used accumulated surpluses to purchase themselves.

Within this increasingly complex system, the law struggled to clarify the status of the slave. In what must be seen as a rearguard action, most (though by no means all) Southern judges held that there could be no contractual agreement about freedom involving slaves and masters: freedom was the 'pure gift' of the owner, as Judge McKinney wrote; it could not be earned.[29] Neither, according to one vein of judicial thinking, could freedom be considered a 'legacy' to the slave. Locke's doctrine that no man could have a property right in his own person was repeatedly expounded by Southern judges. Judge John Green, in *Maria v. Surbaugh* (1824), asserted that 'no man can take or hold a property in himself. If he could, he might sell himself, and, by his own act, become a slave'.[30] Other cases reinforced the doctrine that manumission was *not* the conferring on a slave of a title to herself or himself. Instead slaves were seen as property up to the conclusion of the assertion of ownership. But here, too, there were contradictions: despite these legal doctrines, a number of states enacted voluntary re-enslavement statutes in the decade before the Civil War, seemingly out of an equation flatly equating race with slavery (the extremist George Fitzhugh argued that it was the South's duty to return *all* blacks to their natural state).[31]

The fact that the slave might, despite legal injunctions to the contrary, be considered a debtor paying off the debt invested in the self is suggested not only by self-purchase agreements, but also by the use of new financial instruments relating to persons. In the South in the period after 1830, insurance bonds were sometimes taken out on slaves to indemnify those who had purchased them with the aim of emancipation – effectively a loan of their redemption price, which they would then work off. The slave insurance (and thus the slave's own body) here acted as a collateral for those who were purchasing their own freedom: 'Judges, mayors, and professors, as well as free blacks and ex-slaves, all solicited policies on recently-purchased slaves they intended to free.'[32] This virtual, financial existence continued a decade after the Civil War as cases involving contacts made before the Thirteenth Amendment were heard in Southern courts.[33]

A set of examples of such practices is provided by *A Narrative of the Life of the Rev. Noah Davis* (1859), in which the minister raised money from congregations in Philadelphia for his own purchase before successively freeing his wife and four of his six children.[34] In the case of his children he took out insurance policies on them or himself, effectively indenturing them as servants to pay off the policies to their benefactors; one daughter's finances were caught up in the 'money panic' of 1857 (58). Throughout Davis's narrative, accounts of complex fund-raising drives, loans, and bonds aimed at the freedom of his family alternate with the ledgers of the Saratoga Street African Baptist Church. The following is typical:

> My salary was only three hundred dollars a year; but with hard exertion and close economy, together with my wife's taking in washing and going out at day's work, we were enabled by the first of the year, to pay the two hundred dollars our dear friend had loaned us, in raising, the six hundred dollars before spoken of. But the bond for three hundred dollars was now due, and how must this be met?

I studied out a plan; which was to get some gentleman who might want a little servant girl, to take my child, and advance me three hundred dollars for the purpose of paying my note, which was now due in Virginia. In this plan I succeeded; and had my own life insured for seven years for five hundred dollars, and made it over to this gentleman, as security; until I ultimately paid him the whole amount; though I was several years in paying it. (42)

Collateralizing his own existence and those of his children, Davis juggles bodies, debts, and amortized labour of the kind involved in slavery itself. The 'Notice to the Public' at the beginning of the text itself offers a summation and a last plea: 'THE object of the writer, in preparing this account of himself, is to RAISE SUFFICIENT MEANS TO FREE HIS LAST TWO CHILDREN FROM SLAVERY. Having already, within twelve years past, purchased himself, his wife, and five of his children, at a cost, altogether, of over *four thousand dollars*, he now earnestly desires a humane and christian public to AID HIM IN THE SALE OF THIS BOOK, for the purpose of finishing the task in which he has so long and anxiously labored' (3). The book itself involves a final transfer of the debt, an equation of book and body as commodity.

The effects of the changes just detailed inform a genre of slave narratives in which slaves negotiated actively with their own financial state. In such narratives, slaves buying themselves accept, perforce, their assigned valuation in a contract like that in ransom insurance: having fallen into captivity, one aims to buy release. Many expressed resentment at having to purchase themselves (or having family members or well-wishers do so), since the abolitionist buying the slave from slavery was, at least momentarily, a slaveholder: 'The idea of making them pay for what is their own by the inalienable gift of their creator, is most absurd,' Frederick Douglass wrote. Nevertheless, Douglass was himself ransomed by Garrison and others; and for many, Douglass included, the desirability of reuniting families could override the principles involved.[35] On a larger scale, Douglass repeatedly praised England's 'sublime' act in ending slavery and compensating sugar planters in the West Indies.[36]

For all that it involved a compliance with the logic of slavery, self-redemption did at least recognize the slave as an economic agent. The narratives of self-redeeming slaves like Equiano, Austin Steward, William Hayden, Peter Still, and Lunsford Lane are marked by constant transactions with their own commodity status: the reader must enter a bewilderingly complex series of quasi-legal claims, promissory notes, webs of inheritance and debt, bonds and loans, fine intentions and base trickery, involving a variety of professions, products, and money-making schemes (trading, rope-making, barbering, selling confectionary, a new tobacco process and pipe, timber), as well as the appeal to abolitionists. Many slave narratives contain what could be called a primal scene of self-amortization, as in Lunsford Lane's *Narrative* (1842):

One day ... my father gave me a small basket of peaches. I sold them for thirty cents, which was the first money I ever had in my life. Afterwards I won some marbles, and sold them for sixty cents, and some weeks after Mr. Hog from Fayetteville, came to visit my master, and on leaving gave me one dollar. After that Mr. Bennahan from Orange county, gave me a dollar, and a son of my master fifty cents. These sums, and the hope that then entered my mind of purchasing at some future time my freedom, made me long for money; and plans for money-making took the principal possession of my thoughts. At night I would steal away with my axe, get a load of wood to cut for twenty-five cents, and the next morning hardly escape a whipping for the offence. But I persevered until I had obtained twenty dollars. Now I began to think seriously of becoming able to buy myself.[37]

The decision to invest labour in oneself, to buy into oneself, is a commitment to a view of the self which accepts a debt attached to freedom. This is a narrative crux which contrasts nicely with Douglass's *Narrative*. Valuation is indirectly present in Douglass's story, but in a negative mode: the climax of his epic battle with Covey is his declaration that he is willing to die rather than be beaten – a refusal which represents a reversal of the principle which makes him fungible: he turns himself at once into the equivalent of a bad cheque or a counterfeit bond, a holder of value which cannot be redeemed, and a body which threatens to refuse the value assigned to it.[38]

As in Lane's example, the reader of the *Narrative of William Hayden* (1846) sees a pathway to freedom which is constantly negotiated and renegotiated, the affective and financial in awkward proximity: 'When, however, it was known that I had only commanded $50, the neighborhood was greatly surprised, and many a dealer in human flesh, would have been anxious to have purchased me; but my good mistress loved me for her dear husband's sake, and not all the wealth of Mexico could have then induced her to part with me.'[39] Hayden frees himself through a financial and contractual act which must be negotiated via a web of white sponsors – in a system in which he can have no official agency:

The cause of my thus speaking so confidently, was the fact of having appointed with the consent and advice of Capt. Garrard, Mr. Timberlake as my guardian, consequently when Mr. Chew called for me, and Mr. Mitchell was directed to get me and sell me for the debt of Mr. Hawkins, I immediately referred them to

Mr. Timberlake, who referred them to Captain William Garrard, who informed them that they dare not touch me, as I was within a short space of being free, by the deed of transfer from his father to Mr. Hawkins, to which he was one of the signers. This was too much for them. (50)

In this and many other episodes, contracts and investments replace the physical struggle described by Douglass – contracts which Hayden agrees to, monitors, manipulates, and finally evades. Though Southern law had no equivalent of the Roman *peculium*, the slave's personal fund, many owners allowed slaves to build up savings, even acting as bankers ('During the winter that I had been with Mr. Philips, I had managed to save upwards of $75. This amount I gave to him, and took his receipt for the same, at six per cent interest', 57). Hayden's biography demonstrates the way in which a tenuous financial existence might be sustained through sheer force of personality and moral suasion, but also through the threat of total loss if a valuable and educated slave who knows his way around becomes too disaffected. What follows is another climactic moment, fraught with emotion, but at the same time articulating an irrevocably economic view of the slave as self-investor:

I had mentioned to him also, in the presence of Mr. McElvain, that I was to have my freedom for $650, and that the $300 for which I wished the writings drawn were the first payments thereon; but that I feared Phillips had some sinister motives in view, and designed to cheat me out of my money and my freedom. Mr. Brent requested that I would go and bring Mr. Phillips to the store, which I accordingly did, after cautioning Mr. McElvain to watch the countenance of Phillips, and see if he could not plainly discover guilt of thought and action. – This, he promised to do. When Mr. Phillips came into the store, I placed myself in front of him and riveted my eyes upon him. He seemed embarrassed, and his face flashed like a living coal. Mr. Brent then told him what I had requested him to do – stating, at the same time he considered it nothing more than right that I should have security for my money, in case of his death; and after some hesitation my master concurred. The writings were then drawn up, and signed by Phillips, and attested by the gentlemen present; Mr. Brent counting out the money to Phillips. (83)

As in so many nineteenth-century novels, the flashing of eyes and flushing of faces represent the interactive energies of social life – though what is at stake is a contract. Indeed, it could be argued that these narratives are often concerned with consistency more at the level of law and finance (of the contract) than at the level of character, given the twisting of the slave between a declared 'honesty' and the need to scheme, and the contradictory appearances of some of the white characters, alternately benevolent and rapacious (which is perhaps another way of saying that slavery calls people into contradictory positions).

Hayden's narrative works within the structure provided by the promise: a testamentary desire of freedom; bankruptcy, broken promises; and the resurrection of the promise as a prophecy. The narrative often jumps forward – most prominently to the day of his legal manumission – only to loop back to the state of slavery. Similar fiduciary structures characterize narratives relating to free black citizens taken into captivity: Solomon Northup's *Twelve Years a Slave* (1853) ends with a welter of appended legal documents, including the 1840 act of the New York legislature which related to those kidnapped into slavery and which made Northrup's original disappearance a crime – a document which makes his narrative a double redemption, both from illegitimate capture and from slavery itself.[40] Narrative, in such cases, becomes a struggle with the negativity of debt. Slavery becomes the time of a suspended promise of freedom, of an identity deferred and spread across a thousand acts of accumulation. It is striking that even though Hayden has already described one emotional recognition scene with his mother as an adult slave, he must be reintroduced to her and rerecognized after he gains his freedom. A fairly common feature of slave narratives, this moment tells of an identity freed at last from negation and debt – a new self, but one whose promise must be held painfully open throughout a narrative in which it is obliterated and deferred.

Consider in this light the commoditization of the self in the earliest and most famous narrative of self-purchase, Equiano Oladauh's *Interesting Narrative* (1789). As we build towards his self-purchase, we see the usual maze of transactions, validating witnesses, setbacks, triumphs. The manumission itself is described in terms of the sublime and the trope of *occupatio*: 'my imagination was all rapture'; Elijah rising to heaven, 'tumult, wilderness and delirium' within his breast; 'Heavens! Who could do justice at my feelings at this moment!'[41] The actual manumission document is then presented, punctuating the text and enabling the new identity of 'Freeman' to emerge. Yet it is curious how much *financial* continuity there is on either side of this rapture. Before his self-purchase he had 'laid out about eight pounds of my money for a suit of superfine clothes to dance in my freedom in' (154). But this is on the promise of a share of a legacy from a dying silversmith which turns out to be non-existent. With his freedom, Equiano does indeed dance in his new clothes, before quickly returning to his old position on the ship to please his patrons. He then enters complex negotiations about whether he might be able to carry bullocks or turkeys on his own account on the next voyage. Forced to trade in turkeys – which turns out to be 'a particular providence' when the cattle die – he 'consented to slave on as before' and the captain gave him 'liberty' to take as many turkeys as he could (162). The point here is not that he is unfree, but that freedom itself involves obligations, debts, negotiations, transfers, permissions, and dangers; his description of himself as returning to 'my original free African state' (159) belies his self-commodification as well as the sustained presence of slavery as a threat (including the threat of galley slavery in the Mediterranean). This continued presence of exchange written into identity is most strikingly illustrated in the same chapter when Equiano's benefactor, the captain, dies on the voyage and Equiano must steer the ship into port. For all that he offers a fulsome description of his grief, he dryly notes a transfer of reputation: 'When the death of the captain became known, he was much regretted by all who knew him.... At the same time the sable captain [i.e., Equiano himself] lost no fame' (164). On either side of manumission, this is a catalogue of losses and gains – and continues to be up to the account of conversion in which Equiano sees he is 'a great debtor to sovereign free grace' (206).

In the narrative of self-redemption, the slave becomes an economic agent, but more importantly he or she enters a particular narrative structure: not simply the deferral of a fully realized self (a feature of all slave narratives), but an accumulation predicated on an economic self-understanding. The slave asserts a control over the timeless world of the thing and enters what Bataille defines as the bourgeois economy of accumulation, hoarding money against a deferred pleasure. For Bataille, this is an economy characterized by cruelty and a loss of self-presence: the worker is forced to renounce the present and to see every action in terms of its utility; to commodify the self.[42] If the slave narrative also allows us to see the element of pleasure inscribed within this sacrificial logic, Bataille's harsh judgment on *homo economicus* also suggests that there is in fact no terminal point at which the self is freed; the debt is simply incorporated into the modern self, most obviously as a loss of self-presence.

DEBT, NARRATIVE, AND THE SUSPENDED SENTENCE

'They is plenty niggers in Louisiana that is still slaves.'
    Willis Winn, Works Progress Administration interview, 1930s[43]

Every American schoolchild knows that slavery 'ended' with Lincoln's Emancipation Proclamation in 1863 – though, of course, it did not 'end', remaining legal in some states which were not part of the Confederacy and requiring the Thirteenth Amendment to 'abolish' it. The structures of racial exploitation return, notoriously, after the period of Reconstruction: as debt peonage; as contract and vagrancy laws feeding a vast empire of hired 'criminal' labour; as a captive Southern workforce which would be turned back from migration north by armed deputies at the state line.[44] Sharecropping is central to this situation, in which the worker toils with the hope of return only if he or she should 'clear' his or her debt to the landowner at year's end, a debt which was often never to be cleared.[45] Economic re-enslavement was central to the denial of political and legal rights.

The actuality of debt was underscored by a metaphorical structure attached to the Civil War itself. In *Scenes of Subjection*, Hartman explores the way in which the emancipation of former slaves (and, indeed, all African Americans) in the period of Reconstruction was conceived – within both white discourse and some African-American writings – in terms of a blood debt. Even in the 1840s abolitionists suggested that 'blood money' or 'ransom money' would have to be paid to the South to end slavery. The coming of the war made that a literal sacrifice, as Charles Chesnutt pointed out in 1904 when he wrote that the debt has been 'paid in blood and treasure ... the life of one strong, white man for every three black men, women and children held in bondage' – adding that the money spent on the war could easily have purchased every slave, so that the blood debt becomes, implicitly, a catastrophic and baffling potlatch.[46] Notwithstanding the direct and indirect black contribution to the war, notwithstanding the huge historical residue of stolen labour within slavery, notwithstanding its huge legacy of suffering, the former slave was nevertheless seen in terms of the metaphorical debt created by the white blood spilt on the battlefields of Manassas and Gettysburg – and thus as the bearer of a freedom provisional and liable to be rescinded, or as something that must be paid for with a further term of labour and subordination. As Hartman comments on the cultural metaphors, '[T]o be free was to be a debtor – that is, obliged and duty-bound to others'.[47] Orlando Patterson's comments on slavery proper suggest the continuity here: 'The condition of slavery did not absolve or erase the prospect of death. Slavery was not a pardon; it was, peculiarly, a conditional commutation. The execution was suspended only as long as the slave acquiesced in his own powerlessness. The master was essentially a ransomer.'[48]

In this situation, slavery remained under erasure, as an active trace within historical memory, rather than simply being abolished. The Louisiana Civil Code's section dealing with slaves begins:

Art. 155. – There are in this state two classes of servants, to wit the free servants and the slaves.

This is followed by a long list of articles relating to each class. After the South's defeat, the slave articles were not immediately struck out in the 1867 edition, but were supplemented:

An Act to amend Article 155 of the Civil Code of Louisiana. – Approved, Jan 31, 1864.

Sect. 1 *Be it enacted, & c.,* That article one hundred and fifty-five (155) of the Civil Code of Louisiana ... be so amended as to read thus: 'There is only one class of servants in this state, to wit, free servants.'

The former slave is a slave reclassified as free.[49] This rhetorical sleight of hand, even if a temporary expedient, points us towards a structure in which the slave promised freedom in the self-purchase narratives acts as a mirror image of the freed slave in a state of figural 'debt'. Other examples reinforce the sense in which, despite abolition, the legal status of the African American shadows that of the slave: North Carolina anti-entice-ment statues designed to prevent a free labour market used wording taken directly from the Fugitive Slave Law of 1793; the classifications of black convict labourers hired out in chain gangs were taken direct from slavery; and so on.[50]

The African American thus continued to be considered in ways which carried the traces of slavery. One landmark in the long argument about the effaced nature of the black subject in law is *Bailey v. Alabama* (1911), a key case in the Supreme Court's very gradual dismantling of peonage laws, hinging on the unconstitutional role of presumptive evidence in cases of broken annual contracts. The state wished to assert that leaving an employment contract was sufficient evidence to support the prima facie presumption of an intent to defraud the hirer (and thus a criminal act which could bind the black worker back into forced labour). But the Supreme Court insisted that it was not a criminal act to break a contract, and thus that the case violated the Thirteenth Amendment: there could be no presumption about motives, which could encompass a variety of possibilities (exhaustion, disillusionment, frustration, being cheated).[51] At stake was, among other things, a sense of the black subject as a closed book, a pure operator in the racist game of re-enslavement, whose motives and thinking are amenable to an imposed value rather than demanding individual inquiry.

Given this situation, it is understandable that the topic of debt is central to W. E. B. Du Bois's turn-of-the-century analysis of America's race relations. There is the 'slavery of debt' Du Bois chronicles in sharecropping:

The keynote of the Black Belt is debt; not commercial credit, but debt in the sense of continued inability on the part of the mass of the population to make income cover expense. This is the direct heritage of the South from the wasteful economies of the slave *regime*; but it was emphasized and brought to a crisis by the Emancipation of the slaves. In 1860, Dougherty County had six thousand slaves, worth at least two and a half millions of dollars; its farms were estimated at three millions, – making five and a half millions of property, the value of which depended largely on the slave system.... The war then meant a financial crash; in place of the five and a half millions of 1860, there remained in 1870 only farms valued at less than two millions.[52]

Debt is vested in a racial system and has become an inheritance ('The Negro farmer started behind, – started in debt.... Once in debt, it is no easy matter for a whole race to emerge'). An overall Southern debt produced by the end of the slave economy is, with considerable irony, reassigned to the African American. But Du Bois also explores debt as a more metaphorical inheritance. *The Souls of Black Folk* begins with a scene of refused exchange which grounds his metaphor of the 'veil' between black and white:

In a wee wooden schoolhouse, something put it into the boys' and girls' heads to buy gorgeous visiting-cards – ten cents a package – and exchange. The exchange was merry, till one girl, a tall newcomer, refused my card, – refused it peremptorily, with a glance. Then it dawned upon me with a certain suddenness that I was different from the others; or like, mayhap, in heart and life and longing, but shut out from their world by a vast veil.[53]

From that refusal an understanding of the structured failure of exchange is born: the African American is not recognized as an agent. The weight of that negative inheritance falls on Du Bois himself in 'The Passing of the First-Born', where his son's death is an index of primal sacrifice: 'But now there wails, on that dark shore within the Veil, the same deep voice, *Thou shalt forego!* And all have I foregone at that command, and with small complaint, – all save that fair young form that lies so coldly wed with death in the nest I had builded.'[54] The foreclosed future is a primary fact of black existence, interrupting even bourgeois accumulation and inheritance.

It is that '*Thou shalt forego!*' which forms what is a constant threat in African-American texts, a collapse into a deathly repetition and equivalence at the level of narrative. If, in its traditional attachment to the rise of the bourgeoisie, narrative in the novel depends, in economic terms, on a hermeneutic equivalent of investment and hope (on 'Great Expectations' fulfilled; on that personal 'growth' of the bildungsroman), then foreclosure is a denial of the possibilities of a forward investment in the self. The subject can only hope to pay its debts, or see them called in, enacting an already prepared narrative enclosure (this is why the capacious ending of Zora Neale Hurston's *Her Eyes Were Watching God* represents such a firm break with tradition: 'So much of life in its meshes! She called in her soul to come and see').[55]

At the centre of the figuration of debt and foreclosure is lynching: the act which confirms the already guilty status of the black, male body, its collapse into ideological negativity. Orlando Patterson argues that in the South the black body itself could act as a figure for moral deficit, for an enslavement to sin which demanded recompense in the sacrificial logic of lynching.[56] Perhaps the most economical linkage of lynching to narrative and temporal collapse is Charles Chesnutt's conjure tale 'Dave's Neckliss' – a tale so savage that it could not, seemingly, be included in the published volume of the tales (it appeared in the *Atlantic Monthly* in 1889, but was not reprinted in *The Conjure Woman* in 1899).[57] It is not, in fact, a conjure story at all, as its metamorphosis is entirely psychological and metaphorical. As Eric J. Sundquist suggests, in the story of Dave, an educated and self-improving slave who is falsely accused of stealing a ham, Chesnutt maps the bitterness of post-Reconstruction violence and denial of rights back into the context of slavery.[58] After the ham is tied, decaying, to his neck, Dave hangs himself in the smokehouse, 'becoming' ham – the commodity – but also articulating a horrible pun on African origins and biblical justifications of slavery: this Son of Ham collapses metaphor into meat. That is the recursive element of the story; its proleptic meaning, which asserts that the underlying structures are still present, is the link to lynching, available as a punishment for 'uppity' (i.e., self-improving) African Americans in the period of its publication. The narrative collapse – a version of what I described in the introduction as typological mapping – suggests an ideology which even the narrator Julius cannot escape, for all that he is, at the level of the frame narration's comedy, figured as outwitting his white employers and getting the rest of the ham from his employer's wife; his weeping as he eats the ham is properly bitter and biblical: 'My tears have been my meat day and night' (Psalm 42).

Representations of foreclosure are accompanied, in terms of character, by the often ironical threat of what Hurston labelled 'reversion to type'.[59] This is the correlative of James Baldwin's comment that 'segregation ... has allowed white people, with scarcely any pangs of conscience whatever, to *create*, in every generation, only the Negro they wished to see'.[60] Examples include Bigger Thomas's counter-factual declaration that he *is* the rapist of Mary in Wright's *Native Son* (1940); Rufus's 'he was black and the water was black' as he plunges from the George Washington Bridge in Baldwin's *Another Country* (1962); and the repeated question 'Is it Now?' – is the endlessly anticipated eruption of racial violence here? – in Chester Himes's *If He Hollers Let Him Go* (1945). In each of these plots, the black male subject operates under a suspended sentence configured by the logic of lynching: he is already guilty of being black in the wrong place, in the vicinity of a white woman. At the level of plot there is a similar foreclosure: Bigger's being destined for death from an early stage in the novel; *Another Country*'s structuring around the suicide of the black male protagonist and subsequent mourning; and in *If He Hollers* Jones's working out his week as foreman, having been demoted at the beginning of the novel (he is sentenced to the wartime draft by a judge at the end of the week). What each of these offers is an evacuation of the subject into the space prepared for it by the surrounding culture, into the deadly tautologies of race.

We can discuss *Native Son* in more detail. Readers are often shocked when Bigger seals his fate less than a hundred pages into the novel: as he declares after killing Mary, he is a dead man walking. The novel's plot simply concerns the evasion and then enactment of that end. The series of five 'Biggers' whom Wright describes in 'How Bigger Was Born', with their variously bad ends, heightens the sense of inevitability: 'Life had made the plot over and over again, to the extent that I knew it by heart.'[61] The novel's sense of foreclosure is reinforced by the emblematic opening scene, in which Bigger hunts and kills a rat in his family's slum room. Wright reported that he could not find an opening and had started instead with the scene in the pool room (a 'beginning' rather than an 'origin', in Edward Said's terms; historical rather than analogical).[62] The scene that eventually came to him fixes Bigger in place, as he will be at his ending – as his protest to his mother, 'Stop prophesying about me' (9), seems to register.

'Stop prophesying about me'. In that phrase, temporality collapses into the static, pre-fixed image. Much of Wright's commentary on *Native Son* in 'How Bigger Was Born' relates specifically to the photographic or microscopic image: the notion of the author developing 'the shadowy outlines of the negative that lay in the back of my mind' (444); this is linked to the 'flash of lightning illuminating the whole dark inner landscape of

Bigger's mind' (445) – a Bigger who is 'sensitized' and 'left stranded' to register the reality of America. The result is 'an image, a breathing symbol' of American life (450). In the text itself, the communist lawyer Max describes Bigger as 'a symbol, a test symbol' who has been 'stained for examination under the microscope' (383). Wright himself registers 'impressions which crystallized and coagulated into clusters' and were 'automatically stored away somewhere in me' (457). In the famous closing paragraph of his essay, he notes that despite the thinness of the American scene lamented by Hawthorne, James, and others, 'we have in the oppression of the Negro a shadow athwart our national life dense and heavy enough to satisfy even the gloomy broodings of a Hawthorne' (462). Wright's text is in this pervasive imagery a photograph, a deictic image whose chemistry crystallizes in the text, a bringing-forth of what is shadowed. 'Lodged in the heart of this moment is the question of power which time will unfold!' is Max's comment in the courtroom.[63]

Figuring Bigger in this way, Wright proposes the technologically mediated image itself (the image *qua* image) as the emblem of foreclosure, of the fixed or typed. One might compare Marx's well-known image of the phantoms of ideology as a *camera obscura* image and the way in which for Theodor Adorno the photographic image is compromised by the presence of the world as it is; its indexical nature precludes any ideological resistance (and entangles itself with the Hebraic ban on graven images).[64] Indeed, the photograph is equated in Adorno's thinking with the mimesis in the insect world described by Roger Caillois – as a collapse into 'context', in which 'life takes a step backwards' towards the ground from which it emerges, away from the human conceived in terms of freedom. The fading into background described by Caillois is regressive: at best a protective typing, at worst a step towards immobility, death, and the inanimate.[65] The biological basis of Caillois's argument and its linkage – via the figure of the mantis devouring her mate – to notions of sacrifice again place the dark images that Wright conjures in the dangerous ground evoked by the strange concluding comments of *Dialectic of Enlightenment*, in which Adorno refers to the snail and to scarring as that which prevents a 'new form of life' from emerging.

As many readers notice, the political power of *Native Son* derives from its gamble, in the production of this image, with the racist stereotype articulated by the state attorney in the case, for whom Bigger is a violent, sub-human rapist and murderer. Max's plea, with its insistence that Bigger *not* be seen as a victim of 'injustice', that 'guilt', 'sympathy', and 'hate' be removed from the picture, is a plea for an understanding beyond that image, which recognizes the plot imposed by debt. Of the mob he says, 'In their hearts they feel that a wrong has been done and when a negro commits a crime against them, they fancy they see the ghastly evidence of that wrong' (390). Max returns that pre-inscribed and foreclosed debt to white society: 'though his crime was accidental, the emotions that broke loose were *already* there' (392). Thus 'his crime existed long before the murder of Mary Dalton'. At his most extreme, Max figures Bigger as a living corpse haunting white society: the already dead who must be killed again – something figured more explicitly in Morrison's *Beloved*.[66] In its challenge to America, the novel deliberately borders on embracing 'reversion to type' as existential truth: Bigger's growth is figured as an acceptance that as a black man he 'is' a killer and his declaration that his killing was an expression of his deepest self – that what appears in the narrative as accident was no accident, that it creates the only meaning his life has. The strategy, risky in its collapse of self into the logic of an image which is owned by others, is to take the logic of foreclosure and forcibly render it a narrative of enlightenment.[67]

The problem of a blocked inheritance was rearticulated at mid-century in Langston Hughes's *Montage of Dream Deferred* (1951) – and the notion of the fulfilment of a 'dream' has a powerful subsequent history, of course, in the rhetoric of Martin Luther King, Barak Obama, and others. But the logic of foreclosure also suggests a more negatively dreamlike quality in which that which is foreclosed returns as an illegitimate exchange. Bigger Thomas is described as moving like someone in a dream, and Himes's *If He Hollers Let Him Go* is structured around a series of five dreams, each enacting some aspect of the violence of racism and its ineluctable logic (the most striking is the penultimate dream's white boy remorselessly killing his black rival with thousands of pinpricks from a tiny knife).[68] The fixated logic of the racial unconscious is thus counterpoised against the other temporal schemes of the novel: the working week at a Los Angeles shipyard in wartime; and the furious torrent of Bob's emotional life within the racial-sexual vortex he inhabits. For Bob, the message is ultimately the static inevitability of foreclosure signalled in the dreams: 'Nigger, you haven't got a chance' (150). And while Himes's narrator explicitly refuses the violent conflict of *Native Son*, the work is structured by the same nightmare logic: a black man destroyed by sexual proximity to a white woman – moreover, in Bob's case we are reminded that self-consciousness about the issue is of little help. At one point in Himes's novel, there is a discussion of Wright's novel at a middle-class dinner party. The socratic dialogue that ensues with the condescending white social worker Leighton drives Bob towards an assertion that only a violent revolution would change white attitudes, irrespective of the chances of its success; finally 'I cut him off with a sudden violent gesture and jumped to my feet. That broke it up' (89). The spasmodic grammatical and physical curtness, with all the atemporality of the reflex, anticipates the final line of the novel: 'Two hours later I was in the army'. One can see why Himes flew from the narrative foreclosure of the protest and prison novel (his early work) to his peculiarly plotless versions of the detective story, culminating in the almost entirely meandering *Blind Man with a Pistol* with its central metaphor of random violence.

A response to the logic of nightmare is also visible in the way Ralph Ellison maps the threat of lynching onto both nightmare and incest in the 'Trueblood' episode of *Invisible Man*. The incestuous Trueblood is, as his name suggests, a classic 'reversion to type' from the white point of view and is rewarded for his tale of degradation. But in Ellison's satire his multistage nightmare exploits the logic of foreclosure. The story parallels the (white) logic of incest which so fascinates the New England philanthropist Norton – a logic of frozen or non-progressive time. When Trueblood, in his dream, is trapped in a 'big white bedroom' with a screaming white woman, it is a future itself which is blocked: he tries to escape through a door in the clock, which becomes a tunnel and machinery suggestive of his daughter's genitals. Driven from racial trauma to the generational foldings of incest, he accepts the logic of his wife's anger: 'It seems to me that all I can do is take my punishment.... You ain't guilty, but she thinks you is'. Trueblood, like Bigger, accepts the crime he commits as constituting the self, singing his blues and deciding 'I ain't nobody but myself', a phrase which anticipates the narrator's own 'I yam what I am'.[69] The same logic is later articulated, more politically, by Brother Tarp when he explains to the narrator why he was imprisoned in a chain gang: 'I said no to a man who wanted to take something from me; that's what it cost me for saying no and even now the debt ain't fully paid and will never be paid in their terms' (312).

Foreclosure and debt in the most literal sense are also explored in the eviction episode of *Invisible Man* (we will return to another aspect of this in Chapter 5). Here, moments of gathered time are displayed as a kind of informal artwork as the evicted elderly couple's goods are scattered on the pavement, a Cornell Box evoking African-American life since Emancipation: freedom papers, a portrait of Lincoln, a breast pump, blues records – items representing the hopes invested in work and children. The narrator sees an insurance policy stamped 'void'. Even the names which

are eventually applied to the old couple, 'Sister and Brother Provo', suggest both a provisionality of tenure and a failure to provide. The 'shame'
which the narrator sees in the scene stems from a collective understanding
of that inheritance: 'even then in their nineteenth-century day they had
expected little' (219). Brother Jack, as he attempts to recruit the Invisible
Man after his speech, relegates the old couple to 'history', but his diag-
nosis of them as 'living but dead' (236) nicely encapsulates their position
in white society as discarded day labourers. The narrator's question to the
crowd – 'Where did their labour go?' – is thus a deeply Hegelian one:
their labour has failed to accumulate capital or make a world; they have
always worked under the sign of debt.

Indeed, one could say that *Invisible Man* deploys the logic of foreclosure as its larger structure, beginning as it does with an anticipatory dream
of descent and ending with the notion of a deferred self which, having
achieved its voice, has at last been freed from the past – from the train
of events set in motion by the prescriptions of others in the sealed letter ('That he, or anyone at that late date, could have named me and set
me running with one and the same stroke of the pen ...', 457). That the
narrator himself comes to believe that 'humanity is won by continuing
to play in the face of certain defeat' (465) testifies to the power of the pre-
scriptive as the text's occasion ('I can neither file nor forget', 467). Ellison
describes a dream of emergence, a hibernation, in which time hovers on
the brink of its own unlocking.

'LOST TIME': FAULKNER AND FORECLOSURE

The implication of Du Bois's analysis of debt, cited earlier, is that foreclosure in the sense of an arrested development applies to the South as
a whole, for all that it has been transferred to the black population. This
is true in both the economic sense (the lost capital invested in slavery)
and the mythic (the Lost Cause of an Athenian civilization). But the
white South lives in an inverse of the situation of the freed slave: as he or
she is released into a 'debt' linked to the South's desire for recompense,
the South as a whole is left with a future which never happened; which
increasingly recedes into the space of denial and a compensatory fantasy.
The most famous explorer of this fixated time is William Faulkner. Jean-
Paul Sartre memorably wrote of a 'decapitation' of the future in his work,
a 'frozen speed at the very heart of things' in which the past floods and
overwhelms every utterance.[70] Faulkner's sprawling hypotaxis is firmly
anchored to a sense of Southern historiography, expressed in terms of the

suspended sentence. I will discuss *Light in August* and *Intruder in the Dust*, though the figure of temporal fixation is visible throughout Faulkner's corpus, most famously in the collocation of smashed watch and incest in *The Sound and the Fury*.

Light in August is an exploration of African-American identity as it is conceived by the South, in terms of both the 'stain' of blackness carried in the blood and the issue of an imposed racial typology. In one sense that identity is effected in the name of race alone, since Joe Christmas is pale-skinned, and 'black' only by rumour and supposition. He nevertheless enacts the destiny laid down for him by that name: sexual violence directed at a white woman and her murder; pursuit; violent death and mutilation. As he flees, he literally steps into the shoes of an-other, the 'black shoes smelling of negro', which he uses to escape the bloodhounds.[71] Joe is in this sense self-haunting: 'there was too much running with him, stride for stride with him. Not pursuers: but himself: years, acts, deeds omitted and committed, keeping pace with him, stride for stride, breath for breath, thud for thud of the heart, using a single heart' (337). Faulkner adopts the bifurcation of Du Bois's formula for the double self ('two warring ideals in one dark body') and renders it a narrative of temporal collapse in which every action Joe undertakes is countered and drives him on: 'And then the white blood drove him out of there, as it was the black blood which snatched up the pistol and the white blood which would not let him fire it' (337). His seeming acceptance of his fate bears no mollification: when the lawyer Gavin Stevens attempts to offer what amounts to a plea bargain after he is captured (an adjustment of debt), he refuses, instead escaping to be shot and castrated by Percy Grimm. Grimm is a figure who is himself foreclosed, belated in relation to the Great War, 'not alone too late but not late enough to have escaped first hand knowledge of the lost time when he should have been a man instead of a child'. The memories which the text anticipates Joe will leave are themselves part of a temporality which struggles to write a future. This is his death:

It [the blood] seemed to rush out of his pale body like the rush of sparks from a rising rocket; upon that black blast the man seemed to rise soaring into their memories forever and ever. They are not to lose it, in whatever peaceful valleys, beside whatever placid and reassuring streams of old age, in the mirroring faces of whatever children they will contemplate old disasters and newer hopes. It will be there, musing, quiet, steadfast, not fading and not particularly threatful, but of itself alone serene, of itself alone triumphant. (349–50)

The subject of the final sentence's 'it' is ambiguous: logically still the 'pent black blood' of an earlier sentence; but as lodged in 'their memories' it becomes a rocket, a river, a reservoir, and a reflection. It is difficult to read this passage and not recall a famous passages in Bergson's *Creative Evolution* – a book intensely admired by Faulkner – which describes 'the twisting of the will on itself' in which 'we catch a glimpse of a simple process, an action which is making itself across an action of the same kind which is unmaking itself, like the fiery path torn by the last rocket of a fire-works display through the black cinders of the spent rockets that are dead'.[72] This, for Bergson, is the cut which forms life from undifferentiated matter, as existing form is folded back into matter. Faulkner's rewriting of the trope suggests the problem of the fixed image in Southern historiography. While he might be accused of creating a white liberal redemption from the Christ-like suffering and sacrifice of a black man, as Grace Elizabeth Hale and Robert Jackson suggest, it is a peculiarly non-dynamic redemption he imagines, enclosed once again in the static world of the symbol rather than opening up a future.[73]

The story is bracketed by the figure of the minister Hightower, who represents the extremes of temporal fixation, in terms of both his inheritance and his personal history: his reference points are the death of his grandfather and his brief tenure as a minister in Jefferson. Of the former, we are told: 'my life died there, was shot from the saddle of a galloping horse in a Jefferson street twenty years before it was ever born' (359). It is 'as though the seed which his grandfather had transmitted to him had been on that horse too that night and had been killed too and time had stopped there and then for the seed and nothing had happened in time since, not even him' (50). His rejection as minister after his wife's infidelity and suicide means that his life exists outside clock time, subsisting on 'the few crystallizations of stated instances by which his dead life in the actual world had been governed and ordered once' (275). Faulkner says of Hightower that 'he would neither tell, nor depart' (56) – tell, that is, the secrets of the Klan members who beat him and left him in the woods nor depart from his place as a visible wound in the body politic. Nonetheless, Faulkner associates with Hightower an ethical pull towards the future, most visible in his occasional midwifery and his association with Byron Bunch, who will succour Lena Grove, the text's Madonna. The question, one might say, is that of what can be 'fore-given' on the senses offered by the Protestant eschatology Hightower preaches: what is inevitable and written into the fabric of individual and social life; what can be suffered and directed towards new life.

Even more striking is Faulkner's unravelling of the pattern of foreclosure sixteen years later in his 'boy's adventure', *Intruder in the Dust* (1948), a novel which recasts many of the concerns of *Light in August* within the more redemptive mode allowed by both a different genre and intervening history – lynchings declined in the late 1930s, and the first firm federal action against the crime finally came in the period 1946–47. Again the novel centres on a character of mixed race who is a potential lynch victim, dead, the text tells us, as soon as he commits the murder he is accused of. This is Lucas Beauchamp, 'son of one of old Carothers McCaslin's, Edmonds' great grandfather's, slaves who had been not just old Carothers' slaves but his son too'.[74] Lucas is, Margaret Walker commented, the only black character in Faulkner to provide a secure point of identification for the African American: 'Dilsey is a type, and Christmas is a symbol, but Beauchamp is almost a man'.[75] Like Joe Christmas, he refuses to recognize race as Yoknapatawpha sees it: '*He's got to admit he's a nigger*' is the folk view of the case (18).

The novel's young protagonist, Chick Mallison, conceives a 'debt' of shame to Lucas and repays his debt by disproving the allegation of shooting a white man in the back, saving him from the lynching that awaits him. Chick's debt is curious in formation, since while Lucas Beauchamp assists him in a freezing river, he does not (despite the blurb) actually save him; the perception of debt seems to do with the gift more generally – for example, with the food Chick eats while he is warming up in Beauchamp's cabin after the rescue. The location of that cabin and its 'ten acres' is significant: a 'black' inheritance in the middle of a large plantation, a wound signalling that which cannot be 'annealed' (a word Faulkner uses three times in the novel): 'no well-used tended lane leaning to tenant or servant quarters and marked by walking feet but a savage gash half gully and half road mounting a hill with an air of solitary independent and intractable too … an oblong of earth set forever in the middle of the two-thousand-acre plantation like a postage stamp in the centre of an envelope' (8). Even the spatial metaphors here are unbalanced – a postage stamp does not inhabit the centre of a letter, though its presence might be said to be central to its status. This is the shape of the debt: the money offered by Chick and refused, becoming another image of the implacability of race:

Because there was the half-dollar. The actual sum was seventy cents of course and in four coins but he had long since during that first few fractions of a second transposed translated them into one coin one integer in mass and weight out of all proportion to its mere convertible value … because now not only his mistake and its shame but its protagonist too – the man, the Negro, the room, the moment, the day itself – had annealed vanished into the round hard symbol of the coin and he would see himself lying watching regretless and even peaceful as day by day the coin swelled to its gigantic maximum, to hang fixed at last forever in the black vault of his anguish like the last dead and waneless moon. (20–21)

A man who has vanished into a coin is an image of fixation with a recollection of slavery inscribed within it. 'Annealed' in its origins means fired, burnt hard: a glancing allusion, one might think, to the lynching which never happens in the novel – in *Light in August* the fire which burns Joanna Burden, 'so that there was only the fire to look at' (216). More generally, it suggests the process of symbolic fixation ever present in the psychology of Faulkner's Southerners; and perhaps also, given Faulkner's fascination with Shakespeare's play, the haunting return promised by Hamlet's father when he says he has gone to his grave 'unhousled, disappointed, unannealed'.[76]

The novel's temporal structures reflect its concern with the pre-written. Its opening offers a series of temporally suspended sentences typical of Faulkner – that is, sentences which contain within them a double movement, an analeptic-proleptic leap forward from the past of enunciation to a non-specified time of action; a leap which, in Bergsonian fashion, gathers the skirts of time around it as it advances, spilling synonyms which convey a rich temporal plenitude:

[T]hat was when he saw Lucas Beauchamp for the first time that he remembered or rather for the first because you didn't forget Lucas Beauchamp. (6)

… enclosed completely now in that unmistakable odor of Negroes – that smell which if it were not for something that was going to happen to him within a space of time measurable now in minutes he would have gone to his grave never once pondering speculating if perhaps that smell were really not the odor of a race nor actually of poverty but perhaps of a condition. (11)

Even in those sections in which the main plot slackens, the same tug of analeptic-proleptic meditation directed at an inevitable future point operates – for example, in the memory of Chick Mallison's coming-of-age rituals in which he anticipates, and fails to encounter, his mother's resistance, instead experiencing her 'invincible repudiation' of what she will always have lost in advance (125). The mood here could be described as anti-subjunctive, dependent on a tense in which all conditionals are offered and foreclosed, a tense informed by what the novel calls 'shock and amazement and anticlimax' (145).

The capacity to 'endure' which Stevens (like Faulkner himself) attributes to the black American is thus contrasted with the Southern adherence to the recursive, to the drag of the past. Oddly, the phase 'suspension of a sentence' (as in the suspended sentence which hangs over Bigger Thomas or Robert Jones) itself features at one moment in the text of *Intruder in the Dust*. The 'he' here is Chick, and the passage describes his disillusion at the 'face' of a white South which will not admit its error:

But certainly he hadn't expected this: – not a life saved from death nor even a life saved from shame and indignity nor even the suspension of a sentence but merely the grudging pretermission of a date; not indignity shamed with its own shameful cancellation, not sublimation and humility with humility and pride remembered nor the pride of courage and passion nor of pity nor the pride and austerity of grief, but austerity itself debased by what it had gained, courage and passion befouled by what it had had to cope with. (193–94)

'Pretermission' is suggestive: it signifies the act of passing over or neglecting to do something; or of omitting from a narrative; or, in law, of disinheriting an heir. Mississippi will not finally ratify the Thirteenth Amendment until 1995. The violence of the past is passed over rather than confronted or seen as debt; it receives no adequate narrative in this tale, no vested recognition. The syntax itself is suspended: the passage just cited is a small section of a key sentence in the story, which flows for more than two pages before an embedded citation (with short sentences) from Stevens which itself runs a page; the main sentence then flows on unstopped for a page more to the end of the paragraph.

The 'suspended sentence' signals the time of the South. Indeed, the embedded citation from Stevens's speech famously concerns the imagination of a suspended time; the moment before Pickett's disastrous charge at Gettysburg; the moment when 'it's all in the balance' and Southern history is not foreclosed. Again this is the image frozen in the air:

For every Southern boy fourteen years old, not once but whenever he wants it, there is the instant when it's still not yet two o'clock on that July afternoon in 1863, the brigades are in position behind the rail fence, the guns are laid and ready in the woods and the furled flags are already loosened to break out and Pickett himself with his long oiled ringlets and his hat in one hand probably and his sword in the other looking up the hill waiting for Longstreet to give the word and it's all in the balance, it hasn't happened yet, it hasn't even begun yet, it not only hasn't begun yet but there is still time for it not to begin. (194)

Chick Mallison's 'gratitude for the gift of his time' in the human chronicle (193) is finally an investment in the ethics of a narrative unfolding which does not simply repeat the past. The oddest aspect of *Intruder in the Dust* is that in order to advance the time of the South – in order to get the narrative to move beyond its fixations and suspensions – Faulkner must yoke his tale to the genre of the boy's adventure, with all its urgency in uncovering a plot to deprive a man of his life. This said, there is a patent artificiality in the set-up: the unlikely team of boy, elderly widow, and sheriff uncovers only what Lucas more or less knew all along, if he had bothered to tell. Moreover, the energy of the tale centres on un-writing rather than the creation of a story: we hear about why Lucas was suspected of the crime and why he did not do it; but only at the end do we hear in passing the story of 'what really happened' between the warring brothers, with little interest in the psychology or mythic resonance of that story. The obvious comparison with *Huckleberry Finn* – the story of a boy who owes a debt to a slave, of a slave who has been given freedom but whose freedom is deferred and over-written, both by Twain and by Tom Sawyer, that deferral becoming a baroque boy's game of ransom and rescue which Huck must ultimately reject – suggests what Faulkner has *not* chosen to investigate, namely the opening towards anything other than pretermission, passing over or noting a debt rather than finally being able to imagine its disconnection from Southern mythology.[77]

Intruder in the Dust ends with a payment which echoes the four coins Chick has offered Lucas for his food. Lucas offers to pay Chick's uncle, the lawyer Gavin Stevens. Stevens refuses payment, because (unlike Chick) he has not believed in Lucas's innocence; but he accepts two dollars in expenses, which Lucas carefully counts out in coins. The novel then ends: '"Now what?" his uncle said, "are you waiting for now?" "My receipt", Lucas said' (247). This demand – whose fulfilment is outside the text's boundaries, since that is all we have – is a final comment on debt and exchange. Lucas has maintained his freedom; Chick and his helper, Mrs. Habersham, have paid their debts; but Faulkner's text hovers on the threshold of a modernity, a final recognition which it cannot quite admit into its borders.

BEYOND DEBT?

The judicial decisions of the post-war world and the civil rights movement began, finally, to reverse the logic of deferral and foreclosure. Orlando Patterson argues that in Martin Luther King and the Southern Christian Leadership Conference, the radical social message of Christ (rather than the Pauline document of sacrifice and atonement) receives its most potent response.[78] Subsequent African-American thinkers have firmly reversed the logic of debt, insisting that it is *to* their communities that a historical debt is owed. A legacy of harm and stolen labour amply justifies that claim, and the discourse of reparation has, since the 2001 Durban conference, gathered considerable momentum and some mainstream endorsement.[79]

Nevertheless, the logic of foreclosure remains latent, even as it is challenged, in this situation. This is not to articulate the conservative claim that reparation is 'backward-looking' (as if the past has no residue and could be 'let go'). Nor is it to deny that the campaign for reparations acts as a powerful rallying cry for political action directed towards the future. Rather it is to comment that the notion of 'debt' necessarily imposes a plot in which redemption and justice are deferred; it articulates a temporal split between action and fulfilment, and represents – in the spectre of the debt's continuation – a melancholy failure of American society to punctuate the time of loss. This too is pretermission.

The Illinois judgment of 2004 which denied African Americans 'third-party standing to assert the legal rights of their ancestors' has, to be sure, no parallel in the novel, and neither is there a fictional statute of limitations to be overcome.[80] The historiographical fiction which is such a prominent strain of African-American writing of the past thirty years has provided a powerful investigation of the occluded legacy of the past which is free to make claims denied elsewhere.[81] Often this legacy is articulated in terms of a debt owed to the black subject. Just as many slave narratives reproduce the document of manumission, modern novels of slavery often dwell on a financial instrument, attached to a narrative of historical excavation. African-American novels which hinge on the 'opening' of a document or execution of a will (broadly considered) include Ishmael Reed's *Mumbo Jumbo* (in which the 'text' of Jes Grew seeks its realization), Gloria Naylor's *Mama Day* (which opens with a sale document), and Toni Morrison's *The Song of Solomon* (in which one inheritance is reclaimed while another is potentially deathly). Central to that plot is the notion of debt and delay: of a gap between intention and execution which itself signals an understanding of black history in terms of stolen inheritance.

A powerful example of this genre is David Bradley's *The Chaneysville Incident* (1981).[82] The novel's plot is an obsessive return to the place of historical trauma, with little of the redemptive fulfilment or sense of healing or a return to the everyday offered by the haunting narratives of Morrison, Carolivia Herron, and other practitioners of historiographical fiction. The narrator, John Washington, an academic historian, returns to the county of his father's death, which is in turn that of his great-grandfather's, and such is the recursive tide of analogical relation between the two that, in narrative terms, the novel barely moves beyond that point. It begins with a dying man and ends with a vision of a whole company of dead slaves, whose grave markers John and his white girlfriend, Judith, literally stumble over.

This narrative fixation on the living past is explored initially through John's inheritance from his bootlegging father, Moses – and through him that of the great-grandfather C. K. Washington, also a bootlegger, who led slaves from captivity through Pennsylvania (the grandfather Lamen's story barely appears in the novel, suggesting the post-Reconstruction era's shadowed status). John's inheritance is conceived in terms of the mystery of the father's death (there are hints of murder, though John eventually understands that it is suicide) and a complex testament, held by a patriarchal white judge, which John does not discover until halfway through the novel. That inheritance is initially expressed through ledger books and debts paid and returned – Moses' considerable local power is based on his accumulated information about prohibition era hypocrisy as well as his wealth – but broadens to include a historical accounting which encompasses the legacy of slavery and its continued presence. At the centre of the book – at the opening of the central binding on page 205, as it happens – is an act of historical understanding in which John opens his father's sealed folio by lamplight in the unwired attic, meditating on how the specifics of lamp and electric light yield different ways of writing and different truths. That understanding ultimately leads the historian away from his sources into fiction. C. K.'s story literally ends with (and thus hinges on) a suspended sentence: a diary entry for 23 December 1859, 'a period at the end of the sentence' (367), and then no more, leaving his fate a mystery. That mystery that can be answered only by the act of imaginative engagement which John undertakes at the novel's end, filling in the gaps by telling Judith the imagined but true story of C. K.'s suicide, faced with the choice of capture or death on his last slave-rescue mission.

Moses Washington in Bradley's novel is, as his name suggests, a prophetic figure concerned with his legacy: 'I sometimes thought he could see into the future', the judge says (201). Yet that ability to see the pattern of time is inextricably linked to a concern with the past – Moses' fascination, since boyhood, with his grandfather C. K. That in turn leads to suicide, conceived as a rejoining of his ancestors. Moses' suicide and the investment involved are never fully explained; indeed, in some ways his death is presented as under-motivated, as a foreclosure in the sense we have discussed. He is a proud autodidact with few friends, who enjoys manipulating others, including his own family. But he is also described as a hunter attuned to the presence of the dead who has been in search of his grandfather since he was sixteen: not in search of the man's traces, his son insists, the gravestones and archival material of the historian, nor in search of his ghost, but in pursuit of *him*, a real presence (387). The final acts of the novel are of self-abandonment: the historian burning his file cards, understanding that his father 'gave' his life to the wind, to the voices of the past.

John, the narrator, does not follow his two ancestors into death, and instead we are offered a hint of rapprochement with Judith, whose status as psychologist and prompter of John's final narrative act ('forget the facts') offers a counter to the narrator's harsh sense of race relations. The novel thus exempts itself from the deathly closure – the drive back to the primal scene of racial violence – which it investigates. And yet the notion of inheritance has been so radically linked to the history of slavery in all that comes before this moment that the reader is left with little sense of a possible development outside the novel's frame. John leaves his father's documents in the cabin he has been living in 'for the next man who would need them' (431), and we wonder who that would be: cyclically, a son from whom he would conceal the story, as his father did? The quest is gendered as masculine, as it is in Morrison's *Song of Solomon*, though in a way that seems unthinkingly patriarchal: mothers barely feature in Bradley's genealogy. Manhood is linked to an ability to force an uncovering of the past, but a future seems harder to see in the novel. If we ask, 'What will John do with his father's inheritance?' in terms of understanding, economics, or social life, there is no clear answer.

There is often a similar moment of 'pause' or suspended time at the ending of African-American novels: the promise to return to the world in *Invisible Man*; the airplane's descent in Baldwin's *Another Country*; the leap which ends Morrison's *Song of Solomon*; the closed book in Bradley's *The Chaneysville Incident*; the moment just before the new century in Naylor's *Mama Day*. Often, these moments signal a narrative uncertainty: a quest relating to the past has been fulfilled, and often a truth has emerged and a debt identified or even partially paid; but the difficulty of moving beyond the narrative of debt is also thematized. Debt binds the subject as trauma itself does; it posits an excess located in the past, a pretermission which cannot be easily undone.

I want to finish with a brief discussion of an African-American text in which debt is reconfigured in particularly interesting ways: as the signature of the human. In Octavia E. Butler's *Xenogenesis* trilogy (1987–89), the earth has been devastated and rendered toxic by nuclear war. Those who awaken in the care of the Oankali owe their survival to the aliens and must accommodate themselves to that debt – a debt whose payment is described by the Oankali themselves in terms of 'trade', by which they mean the coercive genetic intermingling or hybridization they need to

continue (a situation, of course, redolent of slavery).[83] The literalization of
the metaphors of slavery in the situation is projected onto Lilith Iyapo, the
black protagonist of the first volume and mother of the first hybrid child;
it is ultimately also reflected in a group of human separatists who refuse
to acknowledge the debt and are allowed to move off and live in isolation
on Mars. At the same time, the narrative of the trilogy – which spans
three generations of human–alien interbreeding – both refuses debt as its
subject matter in favour of a reciprocal trade in which all are (more or
less forcefully) implicated and refuses a plot in which freedom is achieved
and an essential 'humanity' affirmed. Lilith's initial, desperate concern is
that the next generation will not be human: 'That's what matters. You
can't understand, but that *is* what matters.'[84] But by the end of the trilogy
she is a deeply involved matriarch of a hybrid and continually changing
community which includes a living village and a living spacecraft, with
multi-generational and multi-sexual offspring. This is partly because of
the persistently coercive powers of the Oankali to offer humans pleasure
and closeness, so that 'trade' seems almost a kind of 'Xenophilic' addiction.[85] Nevertheless, the reader of the trilogy is also gently drawn into a
form of 'thinking-alien' in which the human is subsumed to the ongoing
power of life, community, and genetic productivity. At the trilogy's end,
the unhybridized and genetically damaged Mars settlers are a sterile irrelevance, their struggle likely to lead nowhere because of the unaltered and
violent 'contradictions' of human nature; the reader's concern is instead
with a complex family of hybrids with a difficult but open future. That
the debt has been transferred to the earth itself is something of a problem – it will be stripped to equip the next leap into space, as Africa was
stripped of people and resources, one might say – but the point of the text
is the drive towards the survival of life itself, beyond the question of race
or the human.

Butler's work, with its imagination of inter-species productivity and
trade, testifies to the difficulty of removing debt from a text founded on a
history of catastrophe and redemption. It is interesting in this respect that
Butler's final work, the posthumously published vampire novel *Fledgling*
(2005), climaxes in a long trial in which a debt for both intra- and inter-
species racism among its subjects is finally paid (though it is a debt that
remains denied by some and accepted by others).[86] *Fledgling* is akin to
Xenogenesis in that it redistributes the elements of racial history among
different species: vampires, or 'Ina', have always lived in close love relations with groups of humans ('symbionts') whom they effectively capture through their venom but whose lifespans they double (in both these

respects they are akin to the Oankali). Race, properly considered, enters this system as an outside factor, mirroring the way 'race' becomes denaturalized at the end of the twentieth century: the young Shori in the novel is the part-human and 'black' product of genetic experiment undertaken to allow vampires to walk in the sun, her memory destroyed by the newly discovered racist violence of other vampires and their human allies. In a loose parallel with the Middle Passage, she wakes to a world in which her family has been shattered by that violence, and begins to seek both her own past and justice: 'My family was destroyed, and I couldn't even grieve for them properly because I remembered so little' (100). As for other characters in Butler's oeuvre, race is catastrophic as an idea, but also bound up with, rather than separable from, the tangled braids of connection between different 'races'. At the end of *Fledgling* the 'racist' vampires (who are contemptuous of human life as well as Shori and her family) are punished, though it seems Butler planned to write follow-up novels in which that apparent closure would necessarily be complicated.

The first two chapters of this study have dealt with the way in which the slave is forced towards a form of identity which is abstracted, monetized, negotiable; produced by the occlusion of agency and future. In the two chapters which follow, we pursue the consequences of the use of human instruments: ways of thinking which equate machines and slaves and which distinguish the human masters of instruments from instruments themselves – the mind from the tool. We also open, in Chapter 4, a topic which becomes important in the final two chapters of the book: the internal status of the subject of these metaphors and, more generally, the way the inheritance of suffering attached to slavery is conceived. Just as debt cannot readily be disentangled from the history of slavery and its aftermath, the way the self and its trajectory are imagined is marked by that history. In Butler's *Xenogenesis* novels, as in Bradley's work, at the point where a debt might be considered to be paid, identity remains attached to the history of that debt; it is carried within the self in terms of the coercive internal negotiations it has occasioned, which are literalized in the novel as sociobiology or genetics.[87] That internal legacy has imposed a particular burden on those who carry the inheritance of slavery, but as we saw with Du Bois and Faulkner, it is also a more general burden, an indebtedness which evokes the total inheritance of a slave society.

CHAPTER 3

Machines inside the Machine: Slavery and Technology

[C]an we not, black and white, rich and poor, look forward to a world of Service without Servants?

W. E. B. Du Bois, *Darkwater*

Early in Harriet Beecher Stowe's *Uncle Tom's Cabin* the slave George has been hired out for factory work, where he invents a labour-saving device for cleaning hemp. His owner, Harris, visits and George – throughout depicted as a figure of active intelligence, in terms of a racial stereotyping of the 'mulatto' – enthusiastically shows him around, but in doing so creates a sense of unease which culminates in his removal from the factory:

'But, Mr. Harris,' remonstrated the manufacturer, 'isn't this rather sudden?'
'What if it is? – isn't the man *mine*?'
'We would be willing, sir, to increase the rate of compensation.'
'No object at all, sir. I don't need to hire any of my hands out, unless I've a mind to.'
'But, sir, he seems peculiarly adapted to this business.'
'Dare say he may be; never was much adapted to anything that I set him about, I'll be bound.'
'But only think of his inventing this machine,' interposed one of the workmen, rather unluckily.
'O yes! a machine for saving work, is it? He'd invent that, I'll be bound; let a nigger alone for that, any time. They are all labor-saving machines themselves, every one of 'em. No, he shall tramp!'[1]

George is punished for overturning hierarchy ('What business had his slave to be marching round the country, inventing machines, and holding up his head among gentlemen?') and returns to the 'meanest drudgery'. But more fundamentally, he is mocked for exposing his own condition, both representing and challenging it by turning himself into an equivalent of the 'workmen' who might ameliorate their labour (as opposed to his *being* labour). In an argument shaped by Stowe to reflect widespread claims about the ignorance and backwardness of the South, the human

70

machine is preferred to technology, at least in part because technology might displace the human machine. Indeed, in a tradition that derives from Aristotle, the power to direct slaves ('anything that I set him about') is itself figured as *techne*.

What this signals is an entanglement of the slave and machine in which the Lamarckian understanding of technology as inheritance and evolution – the question of adaptation and invention so characteristic of nineteenth-century thinking – is set against the static body of the slave. Slavery blocks technological and economic development, Stowe implies. But correspondingly because the slave is 'a labour-saving machine' the question of human labour and the human scale is imported into techno-logical debate.

In this chapter, I will explore the isomorphism between the slave and the machine, and in particular the uncertainties raised by Aristotle's depic-tion of the slave as an extension of the will and actions of the master. Machines might replace slaves, but is the machine required to remain a slave in some senses? How does the issue of consumption relate to the fig-ure of the slave-machine? I will discuss two traditional ways of thinking about technology: as an extension of the body (the tool or prosthetic sup-plement), on the one hand, and as a substitution for the human, poten-tially outside its scale (the freestanding machine), on the other – though one might keep in mind that this distinction, a commonplace in Marx and others, has been questioned by George Canguilhem, who insists that *all* machines exist in a reciprocal relation to human bodies.[2]

ANCIENT SLAVERY AND TECHNOLOGY

In 1932 the psychoanalyst Hanns Sachs left Berlin, where he experienced the beginnings of Nazi persecution, and settled in Boston. A year later, as if to celebrate his move to the New World, he published a paper enti-tled 'The Delay of the Machine Age'. It appeared in the same issue of the *Psychoanalytic Quarterly* as the first English translation of Viktor Tausk's 1919 paper on the influencing machine, which it aimed to complement.[3] Sachs's paper attempted to explain why the Greeks and Romans had mathematics and science but no real mechanical culture. His explanation is ... well, I will introduce a delay of my own here, and return to it in a moment, because Sachs enters into a major diversion aimed at refut-ing one traditional answer: *slavery*. 'Since so many humans were avail-able for arbitrary and reckless exploitation', the idea he contests runs, 'the stimulus for efforts to displace human labor through the forces of nature

was lacking'. Reviewing the literature, Sachs argues that the Romans were
short of slaves, making them costly; he also notes that, in contrast with
the Greeks, the Romans freed and integrated many slaves. So they *did*
have strong motives to replace human labour.

Sachs counters an argument that has, in various forms, had much support among philosophers of technology, both before and after his paper.
There is a particularly strong French tradition: it was proposed in 1938
by P.-M. Schuhl in *Machinisme et Philosophie*; by André Aymard again
in 1959 in his essay 'Stagnation technique et esclavage'; and perhaps most
forcefully by the philosopher Marc Chapiro in his essay 'Liberty and the
Machine', published in *Diogenes* in 1962. Chapiro argued that only with
the abandonment of slavery does the stimulus to replace labour become
intense, not least because slavery is founded on the Aristotilean contempt
for labour – indeed, for all questions of technique: 'Seneca stressed the
fact that all inventions of his time, like the use of transparent window-
panes, central heating, shorthand, were without exception the work of
the vilest of slaves.'[4] Chapiro notes that many industrial inventions have
been produced by workers and artisans rather than by capitalists: by those
who have a motive to reduce their labours. In this argument labour substitution is central to technological development. In matching fashion,
technological development was seen to eliminate slavery: a proposition
stated at its baldest by Gerald Piel, publisher of *Scientific American*, in
the early 1960s: 'Slavery was the technological underpinning of high civilization and of history until very recent times. Slavery was abolished only
when the biological energy of man was displaced by mechanical energy in
the industrial revolution'. Thus 'slavery became immoral when it became
technologically obsolete.'[5]

Many historians have shared this understanding of ancient slavery as
inhibiting technological development. F. W. Walbank, in *The Decline of
the Roman Empire in the West* (1946), stressed that slavery weakens industry, and more recent writers have echoed that view and broadened it to
later slave systems. M. I. Finley summarized the argument in this way
in 1960: 'most experts seem to be agreed in the present century that slavery was the key factor in restricting scientific progress and particularly in
blocking technological advance in antiquity.'[6] More recently Seymour
Dresher writes, 'Both the classical and the Caribbean worlds, distinguished
by dependence on slavery, were tarnished by demographic, technological
and intellectual stagnation.'[7] At the same time, the idea that the classical
world had no real interest in science and technology in any applied sense
has been contested for its massive simplification of a huge period which

we know only in glimpses – one recent overview of Greek and Roman science and technology, for example, barely pauses to dismiss the slavery hypothesis, while documenting a fairly extensive range of machines.[8] Even in the heyday of the 'slavery' thesis, writers noted the importance of other factors, including the lack of coal and iron in the Mediterranean world. Finley, in a more recent article, suggests that technological innovation in the ancient world had to be related to the connection of wealth to land and political power rather than innovation; the lack of investment capital; and the profitability of servile labour and the scarcity of free hired labour. Nevertheless, he stresses that attitudes are important: 'The pejorative judgements of ancient writers about labour, and specifically about the labour of the artisan, and anyone who works *for* another, are too continuous, numerous, and unanimous to be dismissed as empty rhetoric.'[9] In a lucid discussion which refuses any easy causal relation (either way) between technology and slavery, Aldo Schiavone points out that 'the entire social and mental configuration of the ancient civilizations' is bound up with the issue.[10]

If the knotted arguments here form a constellation rather than a clear causality (as Finley points out, technology in the West stagnated well past the end of the Roman Empire, into the late Middle Ages; and as Schiavone adds, 'the most notable period of technological progress in antiquity … coincided almost completely with the apogee of slavery'),[11] the issue of slavery has unarguably been central to the way labour has been conceived in its relation to technology. What seems to be at stake is often less the truth of the hypothesis about slavery's effects than the inevitability of the yoking of the two terms 'machine' and 'slave'. The human instrument is at the core of notions of an original technicity, as Lewis Mumford stressed in 1934 in *Technics and Civilization*:

Before inventors created engines to take the place of men, the leaders of man had drilled and regimented multitudes of human *beings*: they had discovered how to reduce men to machines. The slaves and peasants who hauled the stones for the pyramids … the slaves working in the Roman galley … these were all machine phenomena.[12]

In 'The Delay of the Machine Age' Sachs, however, firmly rejects the hypothesis of slavery's inhibition of technology. When he does turn to his own explanation of the delay of the machine age, he distinguishes tools, which represent a prosthetic extension of human organs and which antiquity did have (ballistae and the like), from machines which replace men: 'those complicated machines which, once set in motion, do the work alone, so that man ... need only play the role of the master-mind in control'. The question then becomes, why were the latter not developed?

His answer – which I deferred earlier – is offered as a contribution to the psychoanalytic understanding of culture and history. For the ancient world, he proposes, the independent machine was uncanny, an object of fear for 'peoples whose narcissism was more strongly developed than ours and more directly related to the body-ego' – evidence for this narcissism being the Greek interest in the wholeness of the body, the (supposed) narcissism of homosexuality, and religious and aesthetic practices which centred on the figure of man. Noting Tausk's work on the influencing machine in schizophrenia, which represents a delusional and narcissistic projection of the self into the outside world, Sachs stresses that the Greeks, in an opposite manner, rejected any move towards the machine; they rejected any animation of the object, and correspondingly (here I am extrapolating from his argument) they disavowed any notion of technology in the self of the kind represented by Freud's Schreber: they refused to let technology enter the human frame. Hence any machines invented were diverted to play, as in Hero of Alexandria's treatises, and – here the argument loops alarmingly – slaves were used 'as' machines:

If, as Pliny the Elder laments, there had to be alien eyes, alien memory of which the ruling classes pampered by the advances of civilization availed themselves, then at least let them be human eyes and ears – sense organs like their own, but not preterhuman machines.... The slave who was used as a machine was, nevertheless, still an actual human being, not an animated anthropoid automaton. (419)

This refers to an earlier passage in which Sachs notes that there is little sense that slavery is wrong in antiquity, but cites a famous dissenting view from Pliny's *Natural History*: 'We walk with another's feet; we see with another's eyes, we greet by another's memory; we live by another's work ... only pleasures do we keep for ourselves.'[13] The slave threatens to supplant the human; the machine might do so more decisively.

Sachs's argument is at once intriguing and problematic. Pliny's remark, which was in fact about skilled Greek doctors rather than slaves doing manual work, is wrenched from context onto which Sachs's 'there had to be' is imposed: it is simply assumed that slaves and machines are equivalent 'others'. The idea that the machine is a challenge to Greek narcissism is not particularly convincing. Why should a crude machine threaten the perfection of the human body? Why narcissism should not more directly take the route proposed by Tausk – *into* the machine, as in fascist thinking – is not clear. The fear of the automaton – for Freud a doppelganger effect in which the human body is replaced by technology – hardly seems to apply to a railway train. The *psychoanalytic* argument hinges on the uncanniness of the machine as an exteriorization of the human body, as in the influencing machine or the automaton (and this as a narcissistic figure, whether defence for the paranoid or threatening fantasy for others). What governs this tangled set of claims is, in part, the relation of the machine to the human body. The tool, ballistae, and the slave are allowed, because they are seen as extensions of the human body. The freestanding machine threatens it. Why is this? Because it is uncanny, 'an animated anthropoid automaton' – a definition of the machine which seems very peculiar and in the classical period could apply only to crudely animated statues and the like. In fact, what might much more accurately be described as 'an animated anthropoid automaton' in Greek thought is the slave.

There is thus a paradox at the heart of Sachs's argument: our response to one such set of machines is used to explain the absence of another, conceptually different set. The argument confuses locomotives and robots. Sachs begins by assuming that slaves and machines *are* in some ways equivalent (in order to argue that the Roman's shortage of slaves *should* have meant the development of machines, but for inhibition). He ends his argument by saying that because slaves are in other ways *not* equivalent to machines, they can be used to substitute for human labour. So the slave *is and is not* equivalent to a machine. Human and not-human, machine and not-machine, the slave is the contradictory entity which allows the uncanny substitution of the human by the machine to be avoided.

It helps here to go back to Aristotle on slavery and to the two rather separate accounts of slavery which lie implicit in the *Politics*. In one, the slave is naturally a slave and, by virtue of physical and moral superiority, the master is a master; the actions of the slave are an extension of the master's will, and he or she has no independent existence: 'the slave is in a sense part of his master, a living but separate part of his body' (*Politics* 1255b4, p. 73).[14] Latin writers were to describe the slave as *instrumentum vocale*, the speaking instrument. In the other Aristotelian conceptualization of slavery, the slave and the master are further apart; their relation is not 'natural' but produced by law and power, and what defines the relationship is the master's knowledge of how to manage slaves – a *technical* knowledge. But Aristotle adds that an overseer might act for his master, looking after other slaves and freeing the master to pursue philosophy or statecraft (*Politics* 1255b30, p. 75). Since this overseer can himself be a slave, this definition can be held in place only by a technical *praxis*; it cannot be founded on a natural superiority. It in this act of possible delegation that I would place

Sachs's sense of uneasy contradiction: if the slaveholder detaches himself from work to free his mind (and almost tautologically the mind *is* freedom here), then his bodily organs, in Pliny's formula, can become alienated – and what then of the claim to superiority 'in nature'? If a slave can be a slave-manager, what then of the claim to technique?

We might speculate that what if anything was uncanny in the machine for the Greeks was not so much that it compromised narcissism as that it exposed the logic of slavery: the fact that slaves are not machines. Perhaps for this reason, Aristotle is keen to depict the slave as bound to the master as an instrument, an extension of the master's body: the slave is 'one of the tools which minister to action' rather than a productive tool (*Politics* 1254a1, p. 65). Despite the fact that ancient Greeks did use slaves in mining and industry – and, indeed, slaves were central to the whole Mediterranean economy – they are attached by Aristotle to the *household* and its economy. As such, slaves belong (as Hannah Arendt insists) to the world of repetitive labour and consumption rather than production and making. I would propose, then, that the best way to understand Sachs's argument is to see it not as directed at narcissism threatened by the machine, but instead (as the Pliny citation suggests) as *invested in* the slave. The slave confirms the master's power and locates that power close to his body in the household. Where the threat of the freestanding machine might arise is in emblematizing the potential independence of the slave, undermining his or her status as an instrument conceived in terms of the human body.

We might turn here to a largely forgotten account of technology provided by Jack Lindsay, a man of letters, biographer, novelist, and classicist whose work spans the period from his arrival in the United Kingdom from Australia in 1926 to his death in 1990. The magnum opus of Lindsay as a classicist was *Blast Power and Ballistics: Concepts of Force and Energy in the Ancient World* (1974), dedicated to the idea that the Greeks were interested in one particular technology, ballistics, because it was modelled on the force of the gods: striking from a distance like fire from heaven.[15] For Lindsay in what is a classic of Marxist cold war analysis, this is the ultimate source of modern notions of action at a distance: rockets and atomic weapons; one might add both the pleasures of remote weaponry recently described by Paul Virilio and others and even the 'tele-touch' of the Internet, in which one can, at a click, gain possession of a remote object.[16] The implication is that only tools which were akin to the slave – an extension of the human body and its operations – were of interest. The power to make war, the power to direct slaves: these are alike – evidence of *thymos*, of superiority.

Lindsay, when he comes to slavery, follows a familiar route in linking it to a lack of incentive to mechanize. But more interesting is his understanding of the Platonic *eidos* as making the consumer a judge of an item more important than the maker, who is merely imitating an ideal form: 'he does not know its *eidos* (its function, its purpose, its full nature).' For Aristotle, too, 'only the consumer fully appreciates the end or purpose of the object; the craftsman's activity deals with the means' (344, 412). This has two consequences: firstly, a link is forged between a stress on the judgment of the consumer, on the one hand, and the notion of alienated labour, on the other; and secondly, the maker is thus bound to a conservative notion of the pre-existing form, the limits of which he observes: 'And this idea of limits, which has far-reaching effects in the whole realm of thought, comes back to the concept of the craftsman as little more than a thing, defined by his own tools, and the full extension of the concept into the slave as worker, the slave who is juridicially a thing' (412–13) – hence the passage in Aristotle in which a property is 'a mass of instruments' and the slave or assistant is a tool. The Aristotelian account of the thing locked into its own potentiality for fulfilment thus exists, Lindsay suggests, outside 'energy as a dynamical aspect of work', and the result is the lack of a clear account of technological evolution as well as a paucity of technological development (417). Here once again the slave acts as a point of blockage in a general account of technology.

MACHINES REPLACING SLAVES? AMERICAN HISTORY

The argument on 'delay' which Sachs attempted to counter has, of course, a particular American resonance, since a traditional account of the underdevelopment of the South has placed slavery and modernity in tension.[17] This is a field riddled with dispute, but most historians have tended to agree that slave workers were less efficient than their free Northern counterparts; that the cost of slaves produced an inflexible use of investment capital; and that even where slavery was applied profitably to industrial enterprises like mining or steel-making, the need for discipline and stability meant that techniques remained relatively stagnant. There were problems in Taylorizing a workforce whose fundamental conditions of labour involved coercion.[18] Gavin Wright argues that the key element here is the capitalization of the slave: even in areas where slave and free labour can be compared directly, the sheer investment in ownership of slaves precludes the technological development which was the obvious path for Northern proprietors. Wright suggests that the advantage of slavery for the South was the flexibility of labour (slaves could be made to move on to better soil at will, to work through the night at peak times, to work as families, etc.) rather than efficiency per se.[19]

Focusing more generally on Southern ideology, however, John Ashworth identifies inhibiting factors, including 'a widespread concern about industrialization; a fear that it might prove incompatible with the maintenance of southern slave society'. He concludes:

The problems in generating a work ethic, a possible reluctance to entrust slaves with expensive tools and machinery, the difficulties of controlling them in an industrial environment, the higher status attached to the plantation life, and the tendency towards local and plantation self-sufficiency in agriculture [rather than specialization] – some or all of these factors constrained southern industrialization.[20]

There was more diversity in Southern positions than this might suggest, however. As Elizabeth Fox-Genovese and Eugene D. Genovese point out, just as the idea that 'slavery undermined Roman military spirit and contributed to imperial decline' was contested by many Southern intellectuals, so too was the idea that slavery made the South unsuitable for technology.[21] In the period after 1840, many Southern reformers were convinced that the South could develop a strong industrial economy and stressed that it was modernizing fast.[22] The notion that a particular technological innovation (or yoking of slave and machine), Whitney's cotton gin, 'stuck' and prolonged slavery is embedded in Southern myth.[23]

The largest-scale example of industrialization within slavery was sugar production in Louisiana, where shift management, on-site dormitories, and flow production linked to steam power were all used by 1850.[24] Other places where industrial techniques were used included the Maryland Chemical Works, the Tredegar Iron Foundry, and the railroads – often with specific incentives to encourage fast work. But as Richard Follet notes, attempts to impose 'clock time and factory discipline' elsewhere stuttered; slaveholders 'reverted to the whip and either chose the simplest tools for production or, convinced of their slave's indifference to care-intensive work, declined to innovate'.[25] The situation was exacerbated by slaves' reputation for breaking all but the crudest tools and the reluctance of slaveholders to invest (Northern factories made lines of cheap tools especially for the Southern market). Slaves were often prohibited from engaging in skilled labour; and where they were used in skilled jobs, invention was not encouraged – as in Stowe's novel. To be sure, masters could show more enlightened attitudes (Genoese reports a case of a master overruling a scornful overseer on a slave's innovation), and slaves made significant contributions to the agricultural technology of the South.[26] But technological innovation existed in an uneasy relation to disciplinary needs: slave owners could comment, in a manner akin to George's master in Stowe's novel, that 'the introduction of new and better equipment merely made both white overseers and black laborers lazy'.[27] As Nicholas Bromell comments, for the slave there was no experience outside slavery, outside instrumentality.[28]

Perhaps the oddest version of the technology thesis – perhaps best thought of as an attempt to deflect it – occurs in the work of George Fitzhugh, the maverick apologist for slavery whose vision of cannibalism was noted in Chapter 1. In *Sociology for the South* (1854), Fitzhugh argues that it is *trade*, not slavery, which produces Southern underdevelopment, since trade is itself a kind of dependence or slavery – a reliance on others to do one's work. His example is not the American, however, but the *African* who 'ceases to smelt iron when he finds a day's work in hunting for slaves, iron or gold, will purchase more and better instruments than he can make in a week'.[29] In this curious chain of argument African slaving is, incidentally, a substitute for technology; it inhibits technique because it is trade, not because it replaces labour. At the same time, Fitzhugh's story acts as an unwitting metaphor for the South as a whole, addicted to slaving and luxury rather than its own development.

Unsurprisingly, the equation of slave body and machine also runs through abolitionist discourse – the idea that, in another version of the logic of substitution, machines would drive out slavery. As David Brion Davis points out, Aristotle's 'shuttle' passage was 'seized upon by nineteenth-century reformers' in order to assert the transience of the 'Slave Power'.[30] The inefficiency of slave labour was taken as a given from the arguments of Adam Smith and a variety of abolitionist economists. Mechanization would inevitably mean the need for crude slave labour. The invention of devices 'that transformed the use of animal motor power' has thus been closely linked to abolition.[31] An example is provided by what might be called the mythical origins of the motor car: engineer George Dumbell's pamphlet published in London in 1799 – possibly the earliest discussion of the modern internal combustion engine. Its catchy title runs *The Commercial Aqueduct, a Plan for Improving the Port of London; with a Descriptive Engraving, and Some Remarks on the Panergicon, a Chymical Power, Capable of Being Used to Great Mechanical Advantage in Carrying This Plan into Effect, as Well as Those which Relate to the Intended Docks in the Isle of Dogs and Gravesend Tunnel, and also Capable of Greatly Ameliorating the Slave Trade.* The

'Panergicon' is a liquid fuel, probably the 'spirits of tar' (a by-product
of coking), which Robert Street had patented for use in an engine five
years earlier in London – enabling, according to one standard history of
internal combustion (which overlooks Dumbell's pamphlet), the development of a liquid fuel motor.[32] Dumbell's motor requires no boiler,
condenser, or brickwork; it consists simply of a piston with arm and a
cylinder into which inflammable liquid is injected and exploded. The
resulting portability, he says, will make it particularly useful in replacing
slave labour: 'the unquestionable advantages it will yield to the Planters,
must be deemed very inferior objects when compared with its probable
effects in ameliorating the conditions of slaves, and diminishing the
necessity which is urged for violating the rights of humanity.'[33] If planters in the West Indies argued that slaves were an economic necessity,
then their eventual replacement would simply be a matter of finding the
right machines for the conditions.[34]

Pro-slavery writers were quick to rebut this line of argument, pointing
out that mechanization in the North and the United Kingdom produced
the system of subordination they labelled 'industrial slavery', whereas
the South's benevolent patriarchy supposedly involved life-long care. But
even here, the slave remained conceptually aligned with the machine. The
equivalence of slave and automaton was assumed by Edward Everett, the
Governor of Massachusetts, when he noted in 1837 that British steam
power was the equivalent of a million workers:

What a population! So curiously organized that they need neither luxuries nor
comforts; that they have neither vices nor sorrows; subject to an absolute control,
without despotism; laboring night and day for their owners, without the crimes
and woes of slavery ... annually lavishing the product of one million pairs of
hands, to increase the comforts of the fifteen or twenty millions of the human
population.[35]

Technological underdevelopment continued to characterize the post-
Reconstruction South up to the New Deal. As Jay Mandle suggests,
few efforts were made to solve the technological problems involved in a
cotton-picking machine until the First World War created a shortage of
labour – at which point productivity rose steeply from 269 man-hours per
bale in 1920 to 57 man-hours per bale in 1960. Richard Godden comments
that 'machinery could only disrupt a social and political order founded on
the owner's capacity to pay low across the board'.[36] The South was, as one
writer put it in 1935, still the 'machine's last frontier'.[37] In such formulas,
the historical alignment of slave and machine remains unchallenged, and
technology remains linked to the power to direct labour.

WASHINGTON, ELLISON, DU BOIS: MACHINES
INSIDE THE MACHINE

Many writers have pointed out the way in which texts about slavery explore the status of the object, and the animation of the object, implicit in chattel slavery.[38] Less has been said about the more specific question of the status of tool attributed to the slave in the classical theory of slavery. As we have seen, between the tool as autonomous agent and the tool as extension of another's will is the zone of uncertainty created by the slave's human existence – a zone in which Sachs saw a threatened narcissism. I want to explore these issues by turning to African-American writers on technology and their response to the complex web of ideas I have been examining.[39] The end of slavery meant, if nothing else, the end of slaves. African Americans might be violently exploited and deprived of rights, but they could no longer be so nakedly conceived as the instruments of others. In this situation, the question of what relation former slaves would have to the tool or the machine became an urgent one. How would the uncomfortable equivalence spoken of in Stowe's story be supplanted, rendered productive?

One possibility is, of course, the seamless incorporation of the master–slave metaphor within technological discourse. As Ron Eglash notes, this happened as early as 1904, when the master–slave distinction was used in double-pendulum clocks: the 'free pendulum' in the vacuum (not powering a dial) has the precision and 'corrects' the working one, and is thus the 'brains' of the system. From there, the metaphor made its way into descriptions of feedback systems in hydraulics, braking, and (in 1964) computing ('master' and 'slave' drives), where it has been subsequently attacked and even banned. Eglash sees in the metaphor the reflection of a split between unskilled labour and skilled management.[40] But in a sense this analysis offers us little beyond the metaphorical reproduction of a relation of subordination; a more interesting question relates to the point of view of users of technology.

That question is addressed in the industrial philosophy of Booker T. Washington. If African Americans were characterized as lazy, careless, and unsuitable to modern labour regimes, Washington's stress on industrial training has often seemed to his detractors to all too readily resolve post-Reconstruction anxieties about the feasibility of yoking supposedly resistant or idle former slaves to industrial work practices. But for all that Washington's separatism was reassuring to the white South, his vision of black achievement is significantly different from that of simply providing labour discipline. The stress on mutual endeavour and the network at Tuskegee links it to cooperative movements like the Irish Agricultural Organisational Society (IAOS). The successful black men he cites as examples are most often businessmen or independent master craftsmen or farmers in the Jeffersonian tradition; the latter are often described as stimulating white farmers by their scientific example rather than working for others (Washington refused to train workers for the cotton mills because the pay rates were so poor).[41]

Moreover, Washington's project, for all that it rejected what he saw as purely academic study (i.e., abstract modes of thought which seek to detach themselves from making), can be seen as articulating a version of philosophical pragmatism in which meditation on the tool is central to the slave's struggle towards autonomy. He writes: 'We said that as a slave the Negro was worked; as a freeman he must learn to work. There is a vast difference between working and being worked.... The whole machinery of slavery was not apt to beget the spirit of love of labour.'[42] Freed labour must be re-evaluated in terms of its relation to the instrument, just as the threatened replacement of black labour by machinery – the washer-woman by the stream laundry – must be confronted by an engagement *with* technology.[43] Washington constantly seeks to draw from technology its interlocking with the world; he seeks to reclaim labour from a system which had divorced thinking from making, directing from being an instrument. In *Up from Slavery* he argues with the minister who insists that labour is a curse; with his students who wish to free themselves from work 'with their hands'; with the parents who seek a more purely academic curriculum; and, of course, with W. E. B. Du Bois.[44] Industrial training will sustain the school financially and morally; students will learn 'beauty and dignity' in labour and lift it from 'mere drudgery and toil'. A Moses of labour, he leads his pupils into the fields: 'My plan was not to teach them how to work in the old way, but to show them how to make the forces of nature – air, water, steam, electricity, horse-power – assist them in their labour' (*US*, 110).

Washington's works thus offer a reappraisal of labour in which he seeks to dissolve the opposition between tools and those who direct them; not simply reclaiming technology for the African-American community, but putting it to work in the service of the idea. He constantly articulates a pragmatism in which the results of thought are tested in the real – visible in his controversial doctrine of 'dovetailing', in which the Institute's academic departments were encouraged to use examples derived from the workshops.[45] In *Up from Slavery* he suggests that one of the school's strongest supporters, Lewis Adams, 'derived his unusual power of mind from the training given his hands in the process of mastering well three trades within the days of slavery' (*US*, 89). *Working with the Hands* (1904) articulates that movement between hand and head even at the level of its chapter headings: 'Welding Theory and Practice'; 'Head and Hands Together'; 'Some Tangible Results'. His autobiographical writings apply this thinking to his own development; his first job was an opportunity to 'get in touch with the real things of life': 'there [in work] my mind was awakened and strengthened' (*WH*, 10). The tool becomes not an extension of the will of another, but an internalized power to grasp the world through thought: 'there is an indescribable something about work with the hands that tends to develop a student's mind' (*WH*, 58); 'there is something, I think, in the handling of a tool that has the same relation to close, accurate thinking that writing with a pen has in the preparation of a manuscript' (*WH*, 59); 'we wanted to teach men and women to put brains into the labour of the hand' (*WH*, 17). In *My Larger Education* he writes: 'I have gotten a large part of my education from actual contact with things, rather than through the medium of books. I like to touch things and handle them.'[46]

Because work in this way becomes a conscious articulation of self, Washington's writings offer a phenomenology of making, an analysis of what tools and objects *are* in their interaction with the human. A stool is three rough pieces of board before it is made into something; bricks in piles are what might make a house. He aims to make the students inhabit their labour: the first task of the Institute was to set up a brickworks so that they might make buildings; and older students would reproach new students for marking the buildings they had built themselves (*US*, 111). In *Working with the Hands* Washington writes of the presence of the self in the made object: 'So much for theory, but his diploma of efficient mastery of his trade is built into the walls of the Tuskegee buildings. They show whether he has learned to be a brick-mason, or whether he has merely learned some things about brick-masonry' (*WH*, 73). The book includes compositions written by students in the voice of their tools, so that 'the strengthening influence of contact with a real thing' (64) becomes a literal embodiment:

I am a nice large broom just made Tuesday by Harriet McCray. Before I was made into a broom, I grew over in a large farm with a great many others of my sisters. One day I was cut down and brought up to the broom-making department, and was carefully picked to pieces to get the best straw. I was put in a machine called the winder. (*WH*, 69)

The tool becomes the *instrumentum vocale*, speaking of its own making in the hands of its maker. In this manner, Washington's thought includes a sense of the way in which the instrumentality of the tool might figure black agency in general. Consider the metaphorical underpinnings of the ringing phrases of his 1903 address, 'Industrial Education for the Negro':

In the words of the late beloved Frederick Douglass: 'Every blow of the sledge hammer wielded by a sable arm is a powerful blow in support of our cause. Every colored mechanic is by virtue of circumstances an elevator of his race. Every house built by a black man is a strong tower against the allied hosts of prejudice. It is impossible for us to attach too much importance to this aspect of the subject. Without industrial development there can be no wealth; without wealth there can be no leisure; without leisure no opportunity for thoughtful reflection and the cultivation of the higher arts.'[47]

'Elevation' is literalized; tools become ideals. The laying of 'foundations' in skill and practical knowledge leads to the professions and arts; elsewhere he aims 'to use the thing in hand as a foundation for still higher growth' (*WH*, 25). Washington's formulas take on a Heideggerian quality as he seeks to ground thought in the reality of the 'close at-hand' rather than the 'distant'.[48] It is this to which Charles Chesnutt seems to respond in his comment that 'Mr. Washington finds the entering wedge by which his people can work their way into the body politic in a higher sense that they have hitherto been able to do'.[49]

This is not to say that there are no negative elements in Washington's view of the self-conscious and self-improving tool wielder. Indeed, a form of double consciousness can be found lingering within his formulas, relating to that other aspect of technology we began with: the machine as that which subordinates rather than extends the human, like slavery itself. One symptom is the sense of attenuation in Washington's own writings, in which anecdotes and tropes are circulated and re-circulated so that they take on a certain machined quality and the man vanishes behind the narcissism of his own discursive apparatus; he gives himself up to his own systematizing.

Washington's most famous opponent countered not only his accommodation of the white South, but also his analysis of instrumentality. The relationship between Washington – a former slave, utterly determined in his fund-raising and promulgation of industrial education, only secretly resisting the racist structures of the South – and the highly educated Du Bois is a complex one, as their biographers have stressed, involving personal and institutional, as well as philosophical, differences. Washington's tendency to disparage purely 'academic' study and Du Bois's countervailing stress on the elite education of the 'talented tenth' were at least partly strategic positions; both took pains to offer some support for the other's aims.[50] Nevertheless, the bitter debate that arose between them has had a lasting impact; it is still visible, for example, in Ishmael Reed's polemical introduction to the 2000 Signet edition of Washington's *Up from Slavery*, which mocks the *traison des clercs* Reed associates with African-American studies at Harvard.[51]

Du Bois's understanding of the relation between the African American and the machine is at once less stable and less tense than Washington's. His speeches and writings in the first decades of the century dwell on the problem of black employment, including self-help in the manner promulgated by Washington, but also the question of entry into the pre-existing structures of industry. In 1898, delivering the commencement address at Fisk, he urged 'captains of industry to employ the labor, to direct the work and develop the capacity of negro workmen by industrial enterprise'.[52] In 'The Economic Future of the Negro', a 1906 address, he asks, 'How efficient a labourer is the negro, and how efficient can he become with intelligence, technical training, and encouragement?' His answer is resolutely political: 'the systematic exploitation of black labor has hurt its steadiness and reliability', and racism from unions and others has excluded black workers from skilled positions – a conclusion he often reiterated.[53]

Later in his career, however, Du Bois sought to explicitly counter suggestions that the African American might make an ideal working machine. Leonidas W. Spratt, editor of the *Charleston Standard* and leading proponent of Southern industrial expansion on the back of a reopened slave trade, had declared in 1859 that 'the negro, in his common absence from reflection, is perhaps the best manipulatist in the world'.[54] This is uncomfortably close to Frederick W. Taylor's well-known comment that an 'educated ape' was the best worker in the factory system, mapped onto Senator Vardaman's 1916 declaration that 'a negro may become an obedient effective piece of machinery, but he is devoid of initiative and therefore could not be relied upon in an emergency'.[55] What Du Bois proposes is a continued refusal of instrumentality, like that depicted by Marx, who notes that the slave is careless about and even seeks to damage the tools to which he is compared.[56] In 1904 he could declare, as if agreeing with Washington, that one of the things 'slavery gave the negro' is the 'habit of work'.[57] But in his 1923 essay, 'The Superior Race', he celebrates as one of 'the two finest things in the industry of the West ... the black labourer's Saturday off' (the other is black laughter) – that is, a resistance to the industrial process.[58] In *The Gift of Black Folk* (1924) he attributes to African

Americans a propensity to labour-saving invention, claiming a series of devices, including the cotton gin (produced by 'a Negro on the plantation where Eli Whitney worked'). In the same text he expresses an avowedly racial belief that the African American, as 'a tropical product', 'was not as easily reduced to be the mechanical draft-horse which the northern European labourer became'.[59]

What explains this shift in views is partly Du Bois's increasing weariness at union resistance to skilled black workers: the middle ground (in class terms) had proved elusive, leaving a split between the 'talented tenth' who might escape into the professions and the masses trapped in labouring and domestic service.[60] Three linked chapters of *Darkwater* (1920) zero in on the issue of technology. His essays 'Of the Servant in the House' and 'Of the Ruling of Men' form the outer panels of a triptych, the central panel of which is 'Jesus Christ in Texas', a story of a visitation by the master-servant in whom absolute power and absolute subordination are reconciled. The story of Christ's return – in which he is recognized by the black servants but not by the rector, and sees a black thief lynched – begins in a prison where the hiring of chain gangs by a railway-maker is being discussed; he simply asks, 'It will be a good thing for them?'[61] The question of the use made of others is also present in the bracketing essays: the first focusing on domestic servitude, the second on industrial control. The final essay of the three, 'Of the Ruling of Men', insists that the Civil War was 'a duel between two industrial systems, one of which was bound to fail because it was an anachronism' (79); because of its wasteful use of the human machine. In the first essay, 'The Servant in the House', Du Bois attacks the relationship between race, domestic servitude, and technology in America: the equation in which '*Negroes are servants; servants are Negroes*' (66). Recalling his own brief stint at a hotel, he writes: 'I did not mind the actual work or the kind of work, but it was the dishonesty and deception, the flattery and cajolery, the unnatural assumption that worker and diner had no common humanity. It was uncanny. It was inherently and fundamentally wrong' (65). The 'uncanny' here is like that in Sachs's automata: the other who is not recognized, the animated machine passing the plates. For Du Bois this system continues to be linked to technological backwardness, since the black housemaid is an anachronism:

Not alone is the hurt thus offered to the lowly, – Society and Science suffer. The unit which we seek to make the centre of society, – the Home – is deprived of the help of scientific invention and suggestion. It is only slowly and by the utmost effort that some small foothold has been gained by the vacuum cleaner, the washing-machine, the power tool and the chemical reagent. (68)

This evokes the world of 'service without servants' (69) referred to in the epigraph of this chapter. Du Bois adds to this an analysis which seems to respond directly to Aristotle's account of slavery: 'All this is because we still consciously and unconsciously hold to the "manure" theory of social organization. We believe that at the bottom of organized human life there are necessarily duties and services which no real human being ought to be compelled to do. We push below this mudsill the derelicts and half-men, whom we hate and despise, and seek to build above it – Democracy!' (69) His proposal is simply to reduce the proportion of black servants to an untalented tenth.

In *Invisible Man* Ralph Ellison also explores the splitting of the self between actor and instrument implicit in the work of his predecessors. Ellison's novel is suffused with Washington's presence: its use of his Atlanta speech and its parody of the Tuskegee Institute and of his network of influence are well known, but it is the paint factory episode which offers the more dialectical investigation of the philosophy of the self-directing instrument. To be sure, Ellison's work is inflected by a post-Taylorist shift in thinking about the factory. As Alan Hyde argues, legal constructions of the human body also moved away from the harsh metaphor of the machine after 1929.[62] Studies of industrial relations from the 1930s on tend to stress the need for cooperation rather than directive management, and the system rather than the tool – hence the emphasis in the novel on the two pillars of Leninism: electrical systems, lighting, stolen power, and electro-convulsive therapy, on the one hand; and the Communist Party on the other. Nevertheless, in a text so deeply concerned with the way in which the black subject is reduced to a puppet, set running, and used by various others, an encounter with Washington's philosophy is inevitable.

Ellison's paint factory episode becomes a parody not simply of the construction of whiteness, but of the paranoia implicit in any attempt to master the construction of the body-as-machine. Lucius Brockway, working alone in his basement, identifies with industrial process, believing that he adds a particular quality, a 'sweetening' of the paint which cannot be reduced to engineering. There is a version of Washington in his declaration: 'They got all this machinery, but that ain't everything; *we are the machines inside the machine.*'[63] That formula evokes the behaviourist objection to Cartesian versions of the self as the director of a machine, a small man within: it produces an infinite regress, because the 'controller' can never be a point of origin. Brockway's declaration of a special power in forming the 'base' of the paint involves claiming a particular place in the economy which is linked to the history of slavery – he is at one with his boilers; he claims a foundational relationship with the 'Old Man', the owner of the company: 'I been here since there's been a here – even helped dig the first foundation' (170). He is irreplaceable, dependable, and even understands the racial logic of the product (the slogan he claims as his is 'If It's Optic White, It's the Right White') – but all at the price of being an instrument bound to his position at the 'base'.

That is why he is also mad, paranoid, willing to blow up his own engine room in attempting to kill the narrator. His paranoia is configured by his identification with the machine. Suspicious that he is being replaced by a Tuskegee-trained engineer, he asks about the Invisible Man's education and is somewhat mollified to find it is 'just a liberal arts course. No trades' (171). Brockway is figured as a Tar Baby, smelling of pine and looking 'as though he had been dipped in pitch' (169) – a signal of danger to the African American for whom the tar baby is that which cannot be manipulated by hand or tongue. He elicits the narrator's hidden name (unheard by the reader) and finally blows him up by having him open the wrong valve ('The white one, fool, the white one!' 187). It is as if the whole factory has become an influencing machine informing a hyper-connected paranoia in which every instrument attacks its controller. Brockway is worried that he is being replaced, worried about the unions, anxious about black engineers, even about the marketing of the paint. The machines themselves work in this crisis mode: every dial must be monitored, pressure released constantly, signals relayed. Technological excitability is paralleled by Brockway himself, constantly over-reacting, exploding, and cooling down. The orgasmic destruction which follows his final actions ('a wet blast of black emptiness that was somehow a bath of whiteness', 188) again suggests a narcissistic investment in the machine as phallic object as well as racial coding. The narrator's later reference to the 'hard, mechanical isolation of the hospital machine' which follows reinforces this critique (275). For Ellison, then, the path into technology is almost impossible to dissociate from an engrossing systematicity; all that can be offered by way of resistance is the marginality suggested by the narrator's tinkering with Monopolated Light & Power's cables – sabotage rather than involvement.

One of the classic cases of paranoia elaborated in Edward Kempf's *Psychopathology* (1921) – a standard textbook of its era – is that of a 'negro paranoiac' (case P-1) who builds an elaborate influencing machine, a 'copulation fetich' designed, Kempf suggests, to compensate for his impotence (Figure 3). Kempf annotates the machine's sexual symbolism: its emission of 'manna', its 'perpetual motion', the religious symbolism in which it is wrapped. But one might also note the way in which it serves as a response

Figure 3. 'Copulation Fetich by Impotent Negro Paranoic', from Edward Kempf,
Psychopathology (St. Louis: C. V. Mosby, 1921), p. 428.

to race generally, in its 'mixing' of 'the blood of the world' and its relation
to the patient's precarious employment as a janitor (another basement
figure) with its 'legal cap', and as a response to poverty with grandiose
assertions of personal significance.[64] Brockway's layering of himself in the

machine is similarly both a response to and an emblem, in the turn to
paranoia, of his narcissistic powerlessness and assertive emptiness. He is
trapped in a machine which is at once his own and the instrument of his
imprisonment.

Where Washington internalized the logic of the tool, Du Bois rejected
the equation of worker and machine; he attacked the relation as uncanny
and retrogressive in its mechanization of the subject – a path also followed,
in a more satirical and psychoanalytic vein, by Ellison. Nevertheless, it
could be said that Du Bois ultimately leaves in place the operative relationship informing the slavery–technology complex, siding with the ideal
of intellectual 'mastery', the accomplishments of the college-educated,
and seeing slavery and the tool bound together. In contrast Washington
refuses the master–slave, intellect–tool dynamics of slavery in the name
of a more active reciprocity. That may have involved a strategic down-
valuing of academic study, but it also suggested a path to the future rather
different from that suggested by Du Bois's dialectics, with their constant
encounter with negation. Exploiting the Lamarckianism typically applied
to technological evolution, Washington proposes to free the slave from
the burden of being an instrument.

THE MACHINE AS SLAVE BETWEEN THE WARS:
SLAVE-POWER AND HORSEPOWER

We have seen the slave–machine equation operating in both directions:
slaves replacing machines; machines replacing slaves. A question begins
to take shape – can we think about machinery without slavery? Before
attempting to answer that, we can consider another concept which came
into curious prominence in the 1920s and 1930s: the machine *as* slave. If
Sachs had read popular science magazines – let us imagine he had them in
his waiting room – he could have found that the slave–machine equation
was a commonplace of American culture. As David Nye reports, throughout the 1920s, a period when servants were becoming costly, '[e]lectrical
devices were often presented as replacements for servants', and for domestic servitude generally. 'Housewives must come up from slavery' was the
cry of Mary King Sherman, President of the Federation of Women's Clubs
in 1926.[65] The idea that technology, with its multiplication of manpower
and horsepower, is akin to a huge system of servants or slaves was deployed
in a range of texts praising technological and industrial expansion: by C.
G. Gibbert and J. E. Pogue in *America's Power Resources* (1921) and the
authors of the 'Giant Power' proposals in Pennsylvania and elsewhere; and

by Stuart Chase in *Men and Machines* (1929) and other writers associated with the Technical Alliance and its successor, the technocracy movement, in the 1920s and early 1930s.[66]

One writer formalizes this discourse with particular obsession: the popular historian of technology Silas Bent, author of *Machine Made Man* (1930) and *Slaves by the Billion: The Story of Mechanical Progress in the Home* (1938).[67] *Machine Made Man* deals with a broad field of mechanization: 'we rejoice that the engineer of a ship, by moving a lever, can loose fifty-thousand horse-power; that the day laborer's hand on the controller of a steam shovel commands a thousand slaves' (*MMM*, 2). *Slaves by the Billion* considers domestic devices like refrigerators ('white slaves', replacing the 'Nubian slaves' sent to 'distant mountain tops' to gather snow), cars ('slaves in the garage'), and so on. Discussing the relationship between slavery, technology, and civilization, Bent asks:

Do we really *live* in a fuller scale or a higher plane? I doubt whether anyone nowadays has a higher standard of living than the southern planter before the Civil War. He stood on the backs of black slaves, of course, to reach the heights, just as Greece built her culture on the backs of helots and Rome on the backs of military captives.... Do we live the higher, then, by reason of radio jazz broadcasts, incandescent lights, vacuum cleaners and electric refrigerators? (*MMM*, 5)

Bent answers this question in the affirmative: modern America is more civilized because the 'worker who uses his body' and 'the worker who uses his brain' are closer to each other than in the past (*MMM*, 257). 'Future generations', he writes in *Slaves by the Billion*, 'will attain once again the ideal of ancient Grecian civilization with the difference that it will be enjoyed by the many instead of the few, because it will be borne by mechanism, not human slaves' (*SB*, ix). He points out that women had yet to be released from servitude in the South, since (like Aristotle's overseer) they needed to direct the household: 'the leisure and culture of the plantation was confined mostly to the males' (*SB*, 8).

Bent seems to both obsessively return to and undercut the body–slave–machine equation; he cannot do without it, even as he undermines it, partly because he is still using the term 'slave' in the conflicted Aristotelian sense: as a metaphor for control of the inanimate, an extension of human will, or as a substituting of human labour which might produce technological autonomy. In this, he is like others in the period: the authors of the government report Bent cites; Fritz Lang in *Metropolis*; Karel Čapek in *R.U.R.* The robot rebellion represents the final extension of autonomy of the technological which he fears – the uncanny substitution which becomes total, freed from human will, but marred by the status of being an extension of the human. Čapek's robots are markedly human, even as their inhuman status and simplified biology is asserted; as liberated slaves they are both ruthless and sentimental, independent and Oedipally bound up with their makers, supplanting and repeating the human.

The precise calibration of bodies and machines also bothers Bent, largely because of the problems of scale involved. His chapter on labour, subtitled 'From Slavery to the Factory', begins: 'A government bureau in Washington now estimates that automatic machines put at the beck and call of the average working man the equivalent of fifty servants' (*MMM*, 257). Similarly in *Slaves by the Billion*, 'to illustrate how many more slaves are at our command than in other countries', he produces this equation:

The National Resources Committee, in its first report, says: 'A mechanical horse-power, costing $20 to $50 per year, substitutes for ten to fifteen human slaves.' Ten to fifteen slaves! Inquiries made in an effort to pin down this nebulous sentence led to my assertion that for a dollar a week we may command the efforts of eleven servants. (*SB*, 124)

The slave–power equation cannot work in terms of an imagined exchange of bodies, as industrial energy outruns the human scale: 'The billion horsepower in the family automobile, at any rate, is the equivalent to ten or fifteen billion slaves, many times the population of this globe'. At such moments, Bent seems baffled by his own metaphor of slave-power. In fact, he does not even like *horse*power as a unit, since it has drifted away from its 'proper' location in the actual body of a horse. He claims that 'Watt and Boulton cooked it up to rate the work of Watt's steam engine; by watching the work of dray horses in London breweries, eight hours a day, they found that the average animal could pull continuously at the rate of 2200 pounds: that is, exerted power to lift this weight one foot in one minute' (*SB*, 122–23). But he adds that 'Watt and Boulton arbitrarily increased the figure by half, to 3300 pounds', and claims that this is an astonishing 'error'. This is to say that what might be seen as an arbitrary measure of power *should* be referable back to the natural order, to the work of the actual body, rather than detached from it and made into a subject of calculation and exchange.[68]

This and other references to the horse, like Du Bois's reference to the factory worker as a 'mechanical draught-horse', suggest that the relation between slave and horse requires some discussion.[69] Peter Garnsey comments that Aristotle creates a 'fuzzy' line between slaves and animals, as opposed to firm lines between people and animals.[70] That fuzziness is exploited, but also sustained, in abolitionist claims that slave owners cared better for their horses than for their slaves. Harriet Ritvo's discussion of the characterization of horses in the nineteenth century makes clear that they were often described in terms used for slaves: as noble and loyal, as patient and strong, as exchanging bondage for a sense of the care given them, as vulnerable to abuse.[71] Anna Sewell's *Black Beauty* (1877), the best-seller marketed as '*Uncle Tom's Cabin* for horses', exploits that connection, even if its logic is that the slave is a passive and less than human victim.[72]

At the heart of the horsepower question is the issue of work. Notoriously, in his discussion in *Latter-Day Pamphlets* of the alleged reluctance of liberated slaves in the West Indies to work, Carlyle evoked the image of a black horse given liberty:

> So long as grass lasts, I dare say they are very happy, or think themselves so. And Farmer Hodge sallying forth, on a dry spring morning, with a sieve of oats in his hand, and agony of eager expectation in his heart, is he happy? Help me to plough this day, Black Dobbin: oats in full measure if thou wilt. 'Hlunh, No – thank!' snorts Black Dobbin; he prefers glorious liberty and the grass. Bay Darby, wilt not though perhaps? 'Hlunh! – Grey Joan, then, my beautiful broad-bottomed mare, – O Heaven, she too answers Hlunh! Not a quadruped of them will plough a stroke for me.[73]

As David Levy suggests, the background to this is Adam Smith's claim that humans can be distinguished from animals by exchange: by a universal desire to trade and use language – a claim countered by Edward Gibbon Wakefield, who suggested that some debased human types did not trade. Carlyle, Levy suggests, 'argues for the fundamental identity of the Irish, blacks and horses on the ground that neither horses, blacks, nor Irish will voluntarily trade leisure for wages'.[74] Historically, this is nonsense: the task system widely used in the South meant that slaves could complete allotted tasks and leave time for their own crops; in more relaxed areas this produced a substantial informal economy and slaves who accumulated – with the law turning a blind eye – considerable holdings of livestock and who resisted being required to do additional work in order to pursue their own business.[75] Nevertheless, Africans and horses, for Carlyle, are linked to a non-productive economy which can expand only with the imposition of a discipline which combats the drag of the body.

It is here that the horse–slave equation operates in a more fundamental manner: both horse and slave are linked to the question of what work can be extracted from the body, and the linkage between power and *techne* generally. These issues are present in the obsessions of a major in the French army, R. F. Lefebvre de Noëttes, whose work in the 1920s offers an odd variation on the technology thesis.[76] Lefebvre de Noëttes was convinced that a specific lack of *horsepower* underpinned slavery in the ancient world. He speaks in the terms inherited from the Romans – 'l'antiquité fit-elle un appel sans réserve à "la machine à voix humaine"'[77] (antiquity had an unqualified call on the 'machine with a human voice') – but clearly it is the horse rather than the human which fascinates him (volume 2 of his work, which consists simply of five hundred illustrations, contains less than ten pictures of slaves; the rest are of horses). Examining records of Greek and Roman harnesses, he concluded that they would not have allowed for a load of more than 500 kg on a good road – meaning that slaves were needed to supplement the horse. It was only, he argued, with the modern horse collar, developed in the tenth century, that the waste of effort and the brake on development thus created were finally overcome. The details of these claims have been contested, but what it is notable is Lefebvre de Noëttes's adherence to the horse–slave equation – as if autonomous explanations of technology were impossible, as if the human were yoked to the horse or the slave as extensions of their power.[78]

Bent's similar preoccupation with what a horse can or cannot do reflects his wider preoccupation with the shift in power away from the human scale, into an economy of massive productivity. This is confirmed by Carroll R. Daughtery (later a well-known labour economist) in his 1927 study, *The Development of Horse-Power Equipment in the United States*. Having talked a great deal of horses in the early republic, he marks the take-off of power ratios in the period after the 1860s, with the steam turbine and high-speed generator, and a sixfold growth in power in the period 1899–19. This is, of course, accompanied by a 'decreasing number of work animals since 1909'.[79] The 1910s saw tens of thousands of work-horses vanishing from the streets of London and New York.[80] The theme of Daughtery's study is the expansion of power away from the scale represented by the horse.

One group in particular seems to share Bent's obsession with the slave–horsepower unit in this period, the technocracy movement. Technocracy had its origins in 1931–32, in a period of economic uncertainty in which the Soviet Five-Year Plan seemed to offer a model of the planned economy, though the movement's deeper origins lie in Veblen's *The Engineers and the Price System* (1921).[81] The movement came to national prominence via a series of articles in *New Outlook*, November 1932, beginning with 'What Is Technocracy?' There was a considerable public response and debate in 1933. The technocrats set up an Energy Survey of North America at Columbia and issued various briefing documents intended to prompt a rationalized social calculus.[82] Central to the technocratic project was the redefinition of society in terms of energy. Noting that 'the human engine in an eight hour day is only capable of producing work approximately at the rate of 1/10 horse-power', the *Introduction to Technocracy* (1933) chronicles the rise from the 7-horsepower engine of 1712 to the 1890s marine engine: 'In this type the rate of energy conversion jumped to 234,000 times the rate of the human engine.' Turbines in 1933 are rated at 'approximately 300,000 HP ... 3,000,000 times the output of a human being'.[83] The result is an imbalance between power and persons: 'If the total one billion installed horse-power of the United States were operated to full capacity, its output would be equivalent to the human labour of five times the present world population' (42). In the graphs which are the movement's master documents, it is the years 1915–20 in which 'that low rate engine of conversion, the human being" (23) is displaced as industrial productivity brings a combination of high output and low employment.

As in Bent, that displacement is described in terms of both a release from and a multiplication of slavery. A 1955 briefing notes:

The use of non-muscular energy has freed man from toil, has replaced human labor. A new kind of slave has taken over the old slaves' jobs by the millions. In fact, there are so many of these slaves in North America that they outnumber all the human slaves on the earth by far. These new slaves are very different from the old. They neither buy nor consume the goods they produce; there is no limit to their working hours; they do not tire; and they can accomplish things the old slaves never dreamed of or thought possible.

As you probably have guessed, the new slave is the kilowatt-hour; the old slave is the man-hour.[84]

The aim was to replace the unit of value based on the 'old' slave labour with a new distributionist unit based on an energy allowance. In the flat sentences which characterize the movement's prose (the 'issuing' of facts):

Price System wealth consists of debt claims against the operation of the physical equipment and its resultants. Physical wealth, on the other hand, is produced by converting available energy into use-forms and services. The process of being wealthy is the degradation of the resultants of the above conversions into complete uselessness – in other words, total consumption. To be physically wealthy is not to own a car but to wear it out. Technology has introduced a new methodology in the creation of physical wealth. It is now able to substitute energy for man hours on the parity basis that 1,500,000 foot pounds equals one man's time for eight hours.[85]

This effects the final conversion of slave value – the 'dead' wealth that accrues from the fixed capital of the slave – into a value which is seen as a distributed form of energy, a shift made possible by the breaking of the link between the human body and production.

The philosopher Peter Sloterdijk has recently, and perhaps rather oddly, echoed the technocrats in arguing that the most fundamental way of seeing changes in Western history is to look not at labour or productivity, but at the question of energy and the machine. Here, too, the slave enters the picture, as a figure for an instrumentality without volition:

The key to the transition from human labor to machine labor (and to new human–machine cooperation) lies in the coupling of power systems with execution systems. In the age of physical labor, such couplings remained latent, insofar as the worker himself, as biological energy-converter, formed a unity of power and execution systems.[86]

At the same time, '[e]ngines are perfect slaves, untroubled by any thought of human rights.... They do not listen to abolitionist preachers who dream dreams of a day not far off when engines and their owners will enjoy equal rights and the children of human beings and machines will play together' (349). Sloterdijk's formulas are almost deliberately banal in their attempt to intimate the order of the machine. The machine is in fact an anti-slave, retaining only the fantasy elements of slavery in which the slave is pure instrument. Sloterdijk's machines are explosive 'Titans', 'prisoners beneath the earth'; they are linked to the order of 'unrestricted mobility and a festive wastage of energy' (345), rather than the restricted order of labour – freed, that is, from the limitations of the human body.

So why does slavery continue to operate as a governing metaphor at such moments? I would suggest that its presence is a result of the dual legacy we have traced. On the one hand, the slave is a figure for the technological, for the extension of human power. On the other, the slave is a figure for blockage and the limitations of the human body, for that which might be replaced by technology. As a boundary figure, the slave mediates – and also in a repressed fashion humanizes – the shift from the human and animal scales into a world of expanded energy and the consumer economy, the move towards a demand-led consumer economy chronicled in the 1920s by economists like Simon Patten and John Maynard Keynes.[87] The result is the disruption in energy scales registered by Bent and an accompanying reconfiguring of the status of the human body in which it is associated not with production but with consumption – with an accompanying linkage to the feminine domestic sphere. The slave serves, in this story, to retain the figuration of the human within the technological. This is just the role described by Sachs; indeed, it is to the threatened narcissism of his *own* era, it seems to me, that Sachs is responding, rather than to that of the classical world.

But it could also, more dialectically, be suggested that technocracy draws from the discourse of slavery in order to circumvent the public sphere; in order to work within the economics of the household, in Aristotle's terms. This is an economy founded, in terms of the history of American slavery, on the belief in the slaveholder's right to dispose of his instruments as he wishes – a belief ultimately founded on the Aristotelian stress on the slave master's technique. As Andrew Ross comments, the technocrats 'had no real need for *politics* (as irrational as business), let alone a requirement for democratic politics'; they simply wanted to direct the economy according to their superior intelligence.[88]

We might compare this to the thinking of Hannah Arendt, who insists – markedly against the run of historical thought – that the replacement of slave labour by the machine as imagined by Aristotle does not mean that 'household slaves could be dispensed with. For slaves are not instruments of making things or of production, but of living, which constantly consumes their services.'[89] A service economy cannot be automated. The 'labour-replacement' paradigm is, for Arendt, a mistake:

The discussion of the whole problem of technology, that is, of the transformation of life and world through the introduction of the machine, has been strangely led astray through an all-too-exclusive concentration upon the service or disservice the machines render to men. The assumption here is that every tool and implement is primarily designed to make human life easier and human labor less painful. Their instrumentality is understood exclusively in this anthropomorphic sense. But the instrumentality of tools and implements is much more closely related to the object it is designed to produce, and their sheer 'human value' is restricted to the use the *animal laborans* makes of them. In other words, *homo faber*, the toolmaker, invented tools and implements in order to erect a world, not – at least, not primarily – to help the human life process. The question therefore is not so much whether we are the masters or the slaves of our machines, but whether machines still serve the world and its things, or if, on the contrary, they and the automatic motion of their processes have begun to rule and even destroy world and things. (151)

Arendt's formulas are rooted in the Aristotelian distinction between chrematistics and economy – between the limitless circulation of money and desire, on the one hand, and the needs of the household on the other.[90] The logic of labour replacement is bound up with the figure of the slave: if machines merely replace human labour, Arendt implies, they might be aligned with the slave; if we focus on their world-building potential, they are detached from the human. For Arendt, the consumer economy has created confusion between the world of made objects (production) and the world of nature (consumption), since obsolescence has become cyclic, destabilizing the object (126). This means, in her terms, that as consumers we are all – artists and philosophers apart – serving a world governed by necessity rather than freedom. The abundance produced by power ('millions of slaves') has had the paradoxical effect of enslaving those who are bound to a nature which has been wrapped into the human. Consumption is linked to slavery via this servitude and via the stress on the uses of life. In this bleak vision the replacement of labour by the machine does not lead to higher pursuits:

The guiding model of this [utopian] hope in Marx was undoubtedly the Athens of Pericles which, in the future, with the help of the vastly improved productivity of human labour, would need no slaves to sustain itself but would become a reality for all. A hundred years after Marx we know the fallacy of this reasoning; the spare time of the *animal laborans* is never spent in anything but consumption. (133)

Slavery thus serves to figure the binding of humans into their own technology as its servants, even as actual slaves are liberated. Arendt's distinction between labour and making might be read as a final plea to disentangle the slave from the machine.

The slave stands, then, on the pathway between the machine as tied to the body (the tool or organ extension) and the machine as independent power; between the logic of the part and that of the whole; between the logic of control or discipline and that of autonomy. As we will see again in Chapters 4 and 5 in accounts of making and reproduction, the slave binds technology to the human body, even as that body is negated. But if the threat of autonomy in the machine is the threat of a productivity and power which have exceeded the human scale, which have detached themselves from the natural order, the slave (as figure) serves paradoxically to ameliorate that threat, to humanize technology. The horse–slave equation is the old economy of equivalence and exchange, contrasted with the new economy of overproduction.

My argument has explored a series of doublings in relation to the figure of the slave. To be schematic: in Sachs the slave is machine and not-machine; in American culture more generally the slave is seen as replaced by technology. Machines may become slaves for Bent and others, but the 'billions of slaves' rhetoric of the inter-war years also suggests an anxiety about that metaphor. The slave–machine equation is born with the machine as its pre-condition; it re-enters the picture as a liminal figure whenever the machine breaks with the human, binding the machine back into an image of subordination and repairing a rupture in human narcissism. At the point of the abolition of slavery, the actual replacement of slaves by machines also becomes an issue, in part because the liberated slave bears an uncertain relation to the mechanical; an issue addressed, as we saw, in Washington's pragmatism and the writings of other African-American authors.

The conclusion is that because of the historical proximity of slave and machine, we cannot easily think about machinery without slavery; without questions of subordination, labour replacement, and the presence of the human body, which have so often derived from slavery. But equally, our thinking on this issue is inevitably disturbed by the uncertain status of the slave and by the slave's independence, even where that independence is potential rather than actual. Most fundamentally, the slave signals the instrumentality and power relations which cannot be dissociated from the question of technology and which frustrate any attempt to explain technology as prosthesis. Moreover, the figure of the slave in accounts of technology indicates the presence of what Timothy Clark calls an 'originary technicity', that is, the presence of the technical, prior to any particular technological development, in such fields as human relations and politics, which have been present in Western thought since Aristotle.[91] Machinery without slavery? It might be a good idea, but because we have bodies which are used by others, we are not quite there yet.

CHAPTER 4

The Hands of Others: Sculpture and Pain

The preceding chapter examined the figural status of the slave within debates on technology, but it also reflected on how African-American writers had necessarily dealt with that tradition. In this chapter, we consider a more specialized and more buried form of the same set of metaphors, investigating the way in which slavery relates to two aspects of sculpture in the nineteenth century: firstly, an association between the slave and the use of others as tools; and secondly, a tension between a pristine surface and contained feelings. Again, the place of African-American artists within this picture provides clues to what is at stake. The issues derive from both general considerations – the nature of sculpture – and more local issues concerning sculptural technique, its status, and in some instances its subject matter. What I will depict is often an entanglement between sculpture and slavery rather than any more directly thematic or causal argument. But these examples also involve two questions which energize each of the next three chapters: How is the pain of slavery suppressed or represented? What is its relation to the aesthetic?

The centrepiece of my exhibition, as it were, is the American sculptor Hiram Powers's *The Greek Slave* (Figure 4), arguably the most important sculpture of its period. Created in 1844, it was displayed in London, toured America in 1847–48, created a stir at the Great Exhibition, and achieved a huge popularity in reproductions. Wherever it went, audiences gathered in silence around it, producing responses that can only be described as contradictory: marvel at the purity and apparent detachment of the naked woman it depicted, supposedly waiting to be sold at a Turkish slave market; curiosity and speculation about what was going though her mind; and a more repressed response to the statue's orientalized sexuality. Most recent writings on Powers's statue have followed contemporary abolitionist viewers in placing it directly in the context of American slavery. Kirk Savage describes it as 'the only antebellum work in marble that came close to abolitionism'.[1] Other writers have seen it in terms of the interplay of

Figure 4. Hiram Powers, *The Greek Slave* (modelled 1841–43, carved 1846). Marble, 66 × 19 × 17 inches. Corcoran Gallery of Art, Washington, D.C. Gift of William Wilson Corcoran, 73.4.

empathetic identification and shame, suggesting that its pristine surface allowed viewers to contain feelings about slavery and feminine subjection.[2] I will take a rather different tack, however, placing it in debates about sculpture and its making.

Here are two very different responses to Powers's work. The first is the abolitionist sonnet by Elizabeth Barrett Browning. Powers was a neighbour in Florence, and she seems to have known his mind well enough:

> Pierce to the centre,
> Art's fiery finger! – and break up ere long
> The serfdom of this world! appeal, fair stone,
> From God's pure heights of beauty against man's wrong!

Catch up in the divine face, not alone
East griefs but west, – and strike and shame the strong,
By thunders of white silence, overthrown.[3]

At issue in her poem is an analogy between the statue and the skin: it asks whether the viewer can see past the tempting availability of the naked body and detect the ideal contained within it and, by analogy, the human inside the slave.

The scurrilous second response is from Nathaniel Hawthorne's note-books and, in contrast, insists on the pure materiality of the artwork; it comes from a rival in Rome, dishing Powers to Hawthorne – accusing him of pastiche and commercial exploitation, even a kind of aesthetic slave trading:

He will not allow Powers to be an artist at all, or to know anything of the laws of art, although acknowledging him to be a great bust-maker, and to have put together the Greek Slave and the Fisher Boy very ingeniously. The latter, however, is copied from the Apollino in the Tribune of the Ufizzi; and the former is made up of beauties that had no reference to one another; and he affirms that Powers is ready to sell, and has actually sold, the Greek Slave, limb by limb, dismembering it by reversing the process of putting it together – a head to one purchaser, an arm or a foot to another, a hand to a third.[4]

What the two passages share is the subject of this chapter: a trinity of issues which can be related to slavery: the ordering of the body; the question of the feelings contained in those deemed inanimate objects; and the issue of whiteness itself. But what I will suggest is that we cannot simply see these issues as incidental to the conceptualization of sculpture in the period – applicable accidentally, as it were, to Powers's subject – but instead as knitted into the way it was produced and received. The discussion which follows traverses the work of Wheatley, Hawthorne, and other writers; the mechanic as sculptor in James Watt's sculpture machine; Rebecca Harding Davis's *Life in the Iron Mills*; an infamous libel case in London; and sculpture itself.

LABOUR AND IDEAL MAKING

There is a scandal at the heart of sculptural practice in the nineteenth cen-tury which is hidden in plain sight. It is simply this: *sculptors did not make their own sculptures*. Instead, they made clay models which were then scaled up and transferred to plaster casts, and then cut from stone by skilled Italian workmen. The hands of others produced the work we see. I am speaking of sculptors in marble, the most culturally prestigious material and the one central to the 'Ideal' sculpture that dominates the field from Canova and Thorvaldsen at the turn of the century to the 1870s.

It can, of course, be countered – and art historians almost inevitably do suggest this – that this is no scandal at all: the way in which sculpture is made has always been known. But what I would suggest is that, rather than achieving a stable resolution, the question is constantly raised and disavowed in the period; indeed, its disavowal is a necessary condition for the consumption of art. Moreover, it is a question which – for reasons we will come to – becomes particularly sharpened in the nineteenth century. If Renaissance texts recalled Michelangelo hacking furiously at the stone, and if the modernist Gaudier-Brzeska insisted on forging his own steel tools before working the stone, almost no text about neoclassical sculpture describes a sculptor as a workman. Paradoxically, this economy of reproduction was central to an art which insisted on the ideal conception of the maker: the work of the sculptor might be reproduced in series, scaled down for the drawing room, or broken up into parts – but in all cases sold with the imprimatur of genius attached to it.[5] This simple set of facts generated, as we will see, a great deal of anxiety and defensive commentary. Indeed, there is what I will call a 'sculpture complex' in the period: a network of anxieties which surround the question of sculpture's origin, status, and practice.

Powers's conception of sculpture is firmly in the Ideal tradition. The statue, as he wrote to Browning, is the 'unveiled soul'.[6] Ideal sculpture is characterized by its emphasis on the conception of the artist: the 'real' work is in the mind. As Charlotte Eaton put it in her account of Canova's studio, though with a significant caveat, – '[A] sculptor begins upon much more ductile materials than marble. He forms his model in clay, and this is generally (and ought to be always) entirely the work of his own hands; but before he begins, the statue is perfectly *ideato* – the visionary figure is before him'.[7] The 'look' of Ideal sculpture accords with this abstract conception: unworldly, white, smooth, with none of the evidence of struggle or work on the surface often visible in Michelangelo's sculpture – or even evidence of the material itself, since Powers was famous for pristine surfaces made of the perfect white marble from Seravezza.[8] Indeed, the effacement of work from the art object is central to its status.

In order to understand what is at stake in the emphasis on the ideal, we need to recall the rather ambiguous inheritance which lies behind sculptural neoclassicism. In an earlier chapter we saw that the Aristotelian account of slavery renders the slave a tool, an extension of the master's will, but a tool whose skill and agency must be accounted for. The craftsman is himself akin to the slave. The suspicion of making implicit in these attitudes extends to art itself. As S. H. Butcher put it a century ago, for the Greeks 'the artist was honoured less than his art. His professional skill seemed to want something of a self-sufficing and independent activity'. In the case of the sculptor, in particular, the artificer approaches the status of a labourer.[9] For Aristotle sculpture falls below poetry and other arts: the sculptor is akin to a mere craftsman, offering an imitation which is founded on *techne* but which has problems in forming a *poesis*. These suspicions were reproduced by Roman writers. Plutarch's 'Life of Pericles' includes a disparaging set of remarks directed at craftsmen, especially sculptors. He has been talking about what leads us to emulate acts of virtue:

> In other things there does not immediately follow upon the admiration and liking of the thing done any strong desire of doing the like. Nay, many times, on the very contrary, when we are pleased with the work, we slight and set little by the workman or artist himself. . . . Nor did any generous and ingenuous young man, at the sight of the statue of Jupiter at Pisa, ever desire to be a Phidias, or on seeing that of Juno at Argos, long to be a Polycletus, or feel induced by his pleasure in their poems to wish to be an Anacreon or Philetas or Archilochus.[10]

This distinguishes the mimesis attached to moral actions – the noble example of Pericles – from the 'mean actions' of the craftsman. Echoing Aristotle's remarks about too much skill in music turning 'the body into that of a mechanic', the Periclean nobleman acts and appreciates, while the maker is in contrast aligned with the materiality of the object.[11] As Hannah Arendt notes, this denigration of sculpture 'is still found in the Renaissance, where sculpturing is counted among the servile arts whereas painting takes up a middle position between liberal and servile arts'[12] – thus the sometimes uneasy line between tradesman and genius visible in accounts of Renaissance sculptors and their interactions with powerful patrons. And even in the nineteenth century, it could be pointed out, as one writer did rather disdainfully in the *North American Review* in 1830, that most sculptures were busts of 'prosperous gentlemen', 'mechanical affair[s]' rather than 'great effort[s] of genius' – as if a poet 'spent the greater part of his life in producing obituary verses for a fee'.[13] It is against this background that the more elevated claims of Ideal sculpture are made.

There is also a rather different tradition we can draw on in Aristotle, in which sculpture provides a more positive way of thinking about essence and materiality. In distinguishing among the four kinds of causes – material, efficient, formal, and final – a frequent example in the *Metaphysics*, book 5, is the statue. While the formal cause is the shape into which the bronze is cast, the 'final cause' is the conception embodied in the design of the sculptor. This in turn suggests another implicit parallel in the *Metaphysics*, between the statue and health. Here the distinction is between the contingent shape of the statue and its material, bronze. The fact that a quantity of bronze can form a statue of Domitian, or be melted and reformed to make a statue of Hermes, suggests the process of generation – of giving form to matter. Bodily sickness is seen as akin to a privation of shape, of an achieved bodily making. If 'the form is prior to the matter and more real', the impairment of form is a lack of human presence.[14] The process of generation, of 'becoming or perishing', is exemplified both by sculpture and by the action of semen: something is shaped from clay or from flesh and bones. The human body in this way is linked to the statue, and the healthy body to the sculptor as final cause, the giver of shape. But this in turn bequeaths a problem to Ideal sculpture – how does it see the place of the body in the actual process of creation?

Aristotle's thinking has a huge influence. On might consider, for example, William James writing on the 'Stream of Thought' and reaching for an apposite metaphor:

The mind, in short, works on the data it receives very much as a sculptor works on his block of stone. In a sense the statue stood there from eternity. But there were a thousand different ones beside it, and the sculptor alone is to thank for having extricated this one from the rest. Just so the world of each of us, howsoever different our several views of it may be, all lay embedded in the primordial chaos of sensations, which gave the mere *matter* to the thought of all of us indifferently. We may, if we like, by our reasonings unwind things back to that black and jointless continuity of space and moving clouds of swarming atoms which science calls the only real world. But all the while the world *we* feel and live in will be that which our ancestors and we, by slowly cumulative strokes of choice, have extricated out of this, like sculptors, by simply rejecting certain portions of the given stuff.[15]

Here sculpture remains the paradigm of form-giving, though one might also notice the tension between a heroic individual effort and a more collective one, and also a certain fear of the inertness and blackness of 'mere *matter*' which is related to a distrust of sculpture itself, conceived of as the elimination of the obdurate material of the world.

It is the ambivalent inheritance of these modes of thinking in Aristotle that informs the tradition of neoclassical thinking which begins with Winckelmann. A realignment of the ordering of the arts saw sculpture in a higher place, in fact at the apex of a classical inheritance. The separation of modelling (design) and carving (making) which was inaugurated by Michelangelo and Alberti and continued by Bernini involved a development of the Aristotelian distinction between ideal making and instrumentality. In Ideal sculpture, the sculptor emerges as an artist unsullied by the labour of the mere craftsman. The master, for Aristotle, infuses his soul into the deficient body of the slave, and thus by proxy into the things he makes. The distinction between mind and labour, or master and slave, which is latent everywhere in Aristotle, receives a concrete expression in the actions of the assistants in creating the body of the sculpture. The stress on the ideal accords with this mode of production: as Hannah Arendt comments in her rather Kantian account of the difference between (mere) labour and making, '[I]solation from others is the necessary life condition of every mastership which consists in being alone with the "idea", the mental image of the thing to be.'[16] In the *Critique of Judgement*, Kant defines genius as 'the innate mental aptitude (ingenium) through which nature gives the rule to art'. But crucially, genius's form-giving powers must be linked to a 'mechanical' element which is the discipline of the fine arts (a point Kant repeats), in order that it achieve a concrete presence in the world:

It is not amiss, however, to remind the reader of this: that in all free arts something of a compulsory character is still required, or, as it is called, a mechanism, without which the soul, which in art must be free, and which alone gives life to the work, would be bodyless and evanescent (e.g., in the poetic art there must be correctness and wealth of language, likewise prosody and metre). For not a few leaders of a newer school believe that the best way to promote a free art is to sweep away all restraint and convert it from labour into mere play.

Kant reiterates the point a few pages later: 'there is still no fine art in which something mechanical, capable of being at once comprehended and followed in obedience to rules, and consequently something academic, does not constitute the essential condition of the art'.[17] In sculpture in particular, the relation of the ideal and the mechanical can be figured as a version of the master–slave relation: a relation of delegation or copying in which the ideal is given body in the world.

This is expressed in the process by which marble statues were created. As I noted, the sculptor created a small model in clay; this was then transferred to a plaster model and usually 'scaled up'; and finally teams of skilled Italian craftsmen would create the sculpture from the plaster model, using a variety of drills, chisels, and measuring devices.[18] It was because of the need for these craftsmen that so many neoclassical sculptors lived in Italy. It is interesting in this respect to compare Ideal sculpture with that of the Renaissance. For Michelangelo, the wrestling of form from the raw material of stone involved a stress on heroic labour, represented by the marks of the chisel left on the statue (as opposed to the smooth surface of Ideal sculpture). He was depicted – despite the fact that he delegated some jobs – as attacking the stone, stripping away its flesh to reveal the soul within. He seldom made models in clay or other materials. The fact that so much of what he made was left, often deliberately, *non finito*, suggests that struggle; his unfinished work may have been modelled on the broken bodies of classical sculpture, showing their histories.[19] Among the best-known examples of the *non finito* are the series of statues of slaves created as part of Michelangelo's ultimately abortive project for the tomb of Pope Julius II: *The Dying Slave*, *The Rebel Slave*, and related works seem to signal the sculptor's frustrated subordination to patrons. In contrast, the Ideal sculpture of the nineteenth century stresses surface, poise, and completion: the sculptor has extricated his work from struggle.

The issue that haunts sculpture is thus *labour*. The question of who makes the artwork could always be raised in the nineteenth century. Powers, Flaxman, Storey, Hosmer, and many others were confronted with accusations that they did not make their own work, that it was in fact made by the skilled artisans who hewed the marble or by studio assistants. The accusation could range from plagiarism to the more general dissatisfaction voiced by Hawthorne in his notebook, in words which he would substantially repeat in his art novel, *The Marble Faun*: 'It is not quite pleasant to think that the sculptor does not really do the whole labor on his statues, but that they are all but finished to his hand by merely mechanical people. It is generally only the finishing touches that are given by his own chisel.'[20] More radically, another commentator reported about Powers that he 'never touched a chisel to "The Greek Slave" or any other of his wonderful products. He says that those sculptures which we had so much admired, are entirely chiselled by assistants.'[21] (One way in which the agency of the sculptor was maintained, incidentally, was through the notion of the 'final touch' applied to the work, giving it life – a version of Pygmalion in which the sculptor animates, where the assistants only reproduce. The catalogue of a recent exhibition of Ideal sculpture at the Tate Britain reproduces this myth of the final touch – against the run of evidence in many cases – in stating that 'usually the sculptor himself finished the piece and executed the final touch to the surface'.)[22]

Now, it would be wrong to suggest that the skilled craftsmen who populated the workshops at Carrara and elsewhere were slaves; moreover, acting as a studio assistant was part of the training of sculptors. Nevertheless, in its hesitancy Hawthorne's comment echoes Pliny the Elder's famous lament over the use of the hands of others. The process of giving form is lodged within the mind; the body is a tool for copying that ideal form. This is reflected in a view of Greek achievement which tended towards the acceptance of slavery's role: 'It took from the shoulder of the free man a great part of those labours whose success requires the exclusive application of just one of the corporal and spiritual facilities – mechanical skill.'[23] Despite Humboldt's opposition to slavery in the Americas, there is implicit toleration of Greek slavery in his 1793 essay, 'On the Study of Antiquity and That of the Greeks in Particular', from which that comment is taken – a toleration shared with many others. At one limit, this parallels what Page duBois calls 'the political deployment of antiquity in defence of [American] slavery' by scholars such as Basil Gildersleeve, the first professor of Greek and Latin at the University of Virginia.[24]

Comments like Hawthorne's found a response in what is something of a guilty sub-genre of essays defending Ideal sculpture. Articles with titles that are variations of 'How Sculpture Is Made' appear frequently in the period 1830–80, deploying a mode of argument involving both the assertion of an ideal making on the part of the sculptor and a detailed description of the work of the Italian assistants who actually form the marble. The claim that the primacy of the sculptor's conception renders the assistant a mere copyist is repeated again and again. Frances E. Willard provides a generic example in a piece reprinted in various magazines for children, 'How Statues Are Made'. She stresses that 'our genius ... has no idea of spending his valuable time in whipping away at this stubborn block of marble' (the metaphor is interesting, to say the least). Instead he uses the 'handsome young fellows' who hang around in Carrera; 'Let's watch this strong-armed substitute', she suggests all too lovingly.[25] Or here is G. H. Calvert, describing the generative power of Powers's hand in 'The Process of Sculpture' in 1847:

The clay under his hand gradually grew into life, and assumed the elastic, vital look, which no mere anatomical knowledge or craft of hand can give, but which is imparted by the genial sympathy with nature's living forms in alliance with a warm sensibility to the beautiful, – qualities which crown and render effectual the other less elevated endowments for art. Thus, by the most minute manual labor, directed by those high and refined mental gifts, the clay model of the 'Slave' was wrought out; and there the artist's work ended: the creation was complete. The processes whereby it was now to be transferred to marble, though of a delicate, difficult time, requiring labor and time, are purely mechanical, and are performed, under the artist's direction, by uninspired hands.[26]

Even recent writers like Joy Kasson have felt the need to repeat this discourse, writing that assistants were 'controversial' but adding that 'some misunderstood their significance and suggested that sculptors were letting others do their work'.[27] At issue here, of course, is precisely the question of what 'work' (and 'the work') is and who owns it. In this sense, Ideal sculpture accords as much with the logic of late capitalism as it does with romantic accounts of genius, with their stress on struggle: it looks forward to the world of Jeff Koons or Damien Hirst, for whom merely thinking of an artwork is enough to touch it with the artist's name. Powers's statue was produced as a series: using his team of Italian craftsmen he made six full-sized versions of *The Greek Slave*, the last involving some remodelling; and many smaller versions were produced for domestic display. It is this industrialization which offended Hawthorne's interviewee.

Belt v. Lawes

I have said sculpture is haunted, so we can turn for a moment to ghosts. Controversy over the use of assistants, in Britain at least, came to a magnificent climax in *Belt v. Lawes* (1882–84), the last great case to be heard in Westminster Hall, described by one newspaper as 'the most portentous piece of modern litigation' after the notorious case of the Tichborne Claimant.[28] Charles Lawes, a sculptor, used a broadside in *Vanity Fair* for 20 August 1881 to accuse his fashionable rival, Richard Belt, of producing art on which he had not worked – effectively, of running a factory.[29] Belt sued and, after a six-month trial involving forty-three court days and scores of witnesses, was eventually vindicated and awarded a record £5,001 in damages. Lawes's subsequent appeal failed.[30] The trial was spectacular, involving many society figures (mostly clients testifying for Belt) and members of the Royal Academy (for Lawes), and a courtroom cluttered with sculptures which the public could see on viewing days.

The case provides a fascinating illustration of the problems of categorizing the labour of the sculptor. It also provides the first citation in the *Oxford English Dictionary* for 'ghost', meaning 'one who secretly does artistic or literary work for another person' – though clearly the phrase had been in use for some time. The sculptural 'ghost' thus precedes the ghostwriter, for the reason – remarked upon by the trial judge and commentators – that sculpture, with its laborious, multi-stage processes, involves delegation and surrogacy. The *Times* expressed surprise that this trial was the first of its kind and commented that 'often before sculptors have not been visited and called to account by their "ghosts", true or false'.[31] Belt was portrayed in terms of gothic substitution and trickery – with accusations that his 'ghosts', Verhyden and Brock, climbed up a ladder to a concealed cubbyhole at the back of his studio.

What underpinned the trial was class and the issue of who may form the ideal and direct others. Belt had begun as a 'machine boy' for the engineer of the House of Commons and taken art classes at a working men's club; his first sculpture was worked on waste stone with a nail. Lawes, who later inherited a baronetcy, had been a well-known sportsman at Eton and Oxford before deciding to take up sculpture; he and Belt trained in the same studio and he employed Belt briefly. The appearance of many Royal Academicians for Lawes (including Lord Leighton, President) reflected this social divide, as did Lawes's description of Belt as 'a broker of other men's sculpture', 'a statue-jobber and a tradesman' (*H*, 237). The only prominent artist to appear for Belt was William Morris, the apostle of craft and socialism. Belt's portrait, published in *Society* in 1883, shows him as a workman in an apron holding a mallet, with the legend 'My mind alone conceived it: no hand but mine touched it'. In contrast Lawes's portrait, in *Vanity Fair*, shows the haughty aristocrat and sportsman with coat, cane, and gloves.[32]

One issue was whether Belt *could* produce sculpture, so he volunteered to make a bust of his assistant Paglianti in a room adjoining the court. One of the reasons the defence failed was that when he had done so, the Royal Academy cohort rushed the bench to declare that the earlier sculpture of Paglianti on display was far superior and obviously 'ghosted' – when they had not previously questioned its attribution, and a witness had seen Belt make the earlier figure. But the more fundamental problem was a paradox: the Royal Academicians wished to defend an ideal making, using a system of delegation *which they themselves employed*. When Leighton was questioned on his use of an assistant for his famous 'Python', he replied: 'I made a highly finished sketch in clay. It put it into the hands of Mr Brock, who caused it to be set up and descended to various operations for which so skilled a sculptor is not required, but in all cases performed such offices as left the artistic individuality of the work wholly mine' (*H*, 249). The sculptor makes in his head; the worker executes the design. These are exactly the terms in which Belt himself supported an idealized view of sculpture. Asked how much an assistant should do for a competition work, Belt replied, 'The assistant may have as much or more ability than the competitor – it will be the difference between execution and mind.... Many people employ persons superior in art' (*H*, 242). Indeed, he was willing to describe the sculptor as a godlike maker: 'With a mask and a "squeeze" we produce animation. I do not take measurements from living persons and give them to my assistants.... No hand but mine touches these heads from start to finish. Many others do it, but I do not, as a fact; but I do not think it very wrong.... No one has ever put animation or expression into any head for me.'[33] But from Leighton's point of view, Lawes was simply the wrong type of person to make these claims: his was a body which should be directed by others, not one which animates.[34]

Lord Coleridge's dissenting judgment at the appeal hearing focused unerringly on the question of the animation or generation of the work as described by Aristotle. Noting that to some extent the Royal Academy itself had been on trial, he commented:

I have already stated what I conceive to be the true question in this case; it is perhaps better that I should also state what I conceive it was not. It was not whether Mr. Belt could make a passable model, one which to an uneducated or uncultivated eye would pass muster as a piece of sculpture. Most men of the least dexterity of hand could do as much as this. The question was not this, but whether fine works of art, admitted on all hands to be so, were really his work or the works of other men; and as to this, again, whether, in the long course of working upon them, he may not now and then have actually handled the clay, or even carved the marble, but whether the completed work, the art in them when they had art – what I believe logicians call 'the formal cause' of them – that which made them what they are, was Mr. Belt's work or another's.... In sculpture, in the long and various process from the slight clay sketch or drawing to the completed marble, there is so much which is necessarily mechanical, and which a competent carving mason can do just as well as a Phidias or Michelangelo. Help, therefore, up to a certain point, every sculptor from the highest to the lowest has, or may have, with absolute integrity; indeed with universal knowledge and acceptance. But there comes a point in modelling, and I should have supposed, but for what I have heard of Flaxman, there comes a point in the carving too, where mechanism ends and original art begins. I imagine that this point is almost impossible to state in words with any approach to accuracy. (*H*, 256–57)

Coleridge's formulas struggle to distinguish the maker as abstract 'formal cause' from making as craft, equated with the 'mechanism' of reproduction. Is the touch of the hand a mere mechanical process, extraneous to the act of creation, or is it the animating cause? His dissenting judgment was that we must trust the experts – the aristocrats of taste, the academicians – but that is simply to understand the circularity of the argument, the fact that the power to claim authorship is simply power itself.

Faced with the mystique of sculptural labour, it was almost impossible for the judges to say who was 'right'. Lawes lost mainly because of contradictions in his evidence. But one of Belt's key witnesses later admitted lying, and Belt did employ teams of workmen. When he produced a new version of the decayed statue of Queen Anne outside St. Paul's in 1886, for example, he was refused the right to put his name on it by the City Lands Committee after it was revealed that he had made a plaster cast of the original, repaired it, and then delegated the rest.[35] What this tells us is that he had assumed certain rights: creation remains a secret lodged in the interaction of 'hands' – his and those he employed. Indeed, one could argue that after Coleridge's failed stand on behalf of the Academy, the field is open for anyone to claim that power. The issues remain with us: the teams of workers employed by artists like Damien Hirst and his own entanglement in accusations about the use of others' ideas or his drawing ability raise the question of what making *is*; whether it is simply the signature.[36] The extent to which the work of the assistant can be rendered invisible is part of this complex.

It may be objected that what I have provided is an excessively materialistic account of sculpture: as if talking about the mechanics of making could say anything about the work of a Flaxman and its power to move us. One answer to that is personal: I don't find Ideal sculpture, with a few exceptions, particularly emotionally engaging; its material, artefactual state seems troubling – and this is a feeling I think I share with many nineteenth-century commentators. A second response is that the achievement of such sculpture is so manifestly technical and bound up with the circumstances of its making that it seems impossible to disentangle questions of the status of making from the artwork; indeed, as I have suggested, the repression of such questions – of authority to shape and direct, of the use of human instruments – is part of the possibility of certain meanings being attached to the work.

AMERICANS

With this example in mind, we can now move back to Powers and his compatriots. As some contemporary commentators noticed, American sculptors were particularly subject to accusations about the use of assistants. This may reflect lingering doubts about American cultural achievement. James Jackson Jarves stresses the necessity of pragmatic, calculating America to produce an ideal art: to gain skill as a foundation, but then to distinguish craft from genius. In *Art Thoughts* (1869) he distinguishes 'manual processes' like chromolithography from the 'higher functions'; the mere copyist (or 'forger') from the artist who develops a tradition through 'thought' and 'taste'.[37] The leading American sculptor William

Wetmore Storey faced the accusation that 'the images he turns out are not his own; that they are rudely moulded, and then given into the hands of skilled artificers in order to be perfected, and that the credit accruing to him is really due to his subordinates.'[38] In response, the writer of the report on these accusations insisted that the statue is 'made tender' by the 'last loving touches' of the artist: 'No sculptor, we venture to say, completes his idea from conception to its execution, without extraneous and mechanical aid.... It is in the conception and the finish that the sculptor's highest faculties come principally into play.' In Storey's *Conversations in a Studio* (1890) the dialogue dwells almost obsessively on the workman and assistant:

MALLETT ... Nothing of the arrangement, or of the finish, or of the feeling is his, and as the work approximates to completion he becomes useless, and the sculptor works alone....

BELTON. In a word, all that any assistant does is purely mechanical, under the direction of the sculptor. He invents nothing, he designs nothing, and he only copies at best, or prepares the parts for the hand of the sculptor to finish.[39]

Such comments suggest a massive ideological effort whose aim is to insist that the workman is a slave rather than a master, a merely mechanical extension of the forming mind of the artist. (The term 'mechanical' is itself interesting, since it has been suggested that the Elizabethan coinage 'mechanicals' for labourers was a learned translation of the Greek *banausoi*.)

Women artists were also singled out for accusation, since they could more clearly articulate the contradictions involved in the 'sculpture complex': they were not as strong and therefore to be doubted in terms of labour; ideologically suspect in terms of the giving of form. Lydia Maria Child sponsored the African-American sculptor Edmonia Lewis but resisted her move from clay to marble, from common earth to spirit, from reproduction to origination. 'She might have made a very good copyist', she remarked, stressing that her busts from life were not as good as her copies of extant works – echoing many other comments on black writers as clever mimics.[40] Or to take another example, one of the best-known photographs of the American sculptor Harriet Hosmer shows her surrounded by her Italian assistants – all twenty-four of them. It is no wonder, then, that she – like Storey, like Powers – was subject to rumours that her *Zenobia* was the product of artisans. Following Joseph Mozier's anonymous attack in the *Queen* in 1863, Hosmer had to defend herself in print, legally, and in terms of practice. As Charmian Nelson notes, these accusations forced other women sculptors in Rome, including Emma

Stebbins and Edmonia Lewis, into 'the unorthodox and physically strenuous practice of doing their own carving'.[41] Defenders of Hosmer stressed that the modelling and cutting 'is all done by her own hands; even the hard, rough, mechanical portions of the work'.[42]

Hosmer's response to Mozier, 'The Process of Sculpture', was published in the *Atlantic Monthly* in 1864. Uncovering the 'mysteries of the studio', she dispels the notion that 'the artist, beginning with the crude block, and guided by his imagination only, hews out his statue with his own hands', instead carefully detailing the processes of clay modelling and scaling: 'To perform that part assigned him, it is not necessary that the assistant should be a man of imagination or refined taste, – it is sufficient that he have simply the skill, with the aid of accurate measurements, to construct the framework of iron and copy the small model before him.'[43] Those who make the object become objects: the 'assistant modeller forms as necessary part of studio "property" as the living model or the marble-workers' (736). Higher attributes belong to the sculptor: brain, imagination, individuality, originality, beauty, refinement, and style. These are expressed in the full-size clay model. But the next stage, casting in plaster and working on the marble, is again a zone of anxiety: 'many' will be shocked that the sculptor leaves it to the 'scientific' workmen to produce the marble figure, moving on to a 'new creation' rather than wielding the mallet and chisel; many will 'ingeniously discover traces of the sculptor's hand where they do not exist' (735). The metaphor Hosmer elaborates for the activities of the workmen – that of 'translating' the intentions 'stamped' on clay to marble, that of 'mere linguist to the author' (736) – is designed to move the reader away from a focus on making, from hand to 'tongue'. This is firmer ground for the female artist; and indeed, as Hosmer was stigmatized for alleged relations with one of her workman, one can see why she would want to move away from the body as ground of making.

Powers's relation to this discourse is interesting. Despite Calvert's suggestion (quoted earlier) that he did not finish his own pieces, he was unusually involved in the production of his works. Donald Reynolds, in a pioneering essay published in 1977, stressed that Powers adapted the traditional tripartite clay–plaster–marble model of construction, with 'its Platonic distinction between substance and shadow', often sculpting directly in plaster.[44] That is to say that he partially collapsed two stages in the process of copying – though even this is attached by Reynolds to a typically passive-voice account of how 'his conception … *was reproduced* identically in Seravezza marble'. Powers stressed his schooling of and control over of his assistants, 'like instruments in my own hands'.[45] He was also known for his skill as a toolmaker, though for Hawthorne this (like Greek machine-making) is turned towards humour:

Powers took us into a room apart – apparently the secretest room he had – and showed us some tools and machinery, all of his own contrivance and invention. 'You see I am a bit of a Yankee,' he observed.... These inventions, he says, are his amusement, and the bent of his nature towards sculpture must indeed have been strong, to counteract, in an American, such a capacity for the contrivance of steam-engines.[46]

He is, then, an artist who can produce on an industrial scale and yet, supposedly, maintain authorial control over his works, who can contain the oppositions of ideal conception and whipping the marble into shape. But the use of other things – mechanicals, instruments – means that slavery is more than simply incidental to his art.

SCULPTURAL PAIN AND THE OBDURATE TONGUE

Having considered the fact that sculpture involves the mechanization of the bodies of others, we must note a second suggestive connection between sculpture and slavery: pain. Simon Richter has suggested that pain is central to the neoclassical aesthetics inaugurated by Winckelmann. 'The serene surface of ideal beauty,' he writes, 'as well as the equally serene surface of its discourse, simultaneously conceals and is dependent on some form of the dynamics of the infliction of bodily pain.' In this account, the appearance of the body is enabled by a suppressed medical interest in the painful exposure of musculature, and by a classical inheritance centred on such figures as Laocoön, Philoctetes, and Marsayas – the flayed, painfully exposed body of the last representing 'the primal scene of classicism', its hidden secret.[47] Richter points out that the term *Reiz* is central to this ambiguous aesthetic – a term which is initially translated as 'grace' or 'charm' but also comes, after the eighteenth century, to mean 'pain', 'irritation', or 'stimulus' (as in Freud's *Reizschutz*, or 'protective shield'; or *Reizüberflutung*, 'sensory overload').[48] Beauty conceals a freight of pain.

Elaine Scarry argues for a more general equivalence between the externalization of the body in making and pain, pointing out that the alienation of work in both slavery and nineteenth-century capitalism involves a 'fundamental shattering of the integrity of act-and-object in the human psyche; for the body at work was separated from the objects of its work'.[49] The statue, that is to say, often contains or reveals states of bodily torment which in actual experience are unspeakable. (There are parallels here with the account of music I offer in Chapter 5, in which pain is seen as

contained in a sonic envelope.) Scarry's argument is heavily indebted to
Hannah Arendt, for whom the necessity imposed on humans by nature is
matched in human affairs only by torture.[50] Only slaves, Arendt points out,
were commonly tortured in antiquity, since they were 'subject to necessity
anyhow'. The violence imposed on slaves was necessary to establish the
ideal of freedom for Greeks; and consequently the arts 'harbour an element of violence within themselves'.[51] Arendt, while noting the improve-
ments in human life brought about by the suppression of social violence,
unflinchingly links the violence of slavery to the valuation of the arts.

A central demand of slavery itself was that slaves contain their feelings,
remaining mute in their suffering. If one wanted to choose an emblem
for the 'contained' pain bound up in sculptural tradition, at least as it
relates to African-American life, one could do no better than follow Phillis
Wheatley, the first African-American poet of any real achievement. If the
Laocoön is the most famous classical depiction of pain, the thirteen figures
of the Niobe Group are also important, focused on the afflicted mother
rather than the struggling father. They were unearthed near Florence in
1583, influencing Shelley and others. Niobe's story offers a literal understanding of sculpture as pain: after Niobe belittled the goddess Latona
(mother of Apollo and Diana), the two Olympians killed Niobe's seven
sons and seven daughters; Niobe's husband kills himself and she turns
to stone, becoming a weeping outcrop in her homeland in Asia Minor.
Wheatley's version of the story was published as 'Niobe in Distress for
Her Children Slain by Apollo, From *Ovid's Metamorphoses*, Book VI. And
from a View of the Painting of *Mr. Richard Wilson*':[52]

> The queen of all her family bereft,
> Without or husband, son, or daughter left,
> Grew stupid at the shock. The passing air
> Made no impression on her stiff'ning hair.
> The blood forsook her face: amidst the flood
> Pour'd from her cheeks, quite fix'd her eye-balls stood.
> Her tongue, her palate both obdurate grew,
> Her curdled veins no longer motion knew;
> The use of neck, and arms, and feet was gone,
> And ev'n her bowels hard'ned into stone:
> A marble statue now the queen appears,
> But from the marble steal the silent tears.

What would have drawn Wheatley to this story? Jennifer Thorn suggests
that its depiction of tyrannical gods and the denial of a family reflect
Wheatley's own situation in Boston, subordinated to white owners, no

matter how benevolent, in a situation in which African-American servants in the North were discouraged from having children.[53] More generally, the Niobe story offers a commentary on the use of the female slave's body. If one puzzle in Ovid's text is why Niobe continues to boast of her fecundity after her sons are killed, prompting the slaughter of her daughters, that boast finds a resonant context in slavery, dependent on African birth rates (compare Wheatley on the Gambia: 'Her soil spontaneous, yields exhaustless stores; / For phoebus revels on her verdant shores')[54].

Yet like neoclassical sculpture itself, Wheatley's work presents a problem of surface which challenges such interpretations. With their polished exteriors and their 'correctness', her poems plot an entry into polite letters (itself, of course, a political statement). They often deflect critics seeking to find evidence of a direct response to slavery or hints of an African-American aesthetic, since if traces of racial awareness are present, they often exist at an extremely sublimated level. What we are called to do is look at the surface itself: the polish is not simply evidence of craft and education, but also a statement about the containment of the suffering that is attached to her existence. Indeed, one could say that the interplay between suffering and the silence of a surface is Wheatley's topic. Ovid hints at a continued pride and aristocratic indifference in Niobe. In Wheatley this becomes a flat stoicism:

> 'But show the cause from whence your triumphs flow?
> Tho' I unhappy mourn these children slain,
> Yet greater numbers to my lot remain.'

In the transformation passage which follows, Niobe is not turned to stone by a compassionate god (as in some versions of the legend), but reacts internally, as it were, to her pride and grief, sealing up the pain within her.

We can compare the pattern of terms Wheatley uses with those in her two immediate models: Sandys's 1632 version, partially written in America; and Samuel Garth's 1717 compilation for the publisher Tonson, in which book 6 is translated by Samuel Croxall.[55] Sandys uses 'waxing stiffe' to describe Niobe's state; 'eye-balls fix', palate and tongue 'congeal'. Croxall uses 'hardened with woes', 'congealed' and 'frozen', and 'stagnate' blood. Wheatley repeats 'fix'd' and shifts the transferred epithet 'congealed' (used for the tongue in the earlier versions) more literally to 'curdled veins'. Where her translation most clearly stands alone is in the use of three terms. Firstly, where Croxall describes death ('Action, and life from ev'ry part are gone') and both Sandys and Croxall use the word 'dead', Wheatley describes a person who is petrified but *alive*. Secondly, she stresses the fact that Niobe '[g]rew stupid at the shock' of her grief (spelling out the link between trauma and immobility). And thirdly, she uses the word 'obdurate' to describe Niobe's tongue (Croxall uses the word some twenty-five lines earlier, describing her as growing 'obdurate by her load of grief'). 'Obdurate' means hardened, though the *Oxford English Dictionary* lists the literal use of the term as rarer than the notion of hardening in heart or sin. In materializing the term, Wheatley directs us towards a *psychology* more firmly than her predecessors, a psychology linked to slavery ('sullenness,' 'obduracy', 'stupidity' are all terms directed at slaves). A 'soft' tongue is desirable in horses, signalling responsiveness; an obdurate tongue signals the refusal even of lament.

It is in this context that Niobe, the grieving woman who becomes a marble statue, can be read as inaugurating a story in which formal surface signals a contained emotion; in which whatever impels and motivates is locked inside a frozen figure. We may wish to see in Wheatley's version a reference to African-American motherhood, stripped of husband and children; or to African motherhood, proud of fecundity but rendered speechless at the rapacity of those with power. But those references are never explicit; they are sealed off from the reader. Thorn argues that in Wheatley's version of Niobe, 'nothing is learned, no social benefit accrued, no divine order affirmed, by Niobe's suffering and petrification'.[56] Similar tropes are used in later African-American writing, for example, France Harper's 'Eliza Harris': 'Save the heave of the breast and the sway of her hair, / You'd have thought her a statue of fear and despair'.[57]

In this way, the statue – as figure and as Powers's example – does important cultural work, enabling an imagination of pain which is not easily yoked to the kind of problems implicit in the spectacles of violence central to abolitionist discourse.[58] The statue defeats an easy empathy. The issue of pain in ancient statuary was discussed in a piece by Sue V. Beeson entitled 'The Gospel of Pain', which appeared in 1882 in the *Journal of Speculative Philosophy* – the St. Louis–based publication to which we will return at the end of this chapter. Beeson suggests that '[t]he element of pain is found in the art of Greece only after it begins its decline'; it represents a falling into the human and struggle from a position of serene mastery. She refers to the Niobe Group as an example of 'endurance accompanied with intellectual recognition', and to the Laocoön and its distinction between mature and youthful suffering, and stresses that will and pain are locked in a Schopenhauerian struggle in more recent statuary: 'will freezing itself from the environment of the flesh and rising to the ideal conception of the spirit'.[59] In this she echoes Winckelmann (translated in the same journal

Figure 5. Edmonia Lewis, *Cleopatra* (1875–76). Smithsonian American Art Museum, Washington, D.C. Gift of the Historical Society of Forest Park, Illinois.

in this period), who wrote of Laocoön's 'effort to contain and shut up the pain within himself'.[60] The containment of pain was central to readings of Powers's *Greek Slave*, the expressionless statue becoming an index of what it did not say, of a self-overcoming which bespeaks superiority.

One might offer a stony parallel here, the African-American sculptor Edmonia Lewis's statue *Cleopatra* (1875–86, Figure 5).[61] In Lewis's work, pain is not depicted in a classical tension with will: will and struggle have departed, leaving flesh which sinks towards a pure materiality; which refuses to signify – a representation which parallels Wheatley's 'obdurate' tongue. Lewis's statue was created for return to America: for the Philadelphia Centennial Exposition (the American government sent a boat to Rome to pick up the work of the expatriate colony), though

America then lost it for a century until its rediscovery in a Chicago yard in the early 1990s. In contrast to William Wetmore Storey's more contemplative queen in his better-known work – to which Lewis's was surely a response – Cleopatra is depicted slumped in painful despair or death, a massive embodiment of what will not be animated or restored. As the contemporary art critic William J. Clark commented, 'The effects of death are represented with such skill as to be absolutely repellent – and it is a question whether a statue of the ghastly characteristics of this one does not overstep the bounds of legitimate art. Apart from all questions of taste, however, the striking qualities of the work are undeniable.'[62] The skill here parallels Wheatley in presenting a residue of pain which the artwork renders as dead flesh (or inert stone), troubling the viewer with its sense of the human retreating from the flesh – in contrast to the classical view in which the hand of the sculptor has bestowed life.

We will quickly examine two related nineteenth-century uses of the trope of petrification or marmorealization. This is Harriet Beecher Stowe's description of meeting the abolitionist and former slave Sojourner Truth:

[A] tall, spare form arose to meet me. She was evidently a full-blooded African, and though now aged and worn with many hardships, still gave the impression of a physical development which in early youth must have been as fine a specimen of the torrid zone as Cumberworth's celebrated statuette of the Negro Woman at the Fountain. Indeed, she so strongly reminded me of that figure, that, when I recall the events of her life, as she narrated them to me, I imagine her as a living, breathing impersonation of that work of art.[63]

If the former slave seems like a statue endowed with a mesmeric power, at the end of the article she returns to animate a sculpture by William Wetmore Storey which, in Stowe's view, should be on the Capitol. Stowe was an avid spiritualist, and she insists that through her mediumship the spirit of Sojourner enters Storey's work:

[H]er memory still lives in one of the loftiest and most original works of modern art, the Libyan Sibyl, by Mr. Story.... Some years ago, when visiting Rome, I related Sojourner's history to Mr. Story at a breakfast at his house. Already had his mind begun to turn to Egypt in search of a type of art which should represent a larger and more vigorous development of nature than the cold elegance of Greek lines. His glorious Cleopatra was then in process of evolution, and his mind was working out the problem of her broadly developed nature, of all that slumbering weight and fulness of passion with which this statue seems charged, as a heavy thunder-cloud is charged with electricity.[64]

A few days later, Storey models his famous *Libyan Sibyl*. Sojourner is present, Stowe suggests, both in this statue and in the later *Cleopatra*: in the electricity which animates the stone, in the power of painful memory held in the form.

For these writers, stone carries a weight of pain, as if the silent incorporation of labour we have seen in the process of making sculpture also represented a binding up of the sufferings of the past. Recall Browning:

> They say Ideal Beauty cannot enter
> The house of anguish. On the threshold stands
> An alien Image with enshackled hands,
> Called the Greek Slave! as if the artist meant her
> (That passionless perfection which he lent her
> Shadowed not darkened where the sill expands)
> To so confront man's crimes in different lands
> With man's ideal sense. Pierce to the centre,
> Art's fiery finger! – and break up ere long
> The serfdom of this world! appeal, fair stone,
> From God's pure heights of beauty against man's wrong!
> Catch up in the divine face, not alone
> East griefs but west, – and strike and shame the strong,
> By thunders of white silence, overthrown.

This is, paradoxically, an attack on the aesthetics of surface which is embodied in the marble itself: the 'white silence' is that of the figure, but it is also the silence shattered by art, involving the viewer seeing more than is apparent in the artwork and its immediate context. The irony that the 'serfdom of this world' is also embodied in the production of the statue seems part of the poem's power. (One work on nineteenth-century American sculptors borrows 'white silence' for its title.)[65] In Browning's poem, the statue becomes a traumatic container, akin to the sonnet itself.

It is that status of sculpture as a container of suppressed anguish, I believe, which explains why what is arguably the first systematic study of racial depiction in the arts by an African American focuses on sculpture – of all the available arts. Freeman Murray's *Emancipation and the Freed in American Sculpture* (1916) perceptively surveys depictions of African Americans and slavery, and the few available works by African-American sculptors, climaxing in his book in a moving account of his own family history as it is bound up with the famous Saint-Gaudens memorial to the black fighters of the 54th Regiment surrounding Colonel Shaw, erected on Boston Common. His study anticipates some of the links made here, citing Stowe as the instigator of Storey's work, for example. But one might notice that writing of Powers's *Greek Slave*, he is alone among all commentators in *beginning* with the workmen, before citing Browning: 'This statue … was indeed as well "finished" as the sculptor's Italian workmen could make it and was "polished to perfection."[66] Among many other things, he has seen the ghosts.

THE MARBLE FAUN

We can now turn to texts which draw out the connections I have been pursuing between the sculptural imagination, instrumentality, and labour. The most important is Nathaniel Hawthorne's *The Marble Faun* (1860). Recent criticism of *The Scarlet Letter* has tended to describe it as offering a displaced exploration of the 'branding' of identity in slavery and its moral overcoming. In a similar way, *The Marble Faun* is an exploration of the 'labour complex' which I have suggested is bound up with sculpture, distributed over the novel's central grouping of two women and two men: Kenyon, the Ideal sculptor; Hilda, the copyist; Miriam, the artist with the trace of 'darkness' and pain in her past; and Donatello, the Italian model and nobleman whose body encodes both the antique and a native vigour. Race is only a trace in the novel – in speculations over Miriam's origins, in the Africanized figure of Cleopatra which Kenyon constructs – but nonetheless it is present at the text's margins, as it was more generally for the American community in Rome. Moreover, the novel's central preoccupation is the issue of making use of others: Kenyon uses his workmen to execute his will; Hilda is used by the old masters to execute theirs; Donatello executes what he perceives to be Miriam's aggressive desires; Miriam has resisted the will of others and been punished.

The Marble Faun explores the process by which sculpture is made in some detail, nowhere better than in chapter 13, 'A Sculptor's Studio':

Here might be witnessed the process of actually chiselling the marble, with which (as it is not quite satisfactory to think) a sculptor, in these days, has very little to do. In Italy, there is a class of men whose merely mechanical skill is perhaps more exquisite than was possessed by the ancient artificers, who wrought out the designs of Praxiteles, or, very possibly, by Praxiteles himself.... The sculptor has but to present these men with a plaister-cast of his design, and a sufficient block of marble, and tell them that the figure is imbedded in the stone, and must be freed from its encumbering superfluities; and, in due time, without the necessity of his touching the work with his own finger, he will see before him the statue that is to make him renowned. His creative power has wrought it with a word.

In no other art, surely, does genius find such effective instruments, and so happily relieve itself of the drudgery of actual performance; doing wonderfully nice things by the hands of other people.... They are not his work, but that of some nameless machine in human shape.[67]

This is a wonderfully rich passage. A few years earlier James Jackson Jarves had written: 'No machine can model an idea, or fill an hiatus of the imagination. When we succeed in measuring the soul. Then, and not until then, we may be able to reduce sculpture to a mechanical art.'[68] The 'hiatus in the imagination' is precisely the issue here. Does the making of others have an impact on the process? Hawthorne's assistant is like an embodiment of Jarves's figure, a 'nameless machine in human shape'. The Aristotelian figure of the slave as the body which needs the direction of the soul of a master again enters the account of making. From his labour, value is extracted in the name of the ideal. This clearly occasions some ambivalence in Hawthorne: in the chapter describing the sculptors' salon, he cynically describes a business, the working of marble at 'about two or three dollars per pound' into 'certain shapes (by their own mechanical ingenuity, or that of artizans in their employment) that would enable them to sell it again at a much higher figure' (966).

The artisan accordingly creates considerable anxiety. His skill is the link to Praxiteles (supposed fashioner of the original Marble Faun in the Capitoline galleries); it is he who, like Michelangelo attacking the block, 'frees' the ideal object imprisoned in stone. In contrast, the operation of the sculptor is so abstract that it might be a 'word'. This anxiety helps explain the pessimism persistently associated with sculpture in the text. Late in the novel, Kenyon meditates on a fragmentary Venus excavated near Rome, reconstructed as an ideal totality.[69] He finds the head and places it 'on the slender neck of the newly discovered statue': 'The effect was magical. It immediately lighted up and vivified the whole figure, endowing it with personality, soul, and intelligence. The beautiful Idea at once asserted its immortality, and converted that heap of forlorn fragments into a whole, as perfect to the mind, if not to the eye, as when the new marble gleamed with snowy lustre' (1206). This moment is, as Charles Swann suggests, a challenge to the novel as a whole: in a distracted state, Kenyon cannot sustain this ideal vision in the world: '[I]n reality, he found it difficult to fix his mind upon the subject ... the divine statue seemed to fall asunder again, and became only a heap or worthless fragments' (1207). In fact, he is ambivalent about the process of sculpture throughout the novel. As he and Miriam walk through the Capitoline galleries, Kenyon criticizes the Dying Gladiator (now usually called the 'Dying Gaul') for its awkward capturing of a moment of transition rather than ideal repose, time-bound where it should represent 'a moral standstill' (here as elsewhere his terms are largely drawn from Winckelmann). Miriam's satirical comment exposes his fear of the temporal: 'You think that sculpture should be a sort of fossilizing process' (865). She is right to question the marmoreal: his most successful works, the narrator informs us, are clay figures like the portrait bust he makes of Donatello, perfected with an unconscious or automatic ('accidental') gesture, a squeeze of the clay. They approximate the genre which everywhere in Hawthorne signals the fleeting and vibrant: the sketch, like the fragment from an old master which is handed around a salon in the novel, revealing 'the very effervescence of his genius' (967). The closest that the sculptural can come to the sketch is the emphasis on the final 'touch' applied to the clay (989). In this, Hawthorne again echoes Winckelmann, for whom 'the soft medium of the modeller and the sketch on paper ... affords us the true spirit of the artist'.[70]

The only sculpture we see Kenyon actually granting transcendent power is the Laocoön, where he recognizes its weight of pain. The same could be said of the *Cleopatra* (based directly on William Wetmore Storey's statue, which Hawthorne saw in preparation), which is his own magnum opus. With 'full Nubian lips' and the 'repose of despair' (957) written into her surface, the figure gathers up the struggles of a lifetime rather than freezing a moment. Hawthorne's formulas, with their stress on the sculptor as 'poet', attempt to bridge once again the gap between conception and execution:

'It is the concretion of a good deal of thought, emotion, and toil of brain and hand,' said Kenyon, not without a perception that his work was good. – 'But I know not how it came about at last. I kindled a great fire within my mind, and threw in the material – as Aaron threw the gold of the Israelites into the furnace – and, in the midmost heat, uprose Cleopatra, as you see her.' (958)

One problem is that the word 'concretions' was used just a few pages earlier to disparage the shoddy busts of the undeserving: 'the concretions and petrifactions of a vain self-estimate' (951). More importantly, the metaphor of the casting process – 'kindled a great fire' suggests Bernini's famously muscular account of casting his *Perseus* – is used to characterize a mesmerically conceived *mental* process which allows Cleopatra to appear in spectral form ('uprose'), meaning the 'hand' is again problematic. Compare the later making of the actual statue, in which it becomes the fossilized trace of its fiery conception:

Kenyon's Roman artizans, all this while, had been at work on the Cleopatra. The fierce Egyptian queen had now struggled almost out of the imprisoning stone; or, rather, the workmen had found her within the mass of marble, imprisoned there by magic, but still fervid to the touch with fiery life, the fossil woman of an age that produced statelier, stronger, and more passionate, creatures than our own. (1166)

The word 'freed' recurs in descriptions of the marble being worked: it is the workmen who struggle to 'free' the painfully imprisoned queen, to realize the ideal. In contrast, Kenyon wishes to strike what threatens to become 'a mere lump of senseless stone' (1167), devoid of the spiritual. As in the Hegelian account of the master–slave relation, it is the worker – though Hawthorne provides no account of this – who struggles to achieve freedom through his work.

In the episode which follows, Hilda praises Kenyon's bust of Donatello, seeing in its permanent incompletion ('It stood on a wooden pedestal, not nearly finished, but with fine white dust and small chips of marble scattered about it') a realization of the ideal:

Most spectators mistake it for an unsuccessful attempt towards copying the features of the Faun of Praxiteles. One observer in a thousand is conscious of something more.... What perplexes him is the riddle that he sees propounded there; the riddle of the Soul's growth, taking its first impulse amid remorse and pain, and struggling through the incrustations of the senses. (1169–70)

But this bust which supposedly testifies to the 'something more' is functionally unlikely: Kenyon does not hew the marble elsewhere in the novel; he applies his touch to the clay and leaves the rest to assistants. The meaning of the bust is central to the story of Donatello's fortunate fall and Hilda's gradual moral development, but in its attachment to an impossible object it insinuates a gap between conception and the object – the gap where labour stands.

If labour is one issue in the novel, a related one is that of copying: present in the process of making sculpture, but also in the relation between art and antiquity. In imitating the ancients, are sculptors necessarily plagiarists, as Miriam suggests? Hugh Honor argues that neoclassical artists drew a 'sharp distinction' between the 'copy' and the 'imitation'[71] – one that was, as we have seen, necessary to the ideology of genius. One corollary of the idealization of the original is the pervasive nineteenth-century tendency to ascribe all Roman statues to an imputed 'lost' Greek original (often a statue mentioned by Pliny or other authorities). This *Kopienkritique* has been criticized by art historians who point out that the classical world had a pervasive culture of copying, blending, and working from templates.[72] And as Seymour Howard argues, despite Canova's refusal to restore or 'complete' the Parthenon marbles, 'his own "New Classics" were essentially pastiche-like caricatures based upon the eclectic procedures used by restorers and academicians, assembled from "fragments" of ancient masterpieces recombined to make fresh "archaeological" creations, which classically trained specialists praised for their "legitimate" style'.[73] Powers's work is, in the account of the hostile critic encountered by Hawthorne, just such pastiche.

The fear of influence is represented in the novel by Hilda, the budding American artist who comes to Rome and, overwhelmed by the riches of the past, becomes a copyist. In her characterization, a complex form of the master–slave dialectic is enacted. Hilda's copying is depicted as an act of sympathetic engagement, a 'surrender' of the self, but also as a form of potential enslavement: 'The Old Masters will not set me free' (1129). She incarnates process seen from the inside. Where other copyists produce a 'superficial imitation', she 'had been led to her results by following pre-cisely the same processes, step-by-step, through which the original painter had trodden to the development of his idea' (901). She works not like a 'machine', reproducing a surface, but in such a way that the 'life and soul' of the picture are transported – in a way in which, according to the contradictory ideology we have examined, sculptural assistants *must* and also *cannot* work: must so that the touch of the sculptor is realized; can-not because the work is seen as mechanical. Rather than being simply a figure for fidelity, she offers a completion of the work of the 'masters'. Indeed, her activity as an instrument threatens to supplant (at least in one sense) that of the master, in a copybook version of the Hegelian account in which the master is incomplete and the servant the more self-conscious realization of his desire:

In some instances, even ... she had been enabled to execute what the great Master had conceived in his imagination, but had not so perfectly succeeded in putting upon canvas; – a result surely not impossible when such depth of sympathy as she possessed was assisted by the delicate skill and accuracy of her slender hand. In such cases, the girl was but a finer instrument, a more exquisitely effective piece of mechanism, by the help of which the spirit of some great departed Painter now first achieved his ideal, centuries after his own earthly hand, that other tool, had turned to dust. (900)

This is a form of feminine mediumship, with the dead artist as 'control'; another version of the combination of directing spirit and subordinated body as tool which is implicit in slavery.

If Hilda the copyist can be aligned with the sculptural assistant, repro-ducing the superior will of another, what of Miriam, the 'dark' woman whose mysterious origin drives the narrative? One rumoured account of Miriam is that she is 'the offspring of a Southern American planter, who had given her an elaborate education and endowed her with his wealth; but the one burning drop of African blood in her veins so affected her with a sense of ignominy, that she relinquished all, and fled her country'

(870). If this is later dismissed in favour of origins in a southern Italian family and a story of scandal, nevertheless her vein of 'Jewish blood' (1211) racializes that past, making her pain an inherited taint. A trace of racial inheritance is also present in her powerful response to Kenyon's *Cleopatra*. Her art is 'shadowed' by the trace embodied in the 'spectre' which follows her. Her sketches are described as disfigured by a twisting which modifies an initially lofty manner: a 'wayward quirk' which makes her Jael a 'vulgar murderess'; a 'scorn' which makes her Judith a cook looking at a calf's head (887). The moral, the narrator comments, is that 'woman must strike through her own heart to reach a human life': a moral relating to a painful awareness of subordination, a form of the unhappy consciousness. In contrast, she shows Donatello a series of portraits of domestic life in which femininity is entirely unquestioned, but in which she herself is always depicted as apart and in 'deep sadness'. The only work she presents which seems fully realized is a self-portrait which, because it is the place where the narrator displays an investment ('we forbore to speak descriptively of Miriam's beauty earlier in our narrative, because we foresaw this occasion', 892), speaks of a self-consciousness and self-revelation equated with both her painful past and her tragic destiny. Miriam's true subject is herself.

The Marble Faun, Donatello, represents the 'realization' of the ancient statue (the Marble Faun in the Capitoline galleries), as if the statue has struggled to free itself from stone. And in other ways, too, he incarnates a struggle with inheritance and fixation. He seems an incarnation of the past – the race of fauns, the ur-object of sculpture, but also that which resists modelling, so quick are his movements. More crudely, he is also a version of the loose-limbed Italian workmen depicted in so many accounts, the person whose body gives flesh to another's intention. He appears late in the novel dressed as a peasant and often seems more like a workman than the Count of Monte Beni. He is 'anything but intellectually brilliant' (869); and his fixation on executing Miriam's will is so absolute that it leads him to murder. But his linkage to the act is also the catalyst for moral development – another version of the Hegelian movement towards freedom born out of bondage.

Miriam's position signals the pain of history, of subordination and the unhappy consciousness associated with a self-understanding that can find no direct relationship with the world. Hilda's refusal to acknowledge Miriam's pain and her refusal of Kenyon's offering of Donatello's story as a version of the fortunate fall – long an interpretive crux in the novel – are also a refusal to see an American reality, to move beyond the reproduction of the past into a developmental model after her artistic and political flight

from America. She dwells in a tower above the 'corrupted atmosphere' of
the city; expatriation has freed her from the 'shackles' of convention; she
has come to Italy as the place of art, 'as if statues could not assume grace
and expression, save in that land of whitest marble' (697). As Kenyon confirms in his discussion with Miriam, 'Her womanhood is of the ethereal
type, and incompatible with any shadow of darkness or evil' (958). Like
Powers's *Greek Slave*, she refuses darkness and rises above it – she is often
depicted in the novel as a kind of statue herself. But in achieving this
state, she suppresses the pain of both historicity and her own subordination. In that respect Hawthorne's well-known declaration in his preface
to the novel takes on a different aspect:

Italy, as the site of his Romance, was chiefly valuable to him as affording a sort of
poetic or fairy precinct, where actualities would not be so terribly insisted upon,
as they are, and must needs be, in America. No author, without a trial, can conceive of the difficulty of writing a Romance about a country where there is no
shadow, no antiquity, no mystery, no picturesque and gloomy wrong, nor anything but a common–place prosperity, in broad and simple daylight, as is happily
the case with my dear native land. (854)

What if we read this as less about a lack of cultural depth than about the
threatening shadows of American reality? In this sense, the exploration
of statuary in the novel is a displacement of those realities and a realization of all that they represent in terms of bondage and freedom. Kenyon
in *The Marble Faun* remains skewed between the dead flesh of his statue
of Cleopatra and the *non finito* of his Donatello sketch, failing to sustain
an ideal vision which would reconcile the two. This, I would suggest, is
linked to a view of civilization in which a unified act of making seems
impossible; in which the made object is linked to the use of others.

THE INDUSTRIAL SCULPTURE MACHINE

A sense of what is at stake in the 'sculpture complex' is provided by two
further examples, dialectically related, which concern the relationship
between sculpture and the machine. The first is drawn from the life of
James Watt, the Scottish inventor responsible for major developments
in the steam engine, and thus one of the instigators of the Industrial
Revolution. The financing of his company, Boulton and Watt, was, Robin
Blackburn comments, 'perhaps the most famous case of a link between
the triangular trade and the onset of industrialization', with more than
a hundred of their steam engines sold to West Indies sugar plantations.[74]
Nevertheless, Watt was opposed to slavery, and there is some evidence that

the company believed that the supply of machinery would ameliorate the labours of slavery (as well as increase its profits), in the manner noted in Chapter 3.

In old age Watt became preoccupied with a curious project: the notion of a sculpture-copying machine. He worked on it from around 1805 to 1818, less than two years before his death. Beginning with a die-copying machine seen in Paris in 1802, he purchased diamond-cutting pencils and other components, busts of Aristotle and Socrates as examples, and developed a form of artificial alabaster. He wrote out the specification for a patent in 1814.[75] He achieved some success – the 'Parallel Eidograph', as he called it, worked best as a 'diminishing machine' – and his work was developed by later inventors.[76]

Conceived by an inventor, industrialist, and member of the Scottish Enlightenment, Watt's project can be considered a meditation on instrumentality itself: on the relationship between conception and production. The machine replaces – and in a sense stands for – the work of the assistants who make the object. Its invention would vindicate an aesthetic: as one respectful commentator put it, 'A machine ... which is capable of multiplying the labours of the sculptor in the durable materials of marble or of brass was a desideratum of the highest value, and one which could have been expected only from a genius of the first order.'[77] The issue is sculpture as an index of ideal conception, marking the line between the ideal and execution, true making and the tool, perfection and deficiency – and conceiver and the rights of reproduction. The tensions involved are suggested by the report that Watt abandoned his work on hearing of another inventor with the same project – a coincidence which questions the singularity of original creation or 'genius'.[78]

There is thus a kind of logic to Watt's move from the steam engine to his late 'eccentric' interest in the sculpture machine: both supplant the human–tool equation, one at the level of energetics or independence (the freestanding engine), the other at the level of the tool as extension of the human will, as *praxis*. The self-powered engine (form-in-motion) is dialectically inverted in the pure, inert surface of the sculpture (static form) – one might remember Hiram Powers's comment that he had an attraction to both steam engines and sculpture. The mechanical reproducing machine attempts to move between these poles. The slave is bound up with this opposition because it is both machine (animated tool, designed to reproduce the master's will) and human form.

My second example concerns the issue of 'hands' and their masters. In *The Marble Faun*, Miriam has a sculptural double in her studio: a large

'jointed figure', or artist's mannequin, which Donatello suddenly encounters, 'half-startled in perceiving, duskily, a woman with long dark hair,
who threw up her arms, with a wild gesture of tragic despair, and appeared
to beckon him into the darkness along with her' (885). This is both a
figure for the body reduced to mechanism and a representation of the
pain which Donatello comes to share. Here is surely an echo in Rebecca
Harding Davis's industrial novella *Life in the Iron Mills*, published a little
more than a year later. A group of visitors to the steelworks encounter a
statue: 'Mitchell started back, half-frightened, as, suddenly turning a corner, the white figure of a woman faced him in the darkness, – a woman,
white, of giant proportions, crouching on the ground, her arms flung out
in some wild gesture of warning.'[79] This is one of the figures fashioned in
korl, or coking waste, by Hugh Wolfe, a mute unsung Rodin among the
Welsh workmen of the plant, whose hopeless ambition and downfall is the
story's subject.[80] The story has been related persuasively to issues of class
and the status of the natural and industrial body; critics have much less
frequently related the novella to the issue of sculptural making as such.[81]

The novella's opening scene (part of the framing, which is the house of
the narrator) begins with two objects which relate to our topic. The first
is the 'broken figure of an angel pointing upward from the mantle-shelf',
a small, presumably white domestic figure whose wings are 'clotted and
black' with pollution – the figure of sculpture under stress in American
reality, on the eve of civil war. The second is the 'negro-like river' which
flows beside the town and on whose 'face' the author used, as a child, to
'fancy a look of weary, dumb appeal' (40). It is this and a few other flickering traces of race that connect the text's general concern with servitude
and exploited, alienated labour to the issue of slavery. Mitchell, the text's
most developed consciousness, is 'spending a couple of months in the borders of a Slave State, to study the institutions of the South' (51); this was a
period when the use of slaves for industrial labour was developing fast and
when, reciprocally, Southern defenders of slavery pointed out the savagery
of Northern 'wage-slavery'.

Wolfe, the workman who dreams of becoming an artist, struggles to
form 'a clear, projected figure of himself, as he might become' (59), to
make an image of himself as an artist. But the realization of that form
is denied him, as a 'hand' rather than a maker. Indeed, in continuing to
produce sculpture without the authority to do so, he is a paradoxically
sentient sculpture machine, releasing the pain we have seen bound up in
the statue ('ample facilities for studying anatomy' is the mill owner's son
Kirby's sneering comment about the toiling workmen). He inhabits, that

is, the impossible position of the master of arts and the slave of industry signalled by the equation of the factory 'hands' with mechanism. Consider Kirby's outburst:

'If I had the making of men, these men who do the lowest part of the world's work should be machines, – nothing more, – hands. It would be kindness. God help them! What are taste, reason, to creatures who must live such lives as that?' He pointed to Deborah, sleeping on the ash-heap. 'So many nerves to sting them to pain. What if God had put your brain, with all its agony of touch, into your fingers, and bid you work and strike with that?' (54)

For Wolfe, release from manual labour – manumission, as it is called in slavery – involves his movement from being a 'hand' to deploying and representing bodies and hands. Kirby's own rhetoric exposes the logic of the machine and the corresponding logic of sculpture in which the moving hand of genius can be considered pure mind. When the doctor then asks Kirby whether he has a political philosophy, he replies in terms which continue this rhetorical structure in his disavowal of the pain of labour, while also linking it to slavery: 'I do not think. I wash my hands of all social problems, – slavery, cast, white or black' (55).

Wolfe's statue embodies his situation. In its use of waste material, it is at once evidence of his 'wasted' genius and, in its rough and unfinished state, of the lack of a smooth white surface which would signal an ideal status in which labour is detached from and concealed within the aesthetic object. Davis stresses the statue's difference from the whiteness of marble – its roughness, tactility, and materiality: '"Not marble, eh?" asked Kirby, touching it', adding 'What a flesh-tint the stuff has!' Here is how it looks to the 'anatomical eye' of the educated Mitchell:

There was not one line of beauty or grace in it: a nude woman's form, muscular, grown coarse with labor, the powerful limbs instinct with some one poignant longing. One idea: there it was in the tense, rigid muscles, the clutching hands, the wild, eager face, like that of a starving wolf's.... Mitchell stood aloof, silent. The figure touched him strangely. (53)

Rather than the self-enclosure of Powers's statue, in which the history of slavery is sealed up and contained, Wolfe's figure demands an empathetic reading as opposed to a cool appraisal in which the positions of naked object and clothed viewer are poised and balanced. The korl statue has leaky boundaries. It is Mitchell whom it 'touches', and his cry – 'Good God, how hungry it is!' (54) – suggests an answer to the 'dumb' secret, the 'terrible dumb question' which is linked to statuary, to a white silence (the word 'dumb' is used ten times in the text, applied to Wolfe, Debs, and the statue). When Wolfe accepts the money which Debs steals and is condemned to nineteen years of 'hard labor' (sentenced to *be* what he is), he must finally, in his cell, cut himself rather than korl, shaping his own death. The moon wraps his body in a marble-like 'white splendor' and creates a 'deeper stillness' in 'the dead figure that never should move again' (71) – as the blood leaves him, he becomes as sepulchral as Lewis's Cleopatra, the dead residue of toil.

At the novella's end the frame narrator meditates on Wolfe's statue, expressive of his 'mighty hunger', as it sits in her study. But what is involved is also a failure of context: his woman cannot sit among the objects on the table and participate in their meanings; she must be placed behind a curtain from which an arm reaches for a future which it cannot imagine:

The gas-light wakens from the shadows here and there the objects which lie scattered through the room: only faintly, though; for they belong to the open sunlight. As I glance at them, they each recall some task or pleasure of the coming day. A half-molded child's head; Aphrodite; a bough of forest-leaves; music; work; homely fragments, in which lie the secrets of all eternal truth and beauty. Prophetic all! Only this dumb, woful face seems to belong to and end with the night. (74)

The final fate of the statue, sequestered behind a curtain in the study, mirrors that of one of the most notorious artworks of the nineteenth century, Courbet's *L'Origine du mode*. What Courbet's explicit depiction of a woman's genital region shares with Wolfe's statue is the shocking revelation of a primary productivity: *this* is what making with the human body is; *this* is what the body is as an objectified part.

WHITENESS AND THE LOST IDEAL

In the era of slavery, then, labour and pain haunt sculpture; its 'white silence' speaks of subordination. I have not yet spoken of a more crudely racist trace within that structure. We need to recall that for Aristotle it is the idea of the 'perfect', indeed statuesque, Greek body which holds in place the opposition of master and slave, Greek and other, and even man and machine. In the *Politics* he writes:

[S]uppose that there were men whose mere bodily physique showed the same superiority as is shown by the statues of gods, then all would agree that the rest of mankind would deserve to be their slaves. And if this is true in relation to physical superiority, the distinction would be even more justly made in respect of superiority of soul; but it is much more difficult to see beauty of soul than it is to see beauty of body. It is clear then that by nature some are free, others slaves, and that for these it is both just and expedient that they should serve as slaves. (*Politics* 1254b32, p. 69)

While he admits that the bodies of slaves may be in no way deficient in comparison with those of masters, the ideal body acts as a metaphor for the healthy soul. This declaration, which echoes through Nietzsche, Pater, and others, is everywhere reflected in the conceptualization of Ideal sculpture, with its focus on the idealized white body. As Kirk Savage points out in his study of black Americans depicted in nineteenth-century monuments, 'More than any of the other arts, sculpture was embedded in the theoretical foundation of the racism that supported American slavery and survived long after its demise. For racism, like sculpture, centred on the analysis and representation of the human body.'[82] Classical sculptures were used as an index of the perfect form in the analyses of Cuvier and other racial theorists; later, Ideal sculpture was used for the same purpose.[83]

That idealization of the white body finds one terminus in late-nineteenth-century physical culture and the eugenics movement's use of Greek sculpture to emblematize the ideal body: the discus thrower and other sculptures recur in physical culture publications, alongside contemporary bodybuilders in sculptural poses.[84] Charles Lawes, the aristocratic athlete and sculptor who sued Richard Belt, was a judge of Eugen Sandow's 1903 bodybuilding competition.[85] W. E. B. Du Bois responds to this racialization in his essay 'The Superior Race' (1923) when he reports a white friend exclaiming, '"Compare the Venus of Milo and the Apollo Belvedere with a Harlem or Beale Street couple."' Du Bois counters: 'With a Fifth Avenue Easter parade or a Newport dance. In short, compare humanity at its best or worst with the Ideal, and humanity suffers.'[86] Which is to say that the imagined perfection of the Greek body serves to hold in place an assumed superiority founded on an aesthetic ideal.

Part of that set of associations is simply the fact that, as Savage remarks, 'classical sculpture served as the benchmark of whiteness'.[87] The association is acknowledged in Joseph Cephas Holly's 'A Wreath of Holly', published in 1853:

> Thou foul man-scourge! soul crushing slavery,
> > Who feed on hearts, and feasts on brain.
> Oh man! thou living marble statue;
> > What tho' thy brothers cast in bronze?[88]

The neoclassical refusal to consider the colouring of statuary in the ancient world is a form of what David Batchelor calls 'chromophobia'.[89] As one American commentator put it in 1833, 'If color is associated with the idea of transitoriness, *Form* is essentially immortal.'[90] The fact that archaeological discoveries revealed that the Greeks painted their statues was largely repressed: Winckelmann's disciples have even been suspected of scraping off colour; and the Elgin Marbles were subject to a whitening depilation.[91] While Canova tinted some of his statues slightly (reputedly with weak coffee), many English patrons requested the pure stone. And while a few sculptures of black subjects were made in dark stone, they were so rare that they barely feature in the histories.

There is one further aspect of the aesthetics of sculpture which I wish to mention: the question of wholeness and the fragment. Ideal sculpture was often seen in terms of aesthetic categories which stress the autonomy of the artwork as an embodiment of *Geist*; it represents what Kant called a 'purposiveness without a purpose' (*Zweckmässigkeit ohne Zweck*). The unity of the artwork which Winckelmann labelled 'oneness', *Einheit*, is related to that autonomy: its sense of mastery and self-containment. At the same time, we have to recall a truism here: many of the Greek bodies which survive from antiquity are *not* wholes but mutilated: armless, headless, disabled. The shattered inheritance of antiquity thus posed a problem, which was partly resolved by the stress on ideal form.[92] In the nineteenth century, it was a common academic exercise to imagine the restoration of the Venus de Milo or the Belvedere Hercules; this was matched by an aesthetic topos in which the ability to educe the totality from the fragment was a test of the viewer's response (a topos mocked in Balzac's 1831 story, 'The Unknown Masterpiece').

We might relate this tension between struggle and self-sufficiency, brokenness and totality, to the aftermath of slavery in America, the period of 'Reconstruction', which for African Americans was an all too brief period of progress, and for the white South a catastrophe in which its self-styled Athenian civilization was shattered. While the issue may seem potentially trivial, commentary on sculpture reflects that turmoil. One might consider Aristotle's use of the metaphor of the sculptural fragment as a metaphor for the body politic: '[T]he state has a natural priority over the household and over any individual among us. For the whole must be prior to the part. Separate hand or foot from the whole body and they will no longer be hand or foot except in name, as one might speak of a "hand" or "foot" sculptured in stone' (*Politics* 1253a18, p. 60). Totality is again signalled by the idealized body; the fragment by the part, in a linkage which readily provides a metaphor for the South's dismemberment.

A little background is needed here. The influence of German classicism on Southern education was huge: more than half of the University of Virginia's class of 1825 studied German and 'by 1869 the degree of Master of Arts there required knowledge of German and French'.[93] The relevance of antiquity to contemporary political life was keenly debated among Southern intellectuals – many of whom saw it as offering values that might be opposed to those of the (supposedly) utilitarian North.[94] Unsurprisingly, Winckelmann's *History of Ancient Art* found its most fervent readers in America: G. Henry Lodge's translation began to appear there in 1849, before it was published in the United Kingdom; the full four-volume edition appeared *only* in America. The book was discussed in a range of American art journals in the period 1850–90: *Crayon, American Art Review, Art Journal,* and others. But it found its deepest admirers among the St. Louis Hegelians, a group of amateur and professional philosophers gathered around the *Journal of Speculative Philosophy,* edited by William Torrey Harris. Today they are best remembered for having fostered the early careers of the American pragmatists Joshia Royce, John Dewey, and William James (though the work of the pragmatists takes, of course, a very different direction).

Shamoon Zamir sees these scholars as offering a kind of retrospective defence of slavery.[95] On the face of it, that seems an odd claim: the Hegelians were linked to the transcendentalists and were often politically progressive; like many in urban St. Louis, they sided with the North once war was declared. The *Journal's* editor, Harris, saw the Civil War as a necessary and world-historical struggle; moreover, as the superintendent of the public school system, he advocated equal education for African Americans.[96] But Zamir is surely right to the extent that the group tended to produce a selective version of Hegel. Harris's magnum opus, *Hegel's Logic* (1890), for example, avoids Hegel's stress on the vitiating effects of slavery on the master; Joshia Royce's *The Spirit of Modern Philosophy* (1892) produces a strangely Nietzschean account of Hegel in which (admittedly this is to read between the lines) the strong man rather the slave best appreciates the Absolute, the truth which is self-present and unmediated.[97] Certainly we can see in their work an account of the relationship between ruination and recovery which responds to Southern history.

Much of the Hellenism of the *Journal* derived from one member of its founding group, the extraordinary Thomas Davidson, the peripatetic Scottish philosopher who moved restlessly between Europe and North America up to his death in Toronto in 1900, and whose utopian philosophy found one destination in Rosminianism and the 'Fellowship of the New Life', which he organized in London in 1883 (the Fabian Society was an offshoot, making Davidson a progenitor of the Labour Party).

Davidson linked figures as diverse as Emerson, William James, Pope Leo XI, George Bernard Shaw, and Joseph Pulitzer.[98] Aristotle, rather than Hegel, was his philosophical touchstone, and he had a deep-rooted adherence to Greek culture.[99] He and E. S. Morgan translated Winkelmann for the journal; he wrote on the Niobe Group and later, in London, published pamphlets on the Elgin Marbles and the evolution of sculpture. For Davidson, sculpture embodies the dream of a social order: '[T]he individual statue, with its balance and proportion of life, is simply the ordered state of freedom writ small. Just in proportion as Greece advances in true freedom, her sculpture gains life and beauty; yea, and when freedom dies, sculpture dies.'[100] Greek art declines into the monstrous after Phidias and Praxiteles; the Elgin Marbles represent the 'Dream of Pericles' before its shattering in the wars with Sparta.[101]

Davidson's translation of Winckelmann's descriptions of the Belvedere torso (in this period regarded as that of Hercules) appeared in 1868. Winckelmann has just listed the extant parts of the torso and attributed to each a significance – the thighs recalling Hercules' travels; the shoulders his carrying the burden of the heavens; the breast his crushing giants. He adds:

If it appear inconceivable how power of thought can be shown in another part of the body beside the head, then learn here how the hand of a creative master is capable of informing matter with spirit. And while such a head, full of majesty and wisdom, rises before my eyes, the other missing limbs begin to take form in my thought; and efflux from what is before me gathers and produces, as it were, a sudden restoration.[102]

Similar ideas about the relation of part to whole can be found elsewhere in German idealist thought of the period.[103] Jarves reproduces such thinking (on the torso) in *Art Thoughts*: 'Despite its mutilation, it asserts itself as a complete, living being; the whole idea leaps from the broken mass.'[104] And of course, an even more complex version of this story of resurrection is Freud's essay on Jensen's *Gradiva*, which describes a literal re-membering; deriving from the foot and gait represented in an ancient relief a buried memory, a lost totality.

For the St. Louis Hegelians, I would suggest, this debate implied a barely articulated recuperation (or 'reconstruction') of the South's history via a return to classicism, which was central to Southern ideology. In these accounts of the fragment, it is as if the ability to restore and reintegrate the statue within a kind of prosthetic imaginary is a measure of the interpretive the power of the perceiver, or his or her own 'superiority of soul'. This is akin to the enlightened conscious which, for Hegel, emerges from the fragmentation and alienation of the master–slave relationship: from the fragmented self, the idea of a lost Absolute arises. But when Hegel argues that 'by creating a standing reflection of ourselves as universal beings we become such beings', he believes that this understanding emerges historically from the forms created from nature by the slave.[105] This is not what is involved for the St. Louis Hegelians, whose stance heals the wounds of history, keeping intact a supposedly prior narcissism which was bound up with both neoclassicism and slavery.

This interpretation is, I think, underscored by a rather different and more subversive essay on the Venus de Milo translated in the *Journal*, by the German art historian Herman Grimm. Writing in broadly Hegelian terms, Grimm insists on a historical difference between then and now which precludes restoration or a return to the past. He argues that '[t]hose who lived then saw the Goddess with other eyes than we, who look upon the shattered form' and continues:

Time and peoples pursue ways too diverse. The world divides itself into freemen and slaves. People made wars on each other only to extirpate each other – other laws, other family ties, another pity, another ambition, rest and motion than those we apprehend and demand. The poet truly rises above his time, and yet he is unthinkable apart from his own time.... An all-overstretching impulse toward equality of rights, before God and the Law, alone controls today the history of our race.... We are living, those times are dead.[106]

For Grimm it is the impact of history on the work of art, its historicity itself, which is always of interest. He constantly compares the idealized art of Raphael, its 'full light', with the trouble and incompletion he celebrates in Michelangelo. His example in a later article on Raphael translated in the *Journal* is the latter's *Dying Slave*, a statue which embodies struggle and incompletion both in its form and in the historical circumstances of its production – as we noted, for the long-planned and ultimately abortive monument to Pope Julius. His giant statue of Julius himself was, Grimm notes, melted down and made into a piece of artillery: 'So end works of art which are intended to last for centuries.'[107] We might read this as a final ironic comment on the hidden relation between Ideal sculpture and its mirroring of the history and practice of slavery.

THE TRIUMPH OF THE IMAGE

One terminus of thinking about Ideal sculpture – as well as a bridge to modernism – is the sculptor and theorist Adolf Hildebrand's influential 1893 essay, 'The Problem of Form in the Fine Arts'.[108] In his complex dialectic, Hildebrand does away with (or at least disparages) the clay model, since the modeller in clay is bound to the real form he creates rather than a pre-existing idea or form. Perception is to be analysed in terms of the *visual*, a stable and distant view, and the *kinaesthetic*, the actual view close up, imbued with the shifting physical contingency of the body. Sculpture is in his view linked to the visual: to the relief, to a framed, architectural view rather than one which must be seen in the round. The role of the sculptor working in stone is to 'release' or 'free' the pre-existing visual ideal from the stone, as a series of planes suggesting depth, aiming to 'translate its ideal form into a real kinaesthetic idea' (275). He asserts his mastery over the real. The modeller in clay, in contrast, clumsily builds up and responds to volumes: 'the visual impression thus plays only the role of a critic; it has no influence over the initial idea of form' (275).

Hildebrand's theory is in one sense the apotheosis of Ideal sculpture: the ideal sense of the artist is privileged over execution; the actual making of a form is downgraded. His preference for cutting stone quickly rather than modelling in clay mirrors the activities of assistants, while attempting to reclaim that dangerous ground for the artist (indeed, the use of an assistant is nowhere mentioned in his essay). The 'ghost' is dispensed with, along with the mere physicality or objecthood of the sculpture as the ideal image is 'freed'. The sculptor becomes 'master' of materials as he develops a series of forms subordinated to the ideal: 'The more masterly the treatment of the stone, the more decisive and the more definite will be the form that emerges onto the surface. Our instinct demands that a positive form step forth from the general spatial fog as quickly as possible' (274). The stepping-forth imagined here is virtual – an image rather than a statue given life by the 'animating force of our imagination' (261), incipiently a kind of computer-generated image.

Hildeband allows us to see the problem in the abolitionist reading of *The Greek Slave*. In calling for the viewer to see the ideal beneath its skin, and by analogy to recognize the slave as a human being, it articulates a view of sculpture which in its dependence on the ideal must participate in the hierarchy which I have described, in which any move into stone must be a kind of slave work and indeed enslavement for the image. I briefly discussed the whiteness of marble. The question of the colouring of statues arose in particular in relation to the work of John Gibson, whose fleshy *Tinted Venus* (1851–55) was such a *succès de scandale*. Powers's opinion of Gibson's work is illustrative:

It is not necessary, he said; and what is more, should interfere with the object aimed at by Sculpture. What is that? To embody and express the spiritual, the higher nature of man. Now, all expression, he contends, depends on form, not on color. Intellectual energy – physical action, must be described by form alone, color can never give it; but color will humanize, and *mortalize*, and pull down to earth the spiritual portion of humanity that you have been trying to separate from the grosser parts and to exalt. Color, in short, represents the animal man; – form, the intellectual, the spiritual. Imagine, for an instance, the Apollo Belvidere colored.[109]

The whiteness and finish of his own statue allowed it to avoid becoming mixed with the earth of the South and the bodies which worked that earth. Even if its intended message was abolition, *The Greek Slave* was displayed in the South without offence – indeed, jokes were made about the maiden being 'sold' on the block which can be seen as illustrative of a desire to re-enact the logic of the fall into stone in which the statue can be sustained only as an ideal.

We have moved, in this chapter, across a field in which the slave appears as a kind of trace – as the mere craft which might be opposed to an ideal conception; as a figure for unacknowledged or ghostly labour; as the dark figure of all that is repressed by the shining surface of marble, including the pain of a body which is conceptually obliterated. The pathway is ultimately from the ideal conception to the artefact. It is matched, as Hildebrand's thinking suggests, by another pathway: from the artefact to the image. Which is to say that the account of making which has been described here, in which the effacement of labour and subordination is a key component, produces a white surface which is purely optical. That surface is that of the commodity, of the marble produced at a few dollars a pound turned into a dazzling object fit for the palace or living room, with the imprimatur of the idea – or of desire itself – stamped upon it. In this way, too, the metaphor of slavery, of the body as pure labour and as a device for the use of others, haunts both art and commodity culture in the nineteenth century and in our own time. What begins as the element of the human that can be impressed on an inert object in the sculpture ends as an object of our own desire, whether it is Damien Hirst's diamond-encrusted skull or a trainer produced in a Vietnamese sweatshop. What has largely vanished, it seems to me, is the intense ambivalence about this inheritance which characterizes the nineteenth-century accounts of sculpture I have examined.

What would comprise an understanding of making which does not idealize the work of the thinker? The answer lies, surely, in a view which sees every made object as involving a variety of actors, including an inheritance from the past which inheres in technique itself. Bruno Latour describes this as 'Technical Mediation', writing that '[e]ven the shape of humans, our very body, is composed in large part of sociotechnical negotiations and artefacts. To conceive humanity and technology as polar is to wish away humanity; we are sociotechnical animals, and each human interaction is sociotechnical. We are never limited to social ties. We are never faced with objects.'[110] To see the object in this way would be to shift our thinking on a number of issues – not least copyright and artistic making – but would also relate in an interesting way to that view of slavery which sees it as knitted into our modes of making.

CHAPTER 5

The Sonic Veil

> I remember that this minor-keyed pathos used to seem to me almost too sad to dwell upon, while slavery seemed destined to last for generations; but now that their patience has had its perfect work, history cannot afford to lose this portion of its record.
>
> Thomas Wentworth Higginson, 'Negro Spirituals'

In the preceding chapter, I examined the issue of locked-in suffering in sculpture, as well as the slave as a suppressed figure for the work of sculpture, and thus the production of the aesthetic itself. This chapter explores the release of that contained pain as sound and the way it is used in accounts of African-American music. It considers two related propositions. The first is that the residue of slavery is often conceived in sonic terms, as a persistent and echoing presence which can be heard into the twentieth century. The literature of slavery, I will suggest, often seeks out a textual form of that sounding. The second and less obvious proposition, again related to the discussion of reproduction in the preceding chapter, is that notions of sonic reproduction – and in particular technologies of sonic storage – make use of the trace of slavery, both within African-American tradition and outside it, as a continued binding of the human figure into technology.

Perhaps it is best if I say what is *not* directly involved here, which is first of all the history and meanings of spirituals as considered by Dena J. Epstein, Paul Allen Anderson, Eric J. Sundquist, and others. A little closer to my topic is the notion of 'authenticity' repeatedly applied to black music-making, from spirituals in the nineteenth century and the blues in the mid-twentieth to Moby's sampling of Vera Hall and Curt Cobain's famous acoustic gig, the singer 'making it real' with the music of Lead Belly. That romantic and racial notion of the 'authentic', applied in particular to the blues, has been fairly comprehensively demolished as anything other than a mythic structure by Hugh Barker, Yuval Taylor,

Marybeth Hamilton, and other historians.[1] Nevertheless, I am interested in a more particular (but still familiar) aspect of this tradition, in which the sounds of black music are seen as transmitting a legacy of *pain*.[2] The idea that the suffering of the past can be carried by the most transitory of sensory modes is surely worth exploring.

What does it mean to say that the past has a sound? We can begin with the *Ninth Bridgewater Treatise* (1838), the refutation of theological attacks on science published by Charles Babbage, the English mathematician whose 'difference engine' is central to the history of computing. In his essay 'The Permanent Impression of Our Words and Actions on the Globe We Inhabit', Babbage considers the way in which the trace of every utterance and action continues to vibrate in time. This is the dream of nineteenth-century materialism: 'No motion impressed by natural causes, or by human agency, is ever obliterated. The ripple on the ocean's surface caused by a gentle breeze, or the still water which marks the more immediate track of a ponderous vessel gliding with scarcely expanded sails over its bosom, are equally indelible.'[3] Sounds might be recaptured, the traces of any bodily action followed. Babbage's essay culminates in the vision of the earth as a giant storage device. It finds its example in the atrocities of slavery:

The soul of the negro, whose fettered body surviving the living charnel-house of his infected prison, was thrown into the sea to lighten the ship, that his Christian master might escape the limited justice at length assigned by civilized man to crimes whose profit had long gilded their atrocity, – will need, at the last great day of human account, no living witness of his earthly agony.... Interrogate every wave which breaks unimpeded on ten thousand desolate shores, and it will give evidence of the last gurgle of the waters which closed over the head of his dying victim. (116–19)

Babbage's long footnote lists cases of abuse, including the jettison of slaves, citing that of the *Adalia*, which to escape pursuit 'threw overboard upwards of 150 of the poor wretches who were on board' (118), though clearly the notorious *Zong* case (discussed in Chapter 1) also resonates in his memory. When Babbage returns to the topic of recollection in a later essay, entitled 'Thoughts on the Nature of Future Punishments', the implications are even clearer: a transmitted historical guilt might torment those with the organs to register it:

If we imagine the soul in an after stage of our existence, to be connected with a bodily organ of hearing so sensitive, as to vibrate with motions of the air, even of infinitesimal force, and if it be still within the precincts of its ancient abode, all the accumulated words pronounced from the creation of mankind, will fall at once upon that ear. Imagine, in addition, a power of directing the attention of that organ entirely to any one class of those vibrations: then ... will the apparent confusion vanish at once; and the punished offender may hear still vibrating on his ear the very words uttered, perhaps, thousands of centuries before, which at once caused and registered his own condemnation. (164)

The painstaking recording of cases, the detailed evidence which was so important to the abolitionist movement, here finds its ontological correlative: not only must the slave trade be abolished, but its suffering must not, indeed in this automated conscience it *cannot*, vanish; its traces remain present in a way which correlates with more recent notions of inherited historical trauma – since the unconscious is the place where nothing is lost.

But this idea also poses problems. In terms of the thematics of trauma, sound as the engram of pain represents a vanishing, entropic trace, external to the listener, rather than the interiorized permanence of the wound or the permanent marking of the scar. Sound is always lost; it fades away from the cry of its occasion. On the other hand, unlike the scar – which always remains sundered from its making by time and natural process – sound offers the possibility of repetition, albeit a repetition which demands that experience is carried across time, via either a reproductive tradition or a technology of transmission. For sound to be heard again it must be stored, recovered, and sounded anew. Thus it must travel a pathway from the individual and particular to the general and reproducible, moving the ground of analysis from the immediacy of experience to the question of identity, or identities, constituted by access to or identification with a particular past, like that of slavery. (This issue is taken up again in relation to notions of inherited trauma in the final chapter.) For Arthur Schopenhauer, it is music which does this best: directly encoding and transmitting, without the need for language, the travails of the Will; its hopes and disappointments as they are present in the human subject.[4]

One might see Babbage's fantasy as pointing to one direction in the history of slave memory, that of recovery – for example, in the attempts by black scholars and the Works Progress Administration (WPA) in the South to gather the memories of slavery in the thousands of narratives recorded and taken down in the 1930s; or in the more recent preoccupation with the material traces of slavery in museum exhibitions, in the remains of slave ships like the *Henrietta Marie*. Even when we acknowledge what Marcus Wood suggests are the potential pitfalls of interpreting and laying claim to these relics, they seem to resonate – in something like the sense demanded by Babbage – because of the notion of a material remnant bound into memory, as a part of what the novelist Caryl Phillips has called the 'Atlantic Sound'.[5]

WASH POTS AND SORROW SONGS

Slave culture had its own figure for the storage and secreting of noise. The tradition, probably African in origin, of 'catching the sound' – of hanging pots in trees or propping them on the ground at religious meetings or other gatherings – is described in a number of sources. This is Marriah Hines in Virginia, who gave her age as 102 when interviewed by a WPA interviewer: 'On our plantation we had general prayer meeting every Wednesday night at church. 'Cause some of the masters didn't like the way we slaves carried on we would turn pots down and tubs to keep the sound from going out. Den we would have a good time, shouting singing and praying just like we pleased.' Or Fanny Moore, describing North Carolina: 'But de niggers slip of and pray and hold prayer-meetin' in de woods, den dey turn down a big wash pot and prop it up with a stick to drown out de sound of the singing.'[6]

The self-protective turning inward of sound relates to disciplinary regimes, but in its intimacy it evokes what Édith Lecourt calls the 'sonorous envelope' or 'musical envelope', which defines both personal and collective experience – a psychic structure founded in the community of the 'original music-group' in harmony around the baby, sharing, touch, 'a group formation produced as protective barrier and receptacle of sounds, a veritable acoustic womb' around the baby.[7] Vocal music, she suggests, creates 'an altogether privileged zone within the sonorous bath, a zone that has the advantage of offering a pre-form for sonorous experience, which will subsequently become a basis for the elaboration of the corresponding psychic container'. The 'musical face' (as opposed to the 'verbal face') is turned towards the inside, the group – hence the stress on caves in myth, sounding boxes, and 'the problem of control of entries and exits, and of its closure'.[8] The result is the 'shadowed' or dissimulated aspect of black speech that has been described by so many commentators, a powerful tradition in which 'speech is made a reservoir of the hidden and unarticulated', as Eric Sundquist writes of Charles Chesnutt's conjure tales.[9]

The caught sound of the wash pot provides in this sense a sonic emblem comparable to the visual metaphor of the 'veil' which separates the black world from the white in Du Bois and those who follow him – remembering that in Matthew 27 the rending of the veil is a response to a sound,

Jesus's death cry. This is James Weldon Johnson's versions of the folk sermon in *God's Trombones* (1927):

> And the veil of the temple was split in two,
> The midday sun refused to shine,
> The thunder rumbled and the lightening wrote
> An unknown language in the sky.[10]

'Unknown language' serves as a metaphor for black music-making more generally. As Johnson puts it in his introduction to *God's Trombones*, it is the 'marked silent fraction of a beat' in syncopation that carries the meaning in black music-making.[11] The 'sonic veil', if we can call it that, divides the spoken from the unspoken. And if one asks where this secreted sound is released, the religious answer lies in the captive voice of Psalm 137, 'By the Rivers of Babylon': 'As for our harps, we hanged them up.... For they that led us away captive required of us then a song.' As Du Bois recognized, this is a sound fully released only at the moment of redemption:

> Michael haul the boat ashore.
> Then you'll hear the horn they blow.
> Then you'll hear the trumpet sound.
> Trumpet sound the world around.
> Trumpet sound for rich and poor.
> Trumpet sound the jubilee.
> Trumpet sound for you and me.[12]

The first port of call, then, is the tradition of sonic persistence in spirituals.

Though fragmentary accounts of spirituals are present in the antebellum period, it was when Northern volunteers went to the Sea Islands of Georgia to educate recently liberated slaves ('contrabands') that black song-making began to have a systematic impact on American consciousness. Observers reported and transcribed songs in which they heard expressed, seemingly as never before, the sorrows of slavery. This encounter produced the first published collection of spirituals, *Slave Songs of the United States* (1867), edited by William Francis Allen, Charles Pickard Ware, and Lucy McKim Garrison. The subsequent impact of the Fisk Jubilee Singers is a story central to the reception of black culture in America and Europe: audiences heard in their songs a new mode of Christian expression, born of an identification with the sufferings of Israel. As a review of *Slave Songs of the United States* in the *National Anti-Slavery Standard* in 1867 put it, 'These plaintive strains seem to have been wrung from the negroes' life. Debarred from speech, the aspirations that the immortal soul – God's image in Ebony – was endowed with, found vent in music, grotesque often, strange always, but creative, original, striking, rich, pathetic and absorbing.'[13] The suggestion that black folk music was the 'only distinctively *American* music' is often attributed to James Monroe Trotter, the African-American author of *Music and Some Highly Musical People* (1878); it was quickly repeated by F. L. Ritter, Dvořák, and other commentators.[14] And the claim was, of course, elaborated in *The Souls of Black Folk*, in which Du Bois asserted that the 'Sorrow Songs' were 'the singular spiritual heritage of the nation and the greatest gift of the Negro people'. 'Nobody Knows the Trouble I've Seen' begins his book – a song first registered, he points out, on the famous occasion when Sea Island slaves first told their story to sympathetic outsiders.[15] For Du Bois the songs are 'full of the voices of the past' – indeed, the *pain* of the past: 'They are the music of an unhappy people, of the children of disappointment.' As Sundquist has argued, the spirituals which Du Bois uses as epitaphs and considers in his final chapter represent double consciousness itself, anchored in the past while also negotiating a path towards a modern black cultural identity.[16]

It is worth hesitating over the notion of pain, since it takes us back to our opening discussion of Babbage and leads us forward to a series of questions about what it means to transmit feeling. Just as music, in Schopenhauer's account, has the function of recording the travails of the Will, the pain of existence, in early writings on spirituals they were seen as releasing a pain inexpressible in slavery. In the ideology of slave owners, it was a commonplace that slaves were relatively insensitive to pain; spirituals, in contrast, figured pain as bound into their composition. This is a correspondent cited in *Slave Songs of the United States*:

I asked one of these blacks – one of the most intelligent of them [Sergeant Rivers] – where they go these songs. 'Dey make 'em, sah.' 'How do they make them?' After a pause, evidently casting about for an explanation, he said: 'I'll tell you, it's dis way. My master call me up, and order me a short peck of corn and a hundred lash. My friends see it, and is sorry for me. When dey come to de praise-meeting dat night dey sing about it. Some's very good singers and know how; and dey work it in.'[17]

Even those songs composed after Emancipation 'were inspired by slavery', the editors insist (xix): 'The wild, sad strains tell, as the sufferers themselves could, of crushed hopes, keen sorrow, and a dull, daily misery' (xix). Similarly, J. B. I. Marsh in *The Story of the Jubilee Singers* (1875) stressed that behind the singers are the 'disabilities and cruelties' of slavery, memories embodied in the singers themselves: 'At different times twenty-four persons in all have belonged to the company. Twenty of these have been slaves and three of the other four were of slave parentage.'[18]

Listening to this living memory, we learn that the issues of proximity and distance are crucial. As Dena J. Epstein notes, Southern accounts suggest 'two contradictory views of the music: close at hand it was often dismissed as mere noise or uncivilized barbarism, but at a distance it became beautiful, melancholy and nostalgic'.[19] Eliza Frances Andrews's journal for February 1865 reported, 'They are mostly a sort of weird chant that makes me feel all out of myself when I hear it far away in the night, too far off to catch the words.'[20] Thomas Wentworth Higginson's comments in his pioneering 1867 article on the Sea Island singers nicely conveys a dialectic of distance and preservation: 'I remember that this minor-keyed pathos used to seem to me almost too sad to dwell upon, while slavery seemed destined to last for generations; but now that their patience has had its perfect work, history cannot afford to lose this portion of its record.'[21]

What does that 'record' involve? Jon Cruz has argued that white celebration of spirituals involved an 'ethnosympathy' which was quickly drained of its political impulse and that one result was a downplaying of the more active written voice of the slave narratives.[22] This is a fractured area: as Anderson points out, there are conflicting interpretations of the degree of accommodation involved in the melodic packaging of spirituals for white audiences in the performance traditions of the Fisk Jubilee Singers and in concert versions by Harry T. Burleigh, John Work, and others.[23] But Cruz ignores what might be two prior questions: What are the *possibilities* of transmission of a historical and political impulse within a musical tradition? What is involved in hearing the musical traces of another? White listeners like Andrews might be discomforted by the sound of slaves, but as Lawrence W. Levine notes, after the Civil War a sometimes intense embarrassment at 'primitive' religion was also present among black religious leaders.[24] This is more than an aspiration for the cultural high ground, surely; it too is a response to pain.

For Du Bois, as Sundquist shows, spirituals are a tradition he receives and renegotiates from outside the circle of their making. The *locus classicus* here is Frederick Douglass's well-known comment in the second chapter of his *Narrative*, which develops the notion of a distance from which a political meaning emerges: 'I did not, when a slave, understand the deep meaning of those rude and apparently incoherent songs. I myself was within the circle; so that I neither saw nor heard as those without might see and hear.'[25] In his second autobiography, Douglass comments that he had himself been much affected by the 'same *wailing notes*' as he heard from slaves when visiting Ireland during the famine – a directness of sympathy that bespeaks an outsider's entry into a community

of suffering (as well as the connection to Irish emancipation figured
in Douglass's encounter with Sheridan's speeches in *The Columbian
Orator*).[26] Douglass's injunction for 'any one' to go to Colonel Lloyd's
plantation and listen from the 'deep pine woods, and there let him, in
silence, analyze the sounds that shall pass through the chambers of his
soul' is a call for an open response; but it is predicated on being without
the circle. As Sundquist notes, Douglass's distance is a 'mode of artifice
and reflection' which produces both self-possession and a sense of origins.[27] Distance *and* identification are both present in his response to the
pain he hears in the songs of the slaves.

What is heard is, for this reason, potentially problematic, difficult, hidden. Comments on spirituals constantly referred to this veiled quality; the
songs and what they encoded contained, in their performance style (in
their *techne*), imponderables. One of the early references in a musical journal in 1846 referred to the 'queerness' of the songs.[28] As Genovese notes,
'the words "wild" and "weird" recurred among white observers'[29] – other
terms were 'eerie' and 'strange'. But these terms were used by black observers as well as white: Douglass refers to 'wild notes'; Du Bois writes of
prefacing his chapters with musical phrases carrying 'a haunting echo of
these weird old songs in which the soul of the black slave spoke to men'.[30]
The result was problems both of transcription and of transmission.
Commentators repeatedly suggested that black music-making could not
be notated, with African tonal systems seen as a kind of natural sound not
readily translated into the pentatonic system: the editors of *Slave Songs*
suggested that 'like birds, they seem not infrequently to strike sounds that
cannot be precisely represented by the gamut, and abound in slides from
one note to another'. Even what is transcribed is compromised in the
transition from performance to print, since 'the intonations and delicate
variations of even one singer cannot be reproduced on paper' (iv–vi).

For a more developed sense of what is involved here, we can turn to
John A. Work, the African-American author of *Folk Song of the American
Negro* (1915). Work notes stereotypically that 'the Negro possesses a peculiar quality of voice which it is next to impossible to imitate'. Equally
characteristically, having said this he goes on to identify stylistic markers
such as the flatted seventh, the expressive note added to the African scale
as an indication of life in America: 'This flat seven expresses a wild and
overwhelming surprise at the utter strangeness of things.' He also suggests
that one marker is the use of 'a nameless little something represented by
the letter "A", as in 'Judg-a-ment, Judg-a-ment, Judg-a-ment day is rolling
around'.[31] Or again:

Another curious as well as interesting addition made by the American Negro is a real groan that he introduces. There were times when the very depths of pain and sorrow were sounded, the awfulness of which were beyond his power to speak, but the pent-up feelings must find some expression which would as nearly as possible represent in essence the pain itself.[32]

This is the 'um' of spirituals: 'How completely does it give expression to that emotion for which words are too weak!' For many listeners, it seemed to be this strangeness and lack of amenity to formal codification which allowed a sense of latent materials, a hidden presence. Paradoxically, it is the pain hidden within the songs which allows them to be transmitted. As Ronald Radano acutely comments, the slave song in such accounts represents 'a "soundtext" that ... refers to the partials of sound it cannot reveal', a process that allowed America to '"hear" its collective slave past'. In Radano's account, it is the partiality – the much-insisted-upon inadequacy of Western transcription systems for African-derived music – which allowed the songs to function as memory.[33]

That the transmission of that memory is constantly threatened by a loss is seen as latent in the tradition at its very beginnings. The introduction to *Slave Songs of the United States* (1897) notes that 'it seems time at last that the partial collections in the possession of the editors ... should not be forgotten and lost, but that these relics of a society which has passed away should be preserved while it is still possible' (iii). A footnote on the same page notes the possibility of shipwreck: 'Only this last spring a valuable collection of songs made at Richmond, Va., was lost on the *Wagner....* We had hoped to have the use of them in preparing the present work.' The threats to tradition, in this and subsequent discussions, lie in the end of slavery and resulting social changes: former slaves are adopting white modes of religious music-making, and '[i]t is often, indeed, no easy matter to persuade them to sing their old songs, even as a curiosity, such is the sense of dignity that has come with freedom. It is earnestly to be desired that some person ... should make a collection of these now, before it is too late' (x). Marion Alexander Haskell, writing in 1899, noted, 'These spirituals have never been systematically collected, and they bid fair to become, a few years hence, only things of the past.' In all such accounts, it is the effect of the loss of oral tradition and modernity which is registered: 'As the negro becomes educated he relinquishes these half-barbaric, but often beautiful, old words and melodies, and their place is taken by the denominational hymns and the Moody and Sankey songs.' Haskell tells the story of 'Maum Rizpah', the old former slave who always sang 'the same pathetic strain', sung by others only after her death: 'the song would float out on the still night air with a sweetness and pathos that stamped itself indelibly upon the memory of her hearers.'[34] A generation on, in *On the Trail of Negro Folk-Songs* (1925), Dorothy Scarborough cites her mentor, the folklorist George Lyman Kittredge, on the need to gather songs 'before the material vanishes forever, killed by the Victrola, the radio, the lure of cheap printed music'. She describes well-meaning white teachers in Charleston learning songs and transmitting them (as 'racial songs') to black children.[35]

The obvious practical way in which the problems of notating black music – and the problem of loss more generally – could be overcome was through recording technology: the phonograph was a machine which could pluck from the air a dying tradition and make its partials and blue notes available for future generations. Folkloric interest in black music-making had declined in the period after 1880. One factor in its revival was the advent of the recording industry in the late 1900s. The Fisk Jubilee Singers were first recorded in 1909; the Victor, Edison, and Columbia companies vied for the service of available groups, often stressing the authenticity of their sounds.[36] At that point, the ability of spirituals to carry the pulse of past events was reiterated. The title of an article in the *Literary Digest* in 1916, 'Canning Negro Melodies', refers to work songs recorded by George A. Miller (his brother, the tenor Reed Miller, included spirituals in his repertoire): 'The phonograph, with its power of bringing back dumb and forgotten voices in something near their original freshness, performs an invaluable service for us in keeping alive and in our memories the songs of past generations.'[37] The same year saw the Tuskegee Singers issue their first recorded spirituals. They were released by Victor with an announcement again referring to 'weird' harmonies and stressing historical resonance:

Words and melody seem to have been made for one another, so perfectly do they express the sorrow of racial bondage, relieved by vague aspirations and the joy of religious ecstasy.... In the new era of educational progress of the Negro in the South, the spirituals in their oldest and purest form are fast disappearing. Fortunately for future generations the Victor is preserving a number of these characteristic songs, given in their original form, unaccompanied, by the famous Tuskegee Institute Singers of Alabama.[38]

Compare a report in the 4 June 1921 *Chicago Defender* on recordings for Black Swan Records, the first mainstream black label, made by baritone Carroll Clark: 'At my request Mr. Clark sang for me "Swing Low, Sweet Chariot", with its quietly exultant "Comin' for to carry me home!", and though he too is three generations removed from slavery, there crept into his voice more than a hint of the longing for escape from suffering which must have inspired the original to a poignant degree.'[39] Latent here once again is the idea that present in these recordings is *the sound of slavery* itself, the lingering pulse of its pain. This sound might be seen differently by different audiences, but in that technological preservation lies the possibility of a stabilized tradition.

There are dangers in that stabilization, of course. One is the notion that tradition becomes petrified at the moment of its capture (its being 'saved' for the future). Perhaps even more dangerous is the idea that in being translated into media the veiled, inward-facing tradition signalled by the wash pot becomes open to all – an implication of Du Bois's use of spirituals in *The Souls of Black Folk*, where they signal both the hidden depths of history and the cultural 'gift' of a people who might finally be liberated from race into a realm where 'souls walk uncolored'.[40] At that point the issue of ownership and identity might become open, and voice stolen. That is indeed one possibility raised by James Weldon Johnson's *The Autobiography of an Ex-Colored Man* (1912).

THE MUSIC NOT HEARD WITH THE EARS

Johnson's novel, with its unsettling alternation of authenticity and masquerade, passing-as-white and passing-as-black, provides a good testing ground for the idea of black music as stored pain, as well as the idea of a translation of black music-making into the public sphere.[41] The initial musical focus of the novel is ragtime, treated in a highly complex and dialectical way. It is associated, by the Ex-Colored Man in his guise as an adventurer in black culture, with a learned performance style deployed for social and financial gain – in a way which is in dialogue, on the one hand, with contemporary criticisms of it as artificial and hysterical and, on the other, with Johnson's views of ragtime as a product of black culture which has entered the American mainstream; as a mode of musical translation between cultures.[42] In that respect ragtime represents modernity itself: ambiguous, double-sided, hybrid, cerebral, both commercial and veiled in its meanings.

Spirituals, in contrast, are linked in the novel to an ambivalent desire for historical authenticity rather than to the performative style of ragtime. In the episode late in the novel when the narrator travels to the South in search of musical inspiration which he might 'translate' into a universal music, he encounters 'Singing Johnson', who has committed to memory 'the leading lines of all the Negro spiritual songs' (154): 'There is sounded in them that elusive undertone, the note in music which is not heard with the ears. I often sat with the tears rolling down my cheeks and my heart melted within me' (157). Spirituals serve as a metonym of race in the novel: in eliciting such emotion, they are the means of preserving black experience, but they also threaten a potentially uncomfortable proximity rather than distance. The 'educated classes', he notes, are 'rather ashamed of them' because they are 'still too close to the conditions under which the songs were produced, but the day will come when this slave music will be the most treasured heritage of the American Negro' (157).

It is the rawness of that heritage – embodied in the description of the lynching which, just after the encounter with Singing Johnson, finally drives the narrator away from the horrors of race – which makes the issue of distance so central to the text: the question of whose story this is, in terms of identity, can be only a matter of half-heard undertones. As Walter Benn Michaels has argued, the novel brings into sharp focus questions about how race might be defined (if it is definable at all), in terms of essence, performativity, or the gaze of others.[43] In the lynching scene, the narrator is repelled, ashamed by the spectacle of tortured flesh (the 'blood' with which he has identified); but at the same time, as a passer in the scene, he is protected from involvement. Faced with actual pain and the toxicity of racial identification, he abandons his mediatory role. What he is left with is a private sphere in which the meanings that have been associated with race are rendered a private and indeed characteristically sonic trace, lodged as a secret whispered into the ear of his mourned-for wife.

Johnson's poem 'O Black and Unknown Bards' sees in spirituals a chain of transmission from slavery, from 'those who've sung untaught, unknown, unnamed' to the present. For the anonymous voices of the past the song contained within it the 'delay' created by the unspeakable facts of slavery ('You sang far better than you knew'); it can be realized only through transmission and revoicing.[44] It is this unrealized voice that seems to attract Johnson to the well-known poem of the Cuban poet Plácido which he translates (also printing Bryant's canonical translation) in the appendix to his *Book of American Negro Poetry*. This is Johnson's version of 'Plácido's Farewell to His Mother (Written in the Chapel of the Hospital de Santa Cristina on the Night Before His Execution)':

> My lyre before it is forever stilled
> Breathes out to thee its last and dying note.
>
> A note scarce more than a burden-easing sigh,
> Tender and sacred, innocent, sincere –
> Spontaneous and instinctive as the cry
> I gave at birth –

Bryant, Johnson insists, misunderstands the context of the poem, seeing it as an intimate farewell when in fact Plácido never knew his mother, a white Spanish woman who abandoned him at birth: he asks the reader to consider the 'humiliating and embittering effect [of this betrayal] upon a soul so sensitive as Plácido's'.[45] In failing to hear the elusive undertone of racial pain in the poem, even the sympathetic Bryant mistranslates and mistransmits the meaning.

This linkage of lost sounds to the painful maternal disconnections of slavery derives from early accounts of spirituals – conditioned by the centrality of 'Sometimes I Feel Like a Motherless Child' to the tradition – and is present in Johnson's *Autobiography*. Even as a child, the narrator tells us, he 'always played with feeling', a result of 'trying to reproduce the quaint songs which my mother used to sing' (22). In an evocation of the episode in Frederick Douglass's *Narrative* in which Douglass describes himself as weeping as he writes of slave songs, the Ex-Colored Man writes, 'Often when playing I could not keep the tears which formed in my eyes from rolling down my cheeks'. This is an authenticity which is mimetic, a product of the way 'a true artist can no more play upon the piano or violin without putting his whole body in accord with the emotions he is striving to express than a swallow can fly without being graceful'. While this seems to make the Ex-Colored Man a kind of gramophone, transmitting the affective life of others, he denies his own mechanicity at a significant point, when he has to play to his visiting white father, and thus confront one of the sources of his own fracture: 'There is only one thing in the world that can make music, at all times and under all circumstances, up to its general standard; that is a hand-organ or one of its variations' (28). This is to say that he is not a pianola. Distracted, he plays 'listlessly', but when he is praised by the father whose name he cannot say, the affective link with the music is restored; it is technique that 'makes him feel like shedding tears', which restores him to a momentary belief in his role as cultural transmitter.

Throughout the book, the question of the adequacy of the ear is raised, from the whispered (and misunderstood) answer to a question which the Ex-Colored Man shoots into the ear of his friend 'Red' at school to the 'softer tone' with which his teacher reveals he is designated black. So it is unsurprising that it is the note not heard with the ears which carries the trace of what the text sees as race proper. It is the elusive undertone which also informs the 'psychic moment of my life', in which the Ex-Colored Man wins his wife after he walks over to her: 'She continued playing, but in a voice that was almost a whisper, she called me by my Christian name

and said: "I love you, I love you, I love you". I took her place at the piano
and played the *Nocturne* in a manner that silenced the chatter of the company both in and out of the room' (180). The name which we never hear,
the music which mesmerizes and silences an audience, the tension between
what is heard from inside the veil and what from without, all these are
evoked as a version of the sonic envelope in the 'little box in which I still
keep my fast yellowing manuscripts', the box which is the repository of his
dreams, is the place of an unsounded sound, a failed transmission-across-
disconnection which is fundamental to the text's understanding of race.
At its centre is the unspeakable sound of pain, whether the half-repressed
sound of the lynching (those 'cries and groans I shall always hear', 136) or
the tearful encounter with a lost patrimony which is encoded in Chopin.
It is this that renders race in the book an impossible topic, since it cannot
finally be represented at the level of culture or identity.

LEARNING TO LISTEN

Johnson's musician, an outsider to African-American tradition who has
to encounter it via books and native informants, has sometimes been
seen as a reverse passer, as using black musical practice for his own ends.
In 'Superstitions and Folk-Lore of the South', Charles Chesnutt provides
another allegory of the captured voice, telling the story of a woman who
wins a man through her singing, only to have her voice stolen by her rival.
A conjure man discovers the culprit, but they find that 'she had taken the
voice, but did not possess the power to restore it. The conjure doctor was
obdurate and at once placed a spell upon her which is to remain until the
lost voice is restored. The case is still pending, I understand.'[46] Chesnutt
comments that the story 'of catching the voice has a simplicity which stamps
it as original', adding learnedly 'the only analogy of which I can at present
think being the story of later date, of the words which were frozen silent
during the extreme cold of an Arctic winter, and became audible again the
following summer when they had thawed out.' The reference to the episode
from Rabelais – where the words are cries of rage and pain from a battle –
directs us to the *topos* which in its African-American context Henry Louis
Gates labels 'the talking book', a story which expresses the painful transition
from oral to written culture –though in Chesnutt's sly version, in an essay
which he begins by discussing Joel Chandler Harris, the possibilities of theft
are suggested in a rivalry for an African-American inheritance.[47] For writers
using dialect this is an especially pointed issue. What does it mean to 'freeze'
the raw matter of language and steal it for literature?

One indication of the problems involved is Mark Twain's 'A True Story' – his first piece for the *Atlantic Monthly*, published in late 1874. It was based on the actual experience of Mary Ann Cord, taken down that summer.[48] The story is set on a Southern porch, as the frame narrator idly asks 'Aunt Rachel' how it is she has lived sixty years 'and never had any trouble'. Her riposte is a harrowing story of the loss of her husband and seven children (and the eventual finding of one), a challenge both to the mammy stereotype and to the writer's project, as well as an expression of the bitterness of the end of Reconstruction. What is left is in some senses the failure of genre, in a tale that Twain himself admitted 'has no humor in it'.[49] Instead of literature, the skilful reimagining of the different voices of the South represented by *Huckleberry Finn*, we have a flat sonic reproduction of a specific painful history: Aunt Rachel says, 'I's gwyne to tel you, den I leave it to you', and the story's subtitle is 'Repeated Word for Word as I Heard It'.[50]

Twain's story again raises the issue of what one can hear, of what can be transmitted and to whom. Jean Toomer's *Cane* (1923) provides a historically specific meditation on the power of sonic reproduction, produced at the point where both folklorists and record companies were beginning to travel south to capture what they saw as dying traditions. This is evidenced by the versions of spirituals and work songs included in the text. For Toomer, as Paul Allen Anderson has shown, the death of folk forms was an inevitable consequence of modernity.[51] They would be saved, he suggested, only by being taken up into the fruit of a literary culture, as in 'Song of the Sun' in *Cane*:

> O Negro slaves, dark purple ripened plums,
> Squeezed, and bursting in the pine-wood air,
> Passing, before they stripped the old tree bare
> One plum was saved for me, one seed becomes
>
> An everlasting song, a singing tree,
> Caroling softly songs of slavery,
> What they were, and what they are to me,
> Caroling softly souls of slavery.[52]

The elision of 'What they were' and 'what they are to me', and the idiosyncratic extension of the metaphor of the plum, suggest that the past comes alive only as a personal inheritance for the sensitive writer. Toomer asks what racial inheritance *is* for each subject.[53] The anxiety involved is reflected in his comments in a letter on seeing the famous singer and arranger Harry T. Burleigh in pursuit of information on spirituals, where he insists that Burleigh recognizes the trace of his grandfather in him – that he can *see* his black heritage, just as Toomer hopes to hear it in the songs of the South.[54]

Toomer's own mediation of tradition is figured in 'Fern'. At the beginning of the episode, Fern's impact is likened to the singing of a Jewish cantor 'if he has touched you and made your own sorrow seem trivial when compared to his' (16). This may seem an investigation of the typological link between spirituals and the Old Testament, buttressed by the desire to follow her 'Semitic' features to a 'common delta'. But a little further on the narrator (by this point in the story identifiable as a version of Toomer) makes it clear that this is a highly personal version of the pain of the other. He asks who she is and gets only a name from others; in contrast 'at first sight of her I felt as if I heard a Jewish cantor sing. As if his singing rose above the unheard chorus of a folk song. And I felt bound to her. I too had my dreams' (17). In the climactic scene in which the narrator sees that her eyes 'held God' and embraces her, her flight and song express a body 'tortured with something it could not let out. Like boiling sap it flooded arms and fingers' (19). That he hears her in the dusk and rushes to her as she faints renders her a test of his ability to inhabit the suffering of his female subjects. Fern embodies, we are told, the principle which takes 'men' out of themselves, makes them 'lose their selfishness' (18), and implicitly enables a translation of feeling between different realms: Jewish history and black; self and surroundings; God and history. But Fern remains the highly poetic narrator's muse, hovering on the borders of a solipsism in which she can, as a person, be negated, a voice in the darkness like Keats's nightingale singing of Ruth amidst the alien corn. Janet M. Whyde comments that 'the woman's body in Part I is continually transformed into poem/songs in such a way that it becomes the narrative direct link to the African-American's origins'; they are 'not women but shadows of women'.[55] This is true of 'Fern', of course, but it is worth noting the agonistic, fractured nature of this transformation, in which even the closing of 'Fern' – the casual naming of 'Fernie May Rosen' and the bar-room invitation to look her up – place the metaphorical and actual in considerable tension. Other men threaten to run the narrator out of town – the 'they' of the South who implicitly contrast with the Northern readership to whom the final comments are addressed, again suggestive of a lack of shared response to her embodied song.

The issue of the transmission or sharing of voice becomes particularly pressing in the final section of *Cane*, the quasi-dramatic 'Kabnis', which describes the title character's stint as a teacher in the South. At a climactic moment, Kabnis is puzzled by the old 'prophet' Father John's stammering declaration: 'O th sin th white folks 'mitted when they made the Bible lie'. As Charles Scruggs and Lee Vandemarr point out, his voice recalls Fern's 'plaintive, convulsive sounds' (19) as she seems to respond to black suffering.[56] Kabnis interprets his statement as evidence of the old man's fixated, traumatized state, locked in the past: 'Do y think youre out of slavery? Huh? Youre where they used t throw th worked-out, no-count slaves' (115). He has heard Father John mumbling the word 'death' at night and asks, 'Death. What does it mean t you? To you who died way back there in th' sixties. What are y throwin it in my throat for?' (114). The imagination of Father John's abject, fly-covered, and 'foul-breathed mouth' in death figures his utterance as an abject testament, a dis-ease thrown into the throat (115).

Kabnis sees a reversion to pious abolitionism in the old man and rejects this as a past he does not share ('My ancestors were Southern blue-bloods', 108). But more perceptive readers have seen Father John's stuttered phrase as an expression of the impossibility of disavowing the horrors of the past. Lewis, the character in the text often seen as closer to Toomer himself than Kabnis, articulates this position. Almost his final words before he departs into the night, overcome by the 'pain' of the South, are 'The old man as symbol, flesh, and spirit of the past ... you look at him, Kabnis' (108). That eidetic look is anticipated by an earlier episode in 'Box Seat' in which Dan contemplates another old man, in which spirituals as well as visual and sexual memory are evoked:

Dan: Strange I never really noticed him before. Been sitting there for years. Born a slave. Slavery not so long ago. He'll die in his chair. Swing low, sweet chariot. Jesus will come and roll him down the river Jordan ... Old man. Knows everyone who passes the corners.... He saw Grant and Lincoln. He saw Walt – old man, did you see Walt Whitman? Did you see Whitman! Strange force that drew me up to him. (67–68)

There is a vital context to these questions. In the early 1920s, the last generation of former slaves was nearing its end (the WPA slave narratives, taken down over a decade later, were significantly affected by the fact that most of those surviving had been slaves as children: an adult at Emancipation had to live into his or her nineties to record for the WPA). Attempts to document the experiences of former slaves began in the late 1920s with projects inaugurated by Charles S. Johnson and Ophelia Settle at Fisk University (Nashville), by John B. Cade at Southern University (Baton Rouge), and others at Kentucky State University (Frankfort), the results published in the *Journal of Negro History* and elsewhere.[57]

In this context, the old man's throwing his words into the throats of others is exactly the issue. Through him, Toomer marks a crucial moment for oral testament, in which the pain of slavery might be passed on or refused. In the face of what he interprets as the grotesque, Kabnis, who describes himself as coming from a family of Ciceronian 'ORATORS', refuses. We might say that Father John's stammered utterance is a linguistic fragment that resists Kabnis's boast that he can reshape an inherited language. The result is a problem of continuity. As Laura Doyle points out, Toomer often imagines cultural reproduction as modelled, in eugenic fashion, on sexual reproduction.[58] It is in this light that the response of Carrie, and her 'amen' at the end of the story, have to be seen: as the 'carrier' of tradition she allows a future to be born. Nevertheless, the split between the rather vapid final figure of the sun as 'gold-glowing child' and the defeated, voice-carrying male figures, carrying their pain away, suggests that Toomer describes a crisis of tradition which cannot be dealt with outside the text's own mechanics for cultural reproduction (which include a living tradition's entry into literature) – that is, at the level of culture rather than vital impulse. Pain is registered and represented; it underscores the text's claim to enter the historical experience of others. But it is as if what is involved is a loss of its historical location in the body of those who suffer and, concomitantly, its release as a less easily located trauma which the author struggles to represent.

Ralph Ellison's *Invisible Man* is also a novel which takes as one of its central metaphors the reproduction of sound, famously, in its opening evocation of multiple recordings of Louis Armstrong's 'What Did I Do to Be So Black and Blue?' But sonic recollection and reproduction are important throughout the novel, and rather than look at the introduction, I want to return to the eviction episode in chapter 13. There the narrator sees the possessions of the old couple scattered on the street and arranged in a drawer – evocative, as we noted in Chapter 2, of a whole history. But his response is sonic as well as visual:

I turned and stared again at the jumble, no longer looking at what was before my eyes, but inwardly-outwardly, around a corner into the dark, far-away-and-long-ago, not so much of my own memory as or remembered words, or linked verbal echoes, images, heard even when not listened to at home.... And with this sense of dispossession came a pang of vague recognition: this junk, these shabby chairs, these heavy, old-fashioned pressing irons, zinc wash tubs with dented bottoms – all throbbed within me with more meaning than there should have been.[59]

'Looking around corners' emerges as a recurrent trope in the novel, a figure for the ability to see what is hidden: 'Incidents in my past, both recognised and ignored, sprang together in my mind in an ironic leap of consciousness that was like looking around a corner' (414).[60] But one does not, of course, *look* around corners; one *hears* around corners, and what the Invisible Man hears, as much as he sees, is the blues of this couple: 'echoes, images'. When he speaks of dispossession, he is listening to those echoes; the sound, as he puts it later, of those 'too silent for the most sensitive recorders of sound' (354). The descent into the Louis Armstrong recording is a step around that corner, beyond the possibilities of technological reproduction imagined by the novel's narrator and perhaps also its audiophile author, into a music which carries with it a layering of histories. Ellison's piece for *Hi Fidelity* magazine, 'Living with Music', describes his own obsession with building a state-of-the-art system in the 1940s:

All this plunge into electronics, mind you, had as its simple end the enjoyment of recorded music as it was intended to be heard. I was obsessed with the idea of reproducing sound with such fidelity that even when using music as a defense behind which I could write, it would reach the unconscious levels of the mind with the least distortion.[61]

It is striking that technology is figured here as a route to an *unconscious* apprehension, as if Ellison had been reading Walter Benjamin on film as unconscious optics. Like Johnson and Toomer before him, Ellison seeks ways to (or a technology which would enable him to) represent an unsounded sound.

The list of objects scattered on the pavement referred to earlier culminates in 'zinc wash tubs', the resonating containers of sound evoked at the beginning of this chapter. What the Invisible Man hears is the sound of a particular history, intimate and familiar. For Freud, Laplanche and Pontalis note, sound is present in the primal scene as the small noise (*petit bruit*) that initiated it, a noise which can be taken to include 'the history, or legends, of parents, grand-parents, ancestors; the lore [*dit*] or the *noise* [*bruit*] of the family, this spoken or secret discourse, previous to the subject, into which it must come or to which it must have recourse'.[62] Thus it is from his identification with a lost family and the apparatus of family life that history floods the subject. When the Invisible Man does, finally, speak the truth of black experience it is after the death of Brother Tod Clifton, impelled by a baritone voice at Tod's funeral singing 'There's Many a Thousand Gone', echoing the sorrows of slavery: 'It was a song from the past, the past of the campus and the still earlier past of home' (364). Of the old man singing, he says, 'It was as though the song had been there all the time and he knew it and aroused it; and I knew that I had known it too and had failed to release it out of a vague, nameless shame or fear.' Not only does the song sound the past, it gathers in the pain of the present to form an emergent politics; as in the earlier episode there is 'more meaning than there should have been', a submerged throbbing: 'It was not the words, for they were all the same old slave-borne words; it was as though he's changed the emotion beneath the words while yet the old longing, resigned, transcendent emotion still sounded above, now deepened by that something for which the theory of Brotherhood had given me no name' (364–65). Throughout *Invisible Man* it is these images of sonic recovery which impel the narrator to speak. The fact that a technological figure – the gramophone of the opening – regulates their presence is, of course, significant, since it stands in a sense for the highly evolved apparatus of the modernist novel itself, as does Louis Armstrong's bravura rendition of 'What Did I do?' Nevertheless, it is the *petit bruit* which we are called to listen to: the old words and murmurs, 'linked verbal echoes' which carry us back, grounding the text's gramophonic figures in the depth of historical experience contained in that battered wash tub.

RECORDING MACHINES: JOHN LOMAX'S IDENTIFICATIONS

As I have suggested, for African-American authors the traces of the somatic in the sonic represent a way of figuring historical continuity. For white interpreters of recorded music, this is less a matter of an inherited or claimed identity, I would suggest, than the problematics of the technology itself as it relates to history. The period after the First World War saw an explosion of interest in American folk music, whether considered part of a legacy of cultural memory or a resource for exploitation. Cecil Sharp's trip to North Carolina and Kentucky in 1916 produced, with Olive Dame Campbell, *English Folk Songs from the Southern Appalachians* (1917), inspiring a number of state folk-lore societies after the war. At Harvard, George Lyman Kittredge, a student of Francis James Child, applied his work to American song and Reed Smith worked on the materials for *South Carolina Ballads* (1928).[63] Two linked developments were important: a shift away from the notion of 'survivals' – lists of Scottish and English ballads with Child numbers – and a contextualism which saw each place as having its music (rather than the textualism which stressed the dissemination of versions of an 'original'). Both of these developments converged on African-America music and the idea that, as one collector put it, it was 'the greatest single contribution which the South or the nation, for that matter, has made to folk-music'.[64] Sound recording meant a stress on surviving traditions: Robert W. Gordon, first curator of the Folk Song Archive at the Library of Congress, insisting 'on finishing his fieldwork among black singers in Darien, Georgia, before coming to Washington, D.C.'[65]

In the 1920s, record companies like Okeah and Victor also contributed a great deal to the recording of black music, creating differentiated markets for 'Hillbilly' (country) and 'Race' (blues and jazz) records, providing the basis of the obsessions of later collectors, reissues, and histories.[66] At some points in the early 1920s, enthnomusicologists and record companies would be working in the same town at the same time, competing for singers.[67] But from an ethnographic point of view the most significant figures in the recording of black folk music in the twentieth century were John and Alan Lomax, father and son: the father for his pioneering records of black musicians in and out of the Southern penitentiaries and his role in setting up the Library of Congress collections and the recordings of slave narratives in the 1930s; the son for later recordings in the Sea Islands and elsewhere, and for his writings on the theory of folk music. The work of the Lomaxes has been described by many scholars, as has the history of the blues. What I will briefly consider is, once again, the thematics of sonic resonance.

As a junior instructor from Texas, John Lomax spent a year at Harvard in 1906–1907 (the year T. S. Eliot entered the college) and took Barrett Wendell's English 33, the first course in American literature in the country. It was devoted that year to regional literature, prompting Lomax to collect a number of Texas ballads, including 'Home on the Range'. This was the beginning of a lifetime's work.[68] By 1911 Lomax had plans for a six-volume folk song anthology, which then became a study of black music, to which he told Wendell he was increasingly drawn (*LC*, 167). He sent out a circular to newspapers in May 1912 and delivered papers on Negro plantation songs (*LC*, 168–69). However, these efforts dwindled in the 1920s, as work intervened (he moved into bond management). It was only after illness, his wife's death, and losses during the Depression that he returned to the field in June 1932, with an anthology proposed for Macmillan (*LC*, 278). Lomax's work in the 1930s included numerous field trips across the South, to prisons, Jim Crow towns, rural backwaters. He also contributed to the archiving of discs at the Library of Congress, where he became Honorary Curator of the Archive of American Folk Song. By mid-1937, after less than a year's work, the archive held 'some 1,314 cylinder and disc recordings and over four thousand folk tunes' (*LC*, 402). Other songs and performers were discovered and commercialized ('Deep River' was discovered in Prairie View, Texas, in 1932; Lead Belly was famously and fractiously

launched on his career as figurehead of the folk revival). In his later position as National Advisor on Folklore and Folkways for the Federal Writers'
Project he played an important role in the recording of the WPA slave
narratives.

The vicissitudes of recording technology form a large part of his autobiography, *Adventures of a Ballad Hunter*. Lomax aimed to gather what
he understood to be a dying tradition, whose death is bound up with the
very modes of technological reproduction he employs (thus the irony in
his comment on the river songs: 'Soon the gang songs of the black men
would follow suit, as part of the advance of the machine age').[69] Edison's
original cylinder phonograph could both record and play back, but the
quality was poor and cylinders degenerated, prompting a quest for better machines.[70] Lomax was courted by an engineer, Walter Garwick, but
his project failed; the Library of Congress's funds were drying up and its
Amplion machine was sold. The Lomaxes tried Edison, ACLS, and RCA
Victor; finally a Dictaphone Corporation of Philadelphia machine was
donated to him by Janice Reed Lit, an amateur folklorist (*A*, 294–97).
The adventures of the machine include the 'primitive' playback effects
which are a feature of early ethnographic phonography.[71] Lomax wrote
of John Lee of Virginia: 'When Joe heard his voice coming back from the
loud-speaker, he was mightily moved. His body shook, he dashed about
the room shouting over and over, "My soul is wrapped in the care of the
Lord and nothing in this world can harm me!"' (*A*, 156). And as Sin-Killer
Griffin said upon hearing his sermon: '"Mr. Lomax … for a long time I'se
been hearing that I'se a good preacher. Now I know it."'[72]

Indeed, there is a kind of archive fever in the Lomaxes' trips across the
South: the father and his machines, the son and his typewriter, working
through the hot Southern night at a New Orleans speakeasy, taking down
forty-one stanzas of 'Stagolee' (*SW*, 21). They conceived of their technology as (in Alan's more political idiom) 'a voice for the voiceless' (*SW*, 174),
as registering the emotions of the excluded: 'The needle writes on the disc
with tireless accuracy the subtle inflections, the melodies, the pauses that
comprise the emotional meaning of speech, spoken and sung. … Singing in
their homes, in their churches, at their dances, they leave on these records
imperishable spirals of their personalities, their singing styles, and their
cultural heritage' (*SW*, 64). John Lomax, for all that he was suspicious of
his son's leftism, worked with an implicit parallel between folk song and a
kind of bardic memory suitable for technological transmission – a memory which tends to be individual, in contrast to the collective memory of
spirituals (at a prison in Jackson, Mississippi, he notes the limits of the
technology: 'Our machine won't take this mass singing. It overflows the

microphone and drowns the harmony', *A*, 124). In Richmond, Virginia, they find the 'blind bard' they have been looking for, James Howard: 'For, as you know, blindness brings a retentive memory'; 'he sang for us until all our records were filled' (*A*, 126). They said of another singer, 'Clear Rock seems to have caught in his capacious memory the floating folk songs that had been current among the thousands of black convicts who had been his only companions for fifty years. He had a store equal in continuous length to the *Iliad*' (*A*, 179). Lomax's most compelling version of the aboriginal cry is the field holler of Enoch Brown, whom he encounters near his informant Ruby Pickens Tartt's house in Livingstone, Alabama:

I first heard Enoch's call one summer evening as I sat on the porch of the Tartt home. From far off in the darkness, long, lonesome, full-voiced, brooding notes pierced the stillness of a perfect night, indescribable and unforgettable. Starting on a low note, the cry reached a crescendo in such pervasive volume and intensity that it seemed to fill the black void of darkness. The sound came from everywhere and nowhere. Then the cry shaded downward, with the lower notes thrice repeated. Suddenly silence. (*A*, 200)

Later Lomax hears Enoch cry – 'Oh, de blood, oh, de blood, / Oh, de blood done sign my name' – and comments, 'Some day it ought to form the core of a symphony, just as the night bird, Enoch, might serve as a part for some actor in a great American play' (*A*, 201). The elder Lomax's descriptions of black music-making thus gravitate towards notions of a natural music in which the depth of history can be heard, emblematized by 'the wail of the Negro woodsman as a fine tree that he is cutting sways and then falls to the earth with a shuddering crash. Shrill, swift, wavering, the shout swings to a sudden and dramatic conclusion, just as does the tree when the cry ends as the tree surrenders and lies prone on the earth that has fed it. It is the dirge of the dying pine and at the same time a warning signal to other woodsmen' (*A*, 119). 'After we listened for a while, a group of glistening ebony figures, their torsos naked, came and sang the requiem of the falling pine into our recording machine'(*A*, 119).

At the same time, there are significant undertones in John Lomax's story which suggest that the sources of his allegiance to black culture is more personal, born of the proximity of small-town life in the South and a sense of a troubling shared history. He describes his early black friend Nat Blythe, an apprentice nine years older. Between Nat and himself there is two-way traffic from the oral to the written: Lomax taught him to read ('Nat made me a teacher'), while 'From Nat I learned my sense of rhythm … the speaking rhythm of his hands', as well as his first songs (*A*, 11). He recalls: 'I came to love Nat with the fierce strength and loyalty of youth. The day he was twenty-one Colonel Blythe handed him his savings of more than a thousand dollars, and Nat took me to town and had two pictures of me made, one for himself. I still have mine' (*A*, 21). But Nat vanishes, becoming an emblem of loss:

I have never since seen or heard of him. His Negro friends think we was murdered for his money, and his body, bound with baling wire and weighed down with scrap iron, thrown into the Bosque river. As I travelled up and down the South these recent years, I find myself always looking for Nat, the dear friend and companion of long ago. I loved him as I have loved few people. (*A*, 12)

We can see the same figure of the African-American double, the lost brother, in Lomax's story of meeting a prisoner called John Lomax, who says he is from 'Holmes County, Mississippi, near Durant' (*A*, 141) – where the white Lomax was born. Lomax does not explicitly raise the possibilities of biological connection, but nevertheless connection is there: 'That boy's mother may once have rocked me to sleep' (*A*, 141).

A third story is more generic. Lomax's biographer describes his tendency, at Harvard, to rework earlier papers depicting himself as a rough from Texas, including 'the story of a lynching, probably based on an event from his youth, in which a black man on trial for raping a white woman is attacked by a mob, hauled from the courtroom, and hanged. It seemed to be a story he couldn't quite finish or let go of'.[73] The first draft was called 'Ebony Fascits' (*sic*); later drafts were titled 'The Courtroom', 'Mob Vengeance', and 'A Southern Scene'. The lynching scene, and stories in which he himself is threatened by Southern lawmen for his recording activities, bespeak a deep identification with his subjects, even if overlaid with Lomax's Southern patriarchalism and conservatism – a violent story he could not stop seeking out and transmitting.

This story is particular to John Lomax, but it is worth noting that to some extent it mirrors the history of the construction of the blues as 'roots' music in the second half of the twentieth century. When Alan Lomax first encountered the blues in the 1930s, he saw it as a new and largely urban style, reflecting the restless energies of modernity, commercialized and hybrid in its origins, political and self-aware – as news out of the South. But as Marybeth Hamilton points out, Alan too eventually came to accept the myth of the Delta as the 'deep' rural origins of the blues, and the status of the blues as 'a personal music of torment and pain', by implication a part of slavery's legacy, for all that (as Elijah Wald notes) the Delta had not been a slaveholding area.[74] It is that view which licences comments like William Ferris's 'The pain of life for black people in Mississippi has been the catalyst for much of the blues repertoire'[75] – a comment which is not exactly wrong but which entirely absorbs the aesthetics of echo into what was in fact a commercial and technologically mediated style. As we will see, there is a logic to that incorporation.

RECORDING TECHNOLOGY

I now want to turn to what may be a version of the same topic, the way in which African Americans have been inserted into the early histories of sound recording, often as figures for the linkage of sound and technology. The Romans dubbed the slave the *instrumentum vitale*, the 'speaking instrument' or the 'machine with a human voice'. From this simple tag we can elaborate a connection between slavery, sonic reproduction, and the survival of a trace which could be described as the ghost in the machine – the sound of an emotional residue both *within* and *of* the instrumental. Aristotle's comments on music in book VIII of the *Politics* are a useful point of departure, since an implicit connection between the slave and the musician structures his thinking. He stresses that 'learning music must not be allowed to ... turn the body into that of a mechanic, ill-fitted for the training of citizen or soldier'; he also notes that a discerning attitude to music results in the rejection of both crude instruments and 'all those that require manual dexterity'. Professional training produces a state of unselfconscious automaticity in which 'the performer does not perform in order to improve his own virtue, but to give pleasure to the listeners'; it should therefore be assigned to a 'hireling' rather than a citizen.[76] The tendency of music is, then, 'to degrade the players into mechanics', to align the person with the instrument, deployed for the use of others. If one remembers the well-known passage in book I of the *Politics* about how there would be no need for slaves if a plucker could play a lyre of its own accord, then the slave musician is implicit in notions of musical technology. In this complex of ideas, the slave is collapsed into the instrument – a suggestion reinforced by the link between primitive performance and a fetishistic investment of spirit in the instrument often made in the nineteenth century (and later by, e.g., Ernst Bloch).[77] In the anti-slavery collection *Autographs for Freedom* (1854), for example, William D. Snow writes, 'The imagination of the African, like his musical genius, which extracts surprising harmony from the rudest of sources, the clapping of hands, the clanking of chains, the resonance of lasso wood, and perforated shells, seems to invest everything with a resident spirit of peculiar power.'[78]

This is a structure traversed, I would suggest – though in something like the opposite direction – by the use of black performers to authenticate technological reproduction. The role of 'race' records in establishing modern musical styles has been well documented; and the notion 'authentic' performance was central to the work of the Lomaxes as they laid down their corpus of recorded black songs in the 1930s and later. For all that the authenticity effect associated with the blues has been fairly substantially critiqued by recent historians, the use of black style to anchor a new technical departure remains a resource in American culture, with the pain of the performer signalling that which survives the technical order itself. In part this is what Alexander S. Weheliye described as the fact that 'black voices are materially disembodied by the phonograph and other sound technologies, while black subjects are inscribed as the epitome of embodiment through a multitude of U.S. cultural discourses'.[79] What is involved here is thus a dialectic in which the disembodied is given a presence within the technology as the trace of embodiment in general.

Examples of this vocal fetishism can also (as I have suggested elsewhere) be garnered from the early history of film sound in the period of transition, 1928–30. All-black casts were used in a number of the first sound films, including *Dialogues in Dixie* and King Vidor's *Hallelujah*, paralleled by the blackface of *The Jazz Singer*; *Hallelujah* in particular focuses on black religious music-making and the tradition of the spiritual. The idea that black voices (especially collective black voices, in contrast to Lomax's claim) recorded better than white ones was briefly canvassed in the film press, but what seems to have been just as important was establishing a sense of real presence via the rhythmic power and synchronicity thought to inhere in black bodies. The fetishism applied to the black voice in these films synchronizes the visible – bodies marked as black – and the new technology; the 'visual obviousness' of race guarantees its problematic attachment to sound.[80]

We can find an earlier example. 'Blind Tom', or Thomas Wiggins, was a slave born near Columbus, Georgia, in 1849 (Figure 6). He quickly proved to have an astonishing talent at the piano, and by the age of 8 he was performing publicly. He subsequently had a hugely profitable career, making money for his owner, General James Bethune, and other promoters; he performed throughout the United States, in the White House, and in Europe. This continued well after the Civil War, with Bethune asserting rights of guardianship (effectively a commercial enslavement or copyright) over a person who was described as an idiot savant. There were various court cases over control of Tom, a story which Stephen Best has elegantly linked to later debates about property rights in sonic reproduction.[81] Tom had a huge cultural impact: his London programme suggested that he

BLIND TOM.
vright 1880, by John G. Bethune.

Figure 6. *Blind Tom* [Thomas Wiggins]. Prints and Photographs Division, Library of Congress, Washington, D. C., LC-USZ62–84287.

had been seen by more people than any living person, and he was written about by, among many others, Rebecca Harding Davis, Mark Twain, and Willa Cather – the last both in factual accounts and in a fictional version of him ('Blind D'Arnault') in *My Ántonia*. Even George Herriman's early cartoon figure 'Musical Mose' seems to involve a memory of Tom, as he 'impussinates' various nationalities and instruments.[82]

More recent historians have disputed the 'idiot savant' label, pointing out that Tom had considerable musical education and that his compositions are highly skilled period pieces, not the unthinking mimicry attributed to him in his lifetime.[83] Nevertheless, central to his performance were two ideas: fidelity of reproduction and storage. Not only would Tom play any piece he had ever heard, he would improvise an accompaniment to or repeat anything played for him on stage; he could repeat long speeches word for word, though his everyday language was limited. According to one testimonial to Blind Tom, 'He gives recitations in Greek, Latin, German, French, as well as imitations of the Scotch bagpipe, the musical box, the hurdy-gurdy, the Scotch fiddler, the American stump orator, comic speakers, and, in short, any sound he may hear.' That might include natural sounds: the wind and storms.[84] In his London programme (c. 1880) a 'Special Notice' inside the back cover says: 'BLIND TOM can only play what he hears or improvises. Until about two years ago a list of pieces that Tom had heard was kept, numbering nearly 2,000. Unfortunately, this catalogue was lost. Since that period he has heard perhaps 3,000 pieces, and his repertoire now numbers upwards of 5,000, entirely at his memory's disposal.'[85]

Two aspects of the descriptions of Tom are important here: technology and pain. The terms used to describe him place him close to accounts of the developing technological reproduction of sound. That is, Tom is seen, in prosthetic terms, as a mechanism, a player piano. Cather described him as 'a human phonograph, a sort of animated memory, with sound producing powers'; as speaking in 'another man's words'.[86] In *My Ántonia*, Blind D'Arnault mates with the piano as a child, deploying its 'mouth' (the open keyboard) as prosthesis: 'He approached this highly artificial instrument through a mere instinct, and coupled himself to it, as if he knew it was to piece him out and make a whole creature of him.'[87] The gramophone metaphor appears be present, proleptically, even in Mark Twain's early (1869) piece on Tom, where he almost seems a record, spinning as it plays down the music:

When anybody else plays, the music so crazes him with delight that he can only find relief in uplifting a leg, depressing his head half way to the floor and jumping around on one foot so fast that it almost amounts to spinning – and he claps his hands all the while, too. . . . And when the volunteer is done, Tom stops spinning, sits down and plays the piece over, exactly as the volunteer had played it, and puts in all the slips, mistakes, discords, corrections, and everything just where they occurred in the original performance!

If this reading seems to be an example of the recursive process that has been labelled 'remediation', it could even be inflected towards the digital. Twain describes Tom as a perfect Fourier analyser, able to pick out the individual notes from twenty keys struck at once, able to 'separate the web of discord into its individual elements'.[88] Similarly, in an article in the *Atlantic Monthly* Rebecca Harding Davis described Tom as an unknowing ('vacant') instrument, working without musical script, by ear. In fact, Davis describes him in double terms: *both* as a perfect reproducer of tunes and as a receptive genius.[89] On the one hand, he can reproduce a fifteen-minute speech and fail to understand a word. His body appears to be a perfect storage device: 'In what part of the unsightly body-carcass had been stowed away these old airs, forgotten by every one else, and some of them never heard by the child but once, but which he now reproduced every note intact, and with whatever quirk of quiddity of style belonging to the person who originally had sung or played them?' (106). At the same time '[h]is comprehension of the meaning of music as a prophetic or historical voice which few souls utter and fewer understand, is clear and vivid' (108). He is, that is, a 'faithful witness' to the life of music in the sense described by Schopenhauer: its carrying the pulse of being. For Davis the resolution of this paradox – Tom as instrument, Tom as the spirit of music – is carried in the observation that he can accompany any piece on first hearing, playing the base line 'secondo'; he can do this partly because of his instinctive understanding of harmony, 'on which the glowing negro soul can seize, you know'. This is to say that he is a servant of the music, a slave to the tune, as it were, in the manner described by Aristotle. The brilliance of his accompaniment is contrasted with the weakness Davis ascribes to his own compositions, which she sees as pastiche and bricolage. Tom is ultimately a responding device: he can play 'secondo', register the harmonies; in artistic terms he listens to his master's voice rather than originating. (This is, of course, close to the characterization of both Edmonia Lewis and Hilda in the preceding chapter as instruments of higher powers.)

Davis's comments about Tom understanding music as 'a prophetic or historical voice' – that is, as conveying the struggle of the Schopenhauerian Will – takes us back to the issue of pain, since pain is what embodiment is about for Schopenhauer. Cather describes Blind d'Arnault as coming from 'the Far South ... where the spirit if not the fact of slavery persisted'. That spirit is manifested in a bodily enactment of that legacy: 'as music it was something real, vitalized by a sense of rhythm that was stronger than his other physical senses – that not only filled his dark mind, but worried his body incessantly.'[90] He plays as a fetishized 'glistening African god of pleasure', but Cather also stresses a connection between music and pain: he was whipped as a child for approaching the music room. In one of the advertising pamphlets which accompanied his tours, Tom is characterized as a kind of dissociated pain receptor who converts pain into pure form:

He was perfectly delighted by cries of pain. When his mother whipped any of the older children he would laugh and caper, and rub his hands in an ecstasy of enjoyment, and soon would be found whipping himself, and repeating the words of the mother and the cries of the child. He enjoyed so highly the crying of children that he would inflict pain upon them, for the pleasure of hearing them cry; and a constant watch had to be kept on him when he was about younger children.... To this day any exclamation or expression indicative of pain gives him great pleasure; and though he will express sympathy for the sufferer, and prescribe remedies for his relief, he cannot restrain his expressions of pleasure. Doubtless it is the strength and intensity of expression given to sounds produced by pain, that afford the enjoyment.[91]

It is as if Tom responds to the legacy of slavery as pure form, devoid of its subjective content. This mediation between the pains of embodiment and a role as a recording device is, I think, one reason for his presence in *My Ántonia*, reflecting as he does the position of both the frame narrator and Jim Burden, the cosmopolitans transcribing the life struggles of the pioneers who work the soil, carrying culture across America.

In *The Fugitive's Properties*, Stephen Best highlights 'the general move in nineteenth-century American jurisprudence for property to absorb, in its expansion, dimensions of life commonly understood as the province of personhood'; the result was a tendency towards 'property's personification'. 'Mechanical reproduction ... returned civil law to the problem of expropriation and the injurious commodification of personhood.' Slavery, he suggests, 'lends depth' to this story. Best argues that Blind Tom's facility, advertised as unfounded on a proper understanding of the formal principles of music, is 'the novelty of the mechanical reproduction of sound before its technical achievement – an imagining, in short, of acoustic property (of the acoustic as alienable and commodity) in advance of the phonograph and the application of the law of intellectual property to sound'.[92] To this analysis, I would add that Tom's allegedly detached pain receptivity is a way of figuring the formal logic and violence of that process, in which the body and its representation are sundered and rendered commodities, as well as a guarantor of the 'truth' of the musical reproduction.

A number of concluding questions suggest themselves. Why does the persistence of the suffering of slavery find such focus in notions of a sonic residue? And why is this bound to notions of technology? Why should sound be conceived as an engram for painful experience, given that other senses seem more directly involved in both physical pain and memory? There are two initial answers to these questions, I would suggest. Firstly, the transition from inner experience to an outward understanding of pain is most readily imagined as sonic: the cry or groan. Secondly, the very ephemerality of sound – the fact that it is radiated and 'lost' or at best faintly apprehended or echoed – makes it a figure for that which is not easily retained across time, for a memory which does not presume that a ready survival like that of the image (for example) offers an easy route into the sufferings of others and which must be actively re-enacted.

An account of the underlying problematic would run something like this (it is derived in part from a reading of Elaine Scarry's *The Body in Pain*). The making of the body of the slave into a thing enforced – albeit unevenly – by the master is an act of making like no other, because the body itself is a primal element of the act of making. To objectify another is to assume a position like that of the Old Testament God: to violently mark the slave, to deny the slave the status of being, to deny the slave anything other than an embodied existence. It is also to refuse the slave an operative voice: voice is assigned solely to whoever directs the slave (again this is a reification – a theoretical rather than actual status – though one that can be actuated in relation to the insolent or 'mouthy' slave). Finally, and as a consequence, in the ideology of slavery, interiority is surrendered to the situation: the slave has no operative thoughts that need to be exteriorized, no sentience that demands legal recognition.

At that point of negation, voice is shattered, repressed, and denied; it is assigned to the master, on the one hand, and locked up in the slave's body – now rendered object-like – on the other. *Pain*, I have suggested, is central to the notion of the sonic veil. As Scarry suggests, pain – whether in war, torture, or enslavement – registers an unmaking of the world which confers power, as she puts it, on 'an ideology or instance of political authority impatient of, or deserted of, benign sources of substantiation'.[93] It is this locked-up voice which we have seen stored in various cultural artefacts: Ellison's wash tub, the statue of Cleopatra, 'Nobody Knows the Trouble I've Seen'. According to Scarry the 'objectlessness' of pain – the fact that it is not like desire, hunger, or fear in having a referent in the external world – allows it to be compared to the imagination. But it seems to me that another possible comparison, indeed a rather more traditional one, can be made to music, specifically Schopenhauer's account of music as an account of Being, which is in turn a form of pain for the pessimist.

But why the emphasis on the *persistence* of this painful sound, on the notion of the echoing continuation of a 'black sound'? One explanation, and the one which one could apply most readily to the African-American tradition itself, concerns the notion that race itself is bound up with a permanent inscription or marking, as in a range of recent writings on trauma. To carry – or rather to recuperate, since we are, as we have seen, firmly in the realm of repetition, echo, and recovery – and to echo the sound of a painful inheritance is to embody that trauma as it is bound up with the pathos of the expression of a previously suppressed message. Scarry writes: 'Physical pain is not only itself resistant to language but also actively destroys language, deconstructing it into the pre-language of cries and groans. To hear those cries is to witness the shattering of language. Conversely, to be present when the person in pain rediscovers speech and so regains his powers of self-objectification is almost to be present at the birth, or rebirth, of language.'[94]

It is this rebirth of the human from its subordination to an instrumentalizing technology which can be activated, I would argue, when black subjects are inserted into the picture as emblems of reproduction. The story of redemption and release is taken up into technology. The making of voice is instrumentalized, but at the same time its human status is guaranteed by the insertion of the *instrumentum vocale*. It is as if the sonic recording would too easily become a cold surface, like that of the statue in the preceding chapter, without the imagination of the human body in pain. In these examples, the problematic of pain in slavery and its enduring aftermath becomes turned around, as it were, as a way of locating a historical residue that survives the potentially alienating transfer into media. To hear the dead voice of the slave, to hear that pain, is to see a particular notion of transmission guaranteed – though one which must, I would hasten to add, be read dialectically, as itself related to the way we see technology as potentially in tension with a human presence, rendering us its instruments in turn.

In making this argument about the progress of a metaphor, I do not, of course, mean in any way to lay aside the terrible sufferings of those involved in slavery; and indeed, those who heard pain in the 'sorrow songs' did so with good reason. Rather what I am tentatively suggesting is that, detached from that history, the human presence within the media itself is predicated on the notion of the pleasurable survival of the traces of pain. Barraud's famous dog in the HMV logo, faithful after death and listening to 'his master's voice' on the coffin, represents the 'animated memory' (as Cather put it) carried on the cylinder. The sound that is figured as released from those upturned tubs, vibrating in the air for Babbage as he inaugurates the digital age, can be used as a guarantee that we survive our media; that there is really someone there, a human cry. That the burden of that guarantee should fall on the slave and the slave's descendants is surely an irony, but perhaps an inevitable one given that the slave, since Aristotle, has always been there, plucking the string, a figure for both the automatic transmission of music and its origin in a human who gives him- or herself up to the instrument.

CHAPTER 6

Slavery in the Mind: Trauma and the Weather

Somehow it was assumed that the Negroes, of all the diverse American peoples, would remain unaffected by the climate, the weather, the political circumstances – from which not even slaves were exempt.

Ralph Ellison, 'Blues People'

The right tune whistled in a doorway or lifting up from the circles and grooves of a record can change the weather. From freezing to hot to cool.

Toni Morrison, *Jazz*

My topic in this final chapter is the understanding of race and history in terms of what is sometimes called 'trauma theory'. The underlying suggestion of literature written in this mode is that catastrophic events – and perhaps ultimately racial marking itself – leave a hidden historical residue within the self. The result is a state of internalized and fixated mourning, even a kind of melancholia. Such thinking has been a keynote of recent discussions of the memory of slavery, and indeed has been important to the understanding of race in general.[1] In Chapter 2, I used the figure of 'debt' to consider the negation involved in slavery and examined the afterlife of that figure in African-American and Southern narrative. In Chapters 4 and 5, I investigated forms of internalized pain and the way they are implicit in both sculpture and music. Nevertheless, because what is involved in these discussions is the idea that slavery enters the language of the aesthetic as a continuing presence, I also want to consider the dangers of internalizing the metaphor of painful or traumatic inheritance and instead explore a counter-traumatic, counter-melancholic, and politically distinct understanding of history and agency – one that might begin to free the subject from the past. That is an understanding which sometimes accumulates around a trope quite different from the wound, that of weather.

173

I should perhaps say something about this figure at the outset, *qua* figure. Hovering as it does in the realm of the everyday, any discussion of 'weather' plays on the vacuous and risks dissolving into the commonplaces of air. Nevertheless, I *do* want to argue that a particular confluence of features relating to American slavery meant that to speak of the weather became both a way of describing the self and potentially a part of a rhetoric of resistance. Which is to say that as a cultural metaphor the figure negotiates between the seeming universal and the specifics of history, between individual experience and collective understanding.

Here are two passages from the mysterious ending of arguably the most celebrated recent American novel, a novel which has informed a whole discourse on trauma:

Everybody knew what she was called, but nobody anywhere knew her name. Disremembered and unaccounted for, she cannot be lost because no one is looking for her, and even if they were, how can they call her if they don't know her name? Although she has claim, she is not claimed....

By and by all trace is gone, and what is forgotten is not only the footprints but the water too and what is down there. The rest is weather. Not the breath of the disremembered and unaccounted for, but wind in the eaves, or spring ice thawing too quickly. Just weather. Certainly no clamor for a kiss.

Beloved.[2]

Why does Toni Morrison end *Beloved* with a fade into 'Just weather'? What does the 'rest' which is weather mean; and in particular, why is it juxtaposed so strikingly with the painful past of slavery: claiming, naming, and the spectre of the 'loneliness that roams' – with the issues, that is, of historical trauma and historical melancholy? The answer seems obvious enough: Morrison seems to imply that 'weather' represents something beyond a traumatic legacy. Weather is the everyday rather than that which haunts; it is lived experience rather than the melancholy burden of the past. But the issue is more complex, because what we are offered at the end of the novel is so clearly a balance between forces and because weather, rather than simply being a kind of remainder at the end, is present throughout the novel in striking ways.

I will return to *Beloved*, but first I want to make a long tack windward, through the intertwined issues of race, trauma, and weather in America. I begin with Herman Melville's allegory of slavery, *Benito Cereno*, published in 1855–86. At the beginning of the story the Spanish slaver *San Dominick* emerges from the 'troubled grey vapours' of the Atlantic, surrounded by 'baffling' breezes.[3] Boarding the ship, the American innocent

Captain Delano becomes involved in a series of enigmatic dialogues with its captain, Benito Cereno, and his black servant Babo, the uncertainties of which are resolved only at the tale's end, when it suddenly becomes clear that this is an inverted world, that the slaves have taken over the ship and enacted an elaborate masquerade of normalcy with the remaining white crew.

Throughout the story, Delano's intermittent suspicions – in particular his anti-Catholic fears of Don Benito's dark motives – are described in terms of mental weather: coming and going like clouds, casting momentary shadows on his mind, 'black vapours' dispelled in turn by the 'mild sun' of his 'good-nature' (240). If this is a conventional enough way of describing states of mind, in Melville's tale the weather takes on a thematic intensity conditioned by the becalmed state of the ship (the calm itself emblematic of the political impasses of the American 1850s). When Delano reflects on the old sailor who seems to solicit his attention and then avoid his eye, he reflects: 'Ah, these currents spin one's head round almost as much as they do the ship. Ha, there now's a pleasant sort of sunny sight; quite sociable, too.' The 'sunny sight' is a 'slumbering Negress', which he interprets as the African in her natural state. He walks aft:

As ... a chance phantom cat's-paw – an islet of breeze, unheralded, unfollowed – as this ghostly cat's-paw came fanning his cheek; as his glance fell upon the row of small, round dead-lights – all closed like coppered eyes of the coffined, and the state-cabin door.... [A]s these and other images flitted through his mind, as the cat's-paw through the calm, gradually he felt rising a dreamy inquietude. (252)

He dismisses these mental eddies. At the end of the story, mystery seemingly dispelled and Babo executed, Delano's belief that the weather will carry one forward – a belief in the healing powers of natural life – is contrasted with a quite different psychology, associated with Cereno's haunted inability to forget. Delano says:

'You generalize, Don Benito; and mournfully enough. But the past is passed; why moralize upon it? Forget it. See, yon bright sun has forgotten it all, and the blue sea, and the blue sky; these have turned over new leaves.'

'Because they have no memory,' he dejectedly replied; 'because they are not human.'

'But these mild trades that now fan your cheek, Don Benito, do they not come with a human-like healing to you? Warm friends, steadfast friends are the trades.'

'With their steadfastness they but waft me to my tomb, Señor,' was the foreboding response.

'You are saved', cried Captain Delano, more and more astonished and pained; 'you are saved: what has cast such a shadow upon you?'
   'The negro.' (306)

Like *Beloved*, *Benito Cereno* depicts two psychologies, one associated with the becalmed ship and the fixity of trauma – with a shadow that does not pass – and another associated with the clouds, breezes, and shifting contingencies of the everyday. One is associated with Don Benito and Spain, the other with Delano and America. As Eric Sundquist points out, the tale evokes a complex set of associations relating to the 1799 Santo Domingo slave rebellion (the year the tale is set in), Haiti, and American understandings of Latin American politics in the context of slavery (*Benito Cereno* ran in *Putnam's Magazine* in the last three months of 1855, when the journal was becoming more belligerently abolitionist).[4] It seems to signal that any attempt to explain away American slavery as an effect of the weather – as local, as passing without trace – is confounded by its melancholy residue. And what appears to be an effect of the weather – the becalmed ship in disarray – is revealed to be a state of affairs of an ineradicable permanency: the trauma is everywhere, knitted into America.[5]

   One obvious emblem of trauma in the text is the 'Gordian Knot' tossed to Delano by an old seaman, one of the surviving crew, with the cry 'Undo it, cut it, quick'. Delano stands, 'knot in hand and knot in head', unable to understand the clue (254–55). The Gordian knot, used metaphorically by James Madison to describe the Constitution in 1821, was often a metaphor for slavery. In the Senate speech on the 1850 Compromise Bill which he engineered, Henry Clay described the sudden cutting of the knot as a dangerous solution:

Standing armies and navies, to an extent draining the revenues of each portion of the dissevered empire, would be created; exterminating wars would follow – not a war of two, nor three years, but of interminable duration – an exterminating war would follow, until some Philip or Alexander, some Cæsar or Napoleon, would rise to cut the Gordian knot, and solve the problem of the capacity of man for self-government, and crush the liberties of both the dissevered portions of this Union.[6]

Speaking from a more radical position and later in the day, the Massachusetts Senator Charles Sumner both suggested that Lincoln should cut the knot and (later in 1868) offered a qualification similar to Clay's: 'It is not every Gordian knot that can be cut: some must be patiently untied.'[7] Delano's compromise is to ignore the knot until it unravels: in historical terms this is accommodation with slavery, refusing to address its trauma. But there is, of course, a complication here. It is Delano's innocence that keeps him alive: had he seen through the charade he might have been slaughtered. At the same time, his dwelling in the weather is ultimately a refusal to see what is everywhere written, a refusal of a coherence focused on violence. One might say that the traumatic inheritance of slavery is ultimately perpetuated in his inability to understand the melancholy slaver, the man he has saved yet not saved, and in his incomprehension of the mute Babo and his anger. For Melville an understanding of slavery as passing weather, as history without residue, is as impossible as it is for Morrison.

RACE AS TRAUMA

Morrison and Melville raise the question of how we approach the traumatic inheritance of slavery. That has become a huge subject, not least because trauma could almost be described as a dominant model for identity within what Mark Seltzer calls the 'pathological public sphere'. In a range of current writings we are victims of, and wounded by, the processes of primary socialization – by the marks of gender, race, class, sexuality.[8] In such accounts, trauma is represented ultimately in terms akin to those of systems theory: it represents the threatening, de-ontologizing interface at which the individual is haunted by externality.[9] At the same time, the idea of trauma becomes problematic in the move from its original location in the individual embodied human subject to a notion of collective experience. The use of trauma to describe the legacy of the Holocaust, for example, has been contested, for reasons which include its implicit medicalization of experience and the suggestion that history might be subject to 'cure'.[10]

The history of trauma is so well known as to barely need rehearsing. The term referred to actual wounding prior to the late nineteenth century; it was used to describe a psychic wound in the 'railroad spine' debate of the 1860s, which was initially focused on invisible lesions produced by accidents, but then suggested an encounter with technological modernity which fed into psychology generally and later shell-shock debates.[11] Freud was to dismiss the notion of organic origins for hysterical conditions like shell shock. Nevertheless, his view of trauma is never entirely dissociated from its links with the concept of the wound, articulated in the neurology of the *Project for a Scientific Psychology* (1895), and he returned to in *Beyond the Pleasure Principle* (1920) in the notion of a breach in the 'protective shield' guarding the ego. Trauma retains its links to a psychic materialism, founded on a version of the self in which it is defined by the *mark*, the permanent inscription. It is perhaps for this reason that trauma is so readily attached to discrete public events, like 9/11; to catastrophic time rather than the everyday.

Abolitionism itself could be described as central to the birth of a traumatic public sphere in which violent events are seen as informing the psychic life of a nation. Stories about the *Zong* case were extensively circulated in English abolitionist circles, as we noted in the first chapter, reinforcing and building its status as a traumatic example.[12] In the American context, exempla and images – like the story of Margaret Garner and the widely distributed *carte de visite* of the scarred back of the slave 'Gordon' – served a similar function.[13] Freud himself acknowledged the power of such scenes in his paper 'A Child Is Being Beaten', when, considering the scene of fantasized abuse underlying sado-masochistic formulas like that of his title, he suggests that the books of one's childhood may retroactively inform their content:

> It was almost always the same books whose contents gave a new stimulus to the beating-fantasies: those accessible to young peoples such as the '*Bibliothèque rose*', *Uncle Tom's Cabin*, etc. The child began to compete with these works of fiction producing his own fantasies and by constructing a wealth of situations and institutions, in which children were beaten.[14]

This points to a tradition of literary memory and recovery, of the *nachtraglich* as it is applied to abolitionist writings, and to the text of *Beloved* itself as a culmination of that tradition in which its meaning is definitively reinterpreted.

The notion of the historical experience of race itself as trauma depends on an understanding of collective experience which sees it as marked by history. Here is one recent example, focused on slavery:

> As opposed to psychological or physical trauma, which involves a wound and the experience of great emotional anguish by an individual, cultural trauma refers to a dramatic loss of identity and meaning, a tear in the social fabric, affecting a group of people that has achieved some degree of cohesion. In this sense, the trauma need not necessarily be felt by everybody in a community or experienced directly by any or all.[15]

It is all too easy to find this confusing. The metaphoricity of the 'tear' in the 'social fabric', the circularity of a 'group' defined by 'some degree of cohesion', the reliance on a notion of trauma as an event or mark while it is also dispersed unevenly across a social field – all these issues pose fundamental problems. Unless one has a theory of *mechanism* involved in collective memory and its transmission as a wound, seeing slavery as 'cultural trauma' has little analytical significance.[16] At the same time, it

is clear that African-American writers *do* have a more complex and dialectical understanding of what is involved when talking about inherited
pain. One tradition was established by W. E. B. Du Bois, who depicts
the African-American subject as fractured by her or his encounter with
white America. Such a wounding demands the metaphorical presence of
a body: for Du Bois, 'two souls' in 'one dark body, whose dogged strength
alone keeps it from being torn asunder'.[17] For Franz Fanon, the imposition of race is 'an amputation, an excision, a haemorrhage' (the 'amputation' metaphor is also present in Richard Wright's description of Bigger
Thomas, 'Like a man staring regretfully but hopelessly at the stump of a
cut-off arm or leg').[18] The metaphorical 'body' so created carries its history
as a visible cut, bespeaking an identity of self and history. As Fanon comments, analysing the 'morbid body' of race, 'one lies body to body with
one's blackness or one's whiteness, in full narcissistic cry'.[19]

It is noticeable that two ways of thinking about this issue are present
in both Du Bois and Fanon: on the one hand, the traces of memory of
an actual violence written on the body, which takes as unspoken exem-
plum the historical experience of slavery; and on the other, a splitting of
the self founded on the continuing racism of the white gaze: 'this double-
consciousness, this sense of looking at oneself through the eyes of others'
for Du Bois; the child's cry of 'Look, a Negro!' in Fanon.[20] Though the
two clearly overlap, they have different temporal foci, before and after
1865. If abolitionist texts focused on physical violence, later texts more
typically focus on moments like that which ends the first chapter of James
Weldon Johnson's *Autobiography of an Ex-Colored Man*, in which race is
inscribed on the self in a version of the mirror stage: having been told he
is black, the narrator searches his own face for an otherness both feared
and desired.[21] *Beloved* includes both these versions of trauma: both Sethe's
'choke-cherry tree' – the whip scars which she carries on her back, experienced in the intimacy of touch by Paul D. – and, in a rather different episode, the branded mark of ownership on her mother which the
young Sethe sees and wishes to have – causing her mother to strike her in
a refusal of that visual identification.[22]

I suggest that we should understand – and to some extent pick apart –
what is involved in these two different characterizations of racial trauma.
Trauma as wounding suggests a permanency fixated on the past and in
Freudian accounts is characterized by the atemporality of the unconscious itself. Trauma as an effect of the gaze, on the other hand, involves
the everyday flux of temporality: the exchange of glances, the eye travelling to a photograph, a glance turning away, that cry of 'Look!' – things

which come and go as one moves through different environments. Both are invoked by Du Bois in chapter 10 of *The Souls of Black Folk*, where he returns to the notion of 'the double life every American Negro must live … swept on by the current of the nineteenth yet struggling in the eddies of the fifteenth century' – analysing both a fixation on the past and a struggle with the turbulence of modernity.[23]

The notion of history itself conceived in terms of trauma has clear links with the first of these two ways of thinking. The 'Sixty Million and more' of Morrison's epigraph invokes an expanded depth of suffering created by the slave trade – and implicitly Beloved's monologue, with its reference to the Middle Passage, suggests a trans-historical haunting both materialized and allegorized in Beloved as a figure for the past that refuses to die; both a traumatized child and a residue of collective suffering.[24] One reason the implicit parallel between childhood trauma and slavery can work is the notion of a primal scene of violence inflicted on those denied voice; in the case of the Middle Passage those who are stripped of family, society, culture, and language, akin to children – the argument goes – in their necessary unknowingness: 'What Nan told her she had forgotten, along with the language she told it in. The same language her ma'am spoke' (62). Indeed the Middle Passage is central to the historiography Morrison creates because of its status as a terror that leaves no record; the linkage of slavery and childhood means that history can be treated, more pervasively than would ordinarily be the case, under the heading of memory and anamnesis. History is seen as carried within both the individual and the family line, something which must be worked on lest it haunt the present. But it is not difficult to see some of the problems with this thinking as it is moved away from the Freudian model of the family: carried across mixed bloodlines and socially complex histories, what is memory here – a kind of cultural DNA? How could one argue that all African Americans carry trauma, despite region, class, and other historical factors?[25]

I should be clear here: I am not suggesting that Morrison is simplistic about these issues – as the conclusion to *Beloved* suggests, she is intensely aware of what is involved in the question of identifying with the pain of others – the questions of 'passing on' and 'passing over', which suggest that the pain of slavery can neither be disavowed ('passed' on or passed over) or transmitted in a way which simply allows that pain to continue (passed *on*). As W. J. T. Mitchell has commented, the implicit opposition is between a fixation on events and a narrativization which allows them to be dealt with.[26] Moreover, *Beloved* investigates the recursiveness of traumatic narrative; the fact that, as Kathy Carruth puts it, 'for history to be a history of trauma means that it is referential precisely to the extent that it is not fully perceived as it occurs'.²⁷ What I *am* suggesting, however, is that the actual status of the relation between historical event and traumatic inheritance is something the novel takes more or less for granted and that has consequences for the way it depicts race.

To attempt to say more clearly what would be involved in traumatic inheritance, one might turn to the best-known model, within the Freudian tradition, of transmission across generations, that of Nicholas Abraham and Maria Torok. Their notion of the 'phantom' implies a transgenerational haunting that may even, they hint at various points, become embedded within whole communities. For Abraham and Torok the phantom is not the reality of what is lost; rather it is 'an invention of the living ... meant to objectify, even if under the guise of individual or collective hallucinations, the gap produced in us by the concealment of some part of the love object's life'.²⁸ That seems to be a good description of the imagined legacy of slavery as depicted in texts like *Beloved* and Fred D'Aguiar's *Feeding the Ghosts* (which is based on the *Zong* case): they gesture towards an archive that is not realizable, to what Abraham and Torok call 'the gaps left within us by the secrets of others'. But note: for Abraham and Torok, the phantom is *not* a knot that might be unravelled. It *cannot* be 'worked through' or identified with; it can only be recognized as the product of *another's* pain (this is perhaps the best Delano can hope for, or Denver in *Beloved*).

In contrast, trauma theory in its current forms often seems to hinge on notions of a therapeutic encounter which allows the self to grow; which unravels knots and incorporates processed experience. Barnor Hesse comments on the dangers of a 'racialized form of a "possessive individualism"', centred on 'the self-ownership of a debilitating psychological legacy, ascribed racially'. In this scheme, he suggests, '[t]hrough a historically positioned racialized embodiment, the black subject remembers slavery through trauma and the white subject remembers it through guilt'.²⁹ This sounds like those two mainstays of bourgeois existence, guilt and shame, rendered as psychological melodrama, and it gestures towards an easy liberalism in which the more the subject learns of the past, the more he or she is declared to have been freed from it. Should we not, as the work of Walter Benn Michaels often implies, be talking about colour, class, and discrimination in the present, rather than trying to stabilize racial identity in this way?

Race conceived under the sign of trauma thus offers a mixed legacy: potentially a knot which cannot be unravelled; which can only be recognized, with uncertain results – though as we have seen (and this has only been hinted at so far) there is a version of racial trauma which is less knotted and more temporal. More generally, race as trauma is – again putting aside that second, less emphasized version of trauma – a deep and immutable presence, a marking of the self, but hidden, invisible, ultimately secret. We might say that trauma anchors and stabilizes race; it gives it a referent, a point of origin. Paradoxically, though the trauma of slavery is historical and geographically located, the characterization of history *as* trauma renders its effects non-locatable, or locatable only via a problematic allegorical device like that which Morrison's *Beloved* uses. I say problematic because most readers remain uncertain whether the healing which the text offers is effected through the *actual* exorcism of a ghost (what is exorcised is gone) or through the working over of the original story which involves giving that ghost an allegorical power. In part this reflects whom one is thinking about in the novel – Beloved haunts Sethe and must be violently dispelled by the community but is a vehicle of anamnesis for Denver. Nevertheless, readers of Morrison's novel are suspended between these two possibilities, and while it might be tempting to say they are not mutually exclusive, they *are* ontologically distinct: in one the figure of Beloved *is* the trauma, and in the other the vehicle of a therapeutic process. Condition and cure, memory and story: that is perhaps why she is so disquieting. A final point can be made about race as traumatic inscription. In positing a hidden agency within historical experience, it links slavery to the realm which it inhabits in classical thinking, *ananke*, or 'necessity'. For the Greeks, natural law made the slave a slave; the slave is a metaphor for the state of bondage to nature. In contemporary accounts of trauma a certain sense of bondage persists: to deny trauma is simply to enter the realm of repetition-compulsion and melancholia.

RACE AS WEATHER: MINDS AND METEORS

We turn now to the other trope raised by Morrison and Melville: the weather. To think of slavery or race as related to weather rather than as trauma may seem odd, but there is a history of that thinking. Here weather and climate do a paradoxical double duty: as a mark of the local, including local justification for the evils of slavery; and, on the side of its victims, as a way of conceiving resistance and its passing away.

The psychology of weather stands in marked contrast to that of trauma. As Daniel Tiffany points out, the weather is often linked to the internal life of the body, the depiction of the mind in terms of shifting moods.

'Weather' here means meteorology as it is conceived in the Aristotelian tradition: the study of 'meteors', a range of inscrutable natural phenomena including rainbows, volcanoes, snowflakes, as well as what we now understand by weather; most of these objects of attention which leave a trace in modern physics. The 'animal spirits' described by Descartes, Newton, and others are also meteors, part of the 'internal climate' of the body, the wind that blows through the subtle matter which composes us. For David Hume, for example, the self can be described as a pattern of weather, a climate of being, a bundling of embodied contingencies which achieves a characteristic shape:

> Nothing seems more delicate, with regard to its causes, than thought; and as these causes never operate in two persons after the same manner, so we never find two persons who think exactly alike. Nor indeed does the same person think exactly alike at any two different periods of time. A difference of age, of the disposition of his body, of weather, of food, of company, of books, of passions; any of these particulars, or others more minute, are sufficient to alter the curious machinery of thought, and communicate to it very different movements and operations.[30]

The tradition of pneumatic automata which descend from Heron of Alexander to Cardanus, Kircher, and others in the Renaissance reinforces this vision of internal weather, often attaching it to notions of control. Such ideas also relate to Hippocratic medicine, with its reference to climate and airs blowing through the body – a mode of thought given fresh impetus by the work of Priestley and others in the eighteenth century.[31] Arden Reed notes that Baudelaire still 'conceives of interior space in terms of the weather', citing his comments on Hoffmann's 'psychological barometer designed to gauge the different temperatures and atmospheric phenomena of his soul'.[32] Such metaphors, in Tiffany's account, enter modern thinking via mesmeric psychology and the physics of the ether.

The best-known recent exponents of the psychology of weather are Gilles Deleuze and Félix Guattari, for whom being can be conceived in terms of weather and climate: 'local movements and transports of affect'. This is part of their definition of 'haeccity', or being which 'consists entirely of relations of movements and rest between molecules or particles, capabilities to affect and be affects. When demonology expounds upon the diabolical art of local movements and transports of affect, it also notes the importance of rain, hail, wind, pestilent air'.[33] 'For Charlotte Brontë', they argue, 'everything is in terms of *wind*, things, people, faces, loves, words'. In reality, '[y]ou are longitude and latitude, a set of speeds and slownesses between unformed particles, a set of nonsubjectified affects. You have the individuality of a day, a season, a year, *a life* (regardless of its duration) – a climate, a wine, a fog, a swarm, a pack (regardless of its regularity)'.[34] But in contrast to this rather programmatic rhapsody, I would stress that in the tradition I consider here, the self is *not* simply weather; or rather that conception of self is always grounded in the politics of the region and in a dialogue between different versions of the self. For Deleuze and Guattari, the subject is unanchored – dangerously so for Michel Serres, for example, who celebrates weather ('In the beginning are the meteors') while suggest-ing that human relations must inevitably be anchored in the heaviness of the object and the structure of ordered temporality. 'Our relationships, social bonds, would be airy as clouds were there only contracts between subjects,' he writes.[35] As I will go on to suggest, the African-American text – defined, originally, by the status of the human object – avoids mere turbulence, constantly placing the meteor in dialogue with the marking of the self.

Weather thus implies a psychology which contrasts with that of trauma: more local, molecular, unfixated by the temporal knot of trauma. The African-American poet Alice Dunbar-Nelson's 'Thought' (published in 1895) sums up this tradition, as well as suggests its relation to a conception of freedom, describing the 'chain of things' in the mind in this way: 'Now straight, now eddying in wild rings. / No order, neither law compels their moves.'[36] And because it exists in the outside world, it has (as Vladimir Janković points out in his cultural history of English weather) often had political significance.[37] It accumulates over time into what we call a cli-mate, which is both persistent and variable, as well as being collective. We share the weather and talk about it; there is, in the wake of Hurricane Katrina, an explicit racial politics of weather.[38] That politics might include the question of how the weather differentiates among persons: some people sleep in it, on the streets; others barely see it through their tinted glass. A final link in this chain of argument is to propose that race itself might be appear to be a meteor: the function of a climate; a cloud in the sky; visible only in certain lights.

At this point, we will turn to accounts of slavery. I will focus primarily on the nineteenth century, though there is also a twentieth-century his-tory of the trope. If slavery's inheritance has been seen in terms of trauma, its historical justification often invoked weather. For those defending slav-ery in the decades of impassioned sectional debate leading up to the Civil War, the politics of region were crucial. In the tradition of geographical thinking running from Rousseau and Humboldt to Burton, it was a com-monplace that slavery was endemic to the tropical zones; Rousseau noto-riously remarked in *The Social Contract* that 'freedom is not the fruit of

every climate', and therefore is a local experience.[39] The South had long
been seen as a dangerous climate for Europeans, and therefore viable only
in terms of slave labour.[40] The idea that slavery, even if in an abstract sense
wrong, could nevertheless be *locally* justified was admitted even by anti-
slavery thinkers like Montesquieu and became a prominent element of the
pro-slavery argument in the 1830s and 1840s: it was needed in the South
because of the cotton crop and the unsuitability of the climate to white
workers[41] – 'under a hot sun and arid miasma, that prostrates the white
man', as J. H. Hammond put it, slaves were unavoidable.[42] Slaves were
considered 'acclimatized' to their condition: 'Yellow niggers didn't sell so
well', recalled one former slave, since 'Black niggers stood the climate better. At least everybody thought so.'[43] The Southern ideologue Josiah C.
Nott refined this thinking in his influential *Two Lectures on the Natural
History of the Caucasian and Negro Races* (1844), linking climate to poly-
genesis and separate development: 'The white man cannot live in tropical Africa, or the African in the frigid zone.'[44] Forced labour was, others
asserted, the only means of overcoming the natural indolence of dwellers
in hot climates.[45] Even Henry Morley and Charles Dickens, imaging the
end of the institution in their 1852 article, 'North American Slavery' in
Household Words, evoke what George Fredrickson calls 'thermal law':

The time is not far distant when the demand for negroes will be confined wholly
to those districts in which the climate appears to be unsuited for field labour by
white men: even to those districts whites will become acclimatized, but in those,
for some time at any rate, negroes will be needed.[46]

In a parallel way, the localism of slavery was increasingly stressed as sectional
feeling intensified in the 1830s. The judiciary usually agreed: as one judgment
put it, 'The power over Slavery belongs to the States respectively. It is local
in its character, and in its effects.'[47] Louisiana Senator Judah P. Benjamin
(later Confederate Attorney-General) insisted that 'slavery is a subject with
which the federal government has nothing to do'. Decisions such as the
notorious *State v. Mann* expressed the reluctance of legislatures to intervene
in what was seen as a private and local affair: the slaveholder's rule over his
property.[48] And this was largely accepted even in the North: Northern poli-
ticians prior to succession were reluctant to challenge the legality of slavery
in the South and the rights of states to enforce their own slave codes. This
localism was enforced on the bodies of the slaves themselves, who were, particularly after the Nat Turner rebellion, excluded from public places and
limited in movement.[49] Outside the South, however, the question of local
jurisdictions remained an issue. Could slaves who were taken to the North

by their owners be forced to return, as if they carried their status with them; or was slavery so local (as the Massachusetts decision of 1836, *Commonwealth v. Aves*, asserted) that they could be freed by travel?[50]

Slavery might thus be seen, for the South, as linked to the wider issues implicit in meteorology: as in Aristotle's *Meteorologica* with the practicalities of agriculture, under a common sky. As Conevery Valencius has shown, a geographically specific medicine derived from Hippocrates was often applied to the South.[51] Racial theory tended to link race strongly to climate: the indolence and sexuality of the tropics, the vigour of cold climates. Again, the Hippocratic treatise *Airs, Waters and Places* is one point of origin, with its categorization of Asiatics as non-martial and naturally 'the slaves of others', whether tyrants or Greek conquerors – paralleling Aristotle's comments on the lack of spirit (*thymos*) in subservient peoples from hot climates.[52] This climactic slur is patiently refuted by George Washington Williams in the first volume of his *History of the Negro Race in America* (1883), citing David Livingstone in a way which renders slavery an almost individual imposition:

It is remarkable that the power of resistance under calamity, or, as some would say, adaptation for a life of servitude, is peculiar only to certain tribes on the continent of Africa. Climate cannot be made to account for the fact that many would pine in a state of slavery, or voluntarily perish. No Krooman can be converted into a slave, and yet he is an inhabitant of the low, unhealthy west coast; nor can any of the Zulu or Kaffir tribes be reduced to bondage, though all these live on comparatively elevated regions.... But blood does not explain the fact. A beautiful Barotse woman at Naliele, on refusing to marry a man whom she did not like, was in a pet given by the headman to some Mambari slave-traders from Benguela. Seeing her fate, she seized one of their spears, and, stabbing herself, fell down dead.[53]

To be sure, the justification of slavery as climactic localism was a self-serving argument, swept away by the Thirteenth Amendment's extension of universal constitutional protection. But it is interesting that the revival of Southern regionalism in the 1930s often returns to climate.[54] One might compare the way that even in the nineteenth century, with the arrival of a more systematic meteorology associated with Humboldt and others, and the decline of almanacs, weather retains strong links to region. The national weather network established by Joseph Henry at the Smithsonian in 1870 sought a continental perspective, but as Andrew Ross comments, 'In many regions of North America, a tradition of local pride in "state weather" is imbued with the political legacy of "states" rights' – with a corresponding suspicion of 'national weather'.[55]

The turbulent localisms so produced are perhaps nowhere more visible than in Alabama, where the meteors of 1833, 'the year the stars fell' (the Leonid shower of 13 November; Figure 7), are written into the state's official mythology – and bumper stickers.[56] Faulkner makes 13 November 1833 a fulcrum point of his regional myth, along with a slightly earlier 'meteor', the 1811 Mississippi earthquake.[57] Carl Carmer's *Stars Fell on Alabama* (1934) founds its exploration of folkways on meteorology: 'Once upon a time stars fell on Alabama, changing the land's destiny. What had been written in eternal symbols was thus erased – and the region has existed ever since, unreal and fated, bound by a horoscope such as controls no other country.'[58] And Clarence Cason's *90° in the Shade* (1935) displaces race onto climate. Chapter 1, 'It Never Snows', declares, 'Upon the ethnic structure of the South, the sparsity of snow has exerted a tremendous influence.... Like the heat of the sun, the Negro has delimited activity among the whites; like the sun, he has given his energy to the growing of crops for the white man.'[59] Cason, who was shocked by three lynchings in his home town, Tuscaloosa, in 1933, struggles to present race as a matter of climate, even as he notes the possibility of traumatic foreclosure: 'Can it be that this feeling that the Negro has a "place" is a kind of myth in the South; that it is always being forgotten temporarily and then suddenly being remembered, sometimes with violent consequences?'[60]

But if slavery could be understood in terms of climate and localism, what relation does that observation have to the psychology of weather sketched in the preceding section? The first point here is that, as we have noted, abolitionism was committed to a discourse of trauma: to seeing slavery as a wound in the body politic. This meant dismissing the local and focusing on a universal wrong, one which permeated the nation and, indeed, Christendom. Charles Sumner's catch-cry throughout the 1850s was 'Freedom National, Slavery Sectional' – this in response to the Fugitive Slave Act of 1850, which in the eyes of abolitionists illegitimately rendered slavery a national institution. Anti-slavery campaigners felt obliged to refute climactic specificity, William H. Seward insisting in the debate on the Compromise Bill of 1850 that 'there is no climate uncongenial to slavery'.[61] Indeed, the climactic argument always sat uneasily alongside claims that slavery should be extended to new western states.

It is perhaps because of this adhesion to trauma that an initial movement in many texts on race in America, by both black and white authors, is a *rejection* of weather – or indeed the meteor – as irrelevant in the state of emergency which is slavery. A nice example is Josiah Henson's slave

Figure 7. Adolf Völlmy, *Leonid Shower*, 1833. Engraving based on a painting
by Karl Jauslin, from *Bible Readings for the Home Circle* (Battle Creek, MI:
Review & Herald Publishing, 1889), p. 66.

narrative. Henson has freed himself but is returning to Kentucky in 1833
for the underground railroad:

On my way, that strange occurrence happened, called the great meteoric shower.
The heavens seemed broken up into streaks of light and falling stars. I reached
Lancaster, Ohio, at three o'clock in the morning and found the village aroused,
the bell ringing, and the people exclaiming, 'The day of judgement is come!'

I thought it was probably so, but felt that I was in the right business, and walked on through the village leaving the terrified people behind. The stars continued to fall till the light of the sun appeared.[62]

'The right business' precludes too much attention to the signs in the heavens, the great Leonid shower. In *The Accursed Share*, George Bataille describes the psychology and being of slavery in terms of an occultation. 'The slave is a thing for the owner; he accepts this situation which he prefers to dying', and 'the same poverty then extends over human life as extends over the countryside if the weather is overcast. Overcast weather, when the sun is filtered by the clouds and the play of light goes dim, appears to "reduce things to what they are."' This, for Bataille, is the lifeless or bare life of the human reduced to a thing.[63] The *Narrative of William Hayden* (1846) includes a poem, here entitled 'Woman in the Slave World' but taken in fact from a longer work on India published a decade earlier in an Albany periodical called *The Zodiac*:

> Amid the trackless waste how may she fare,
> Where an impure Religion's meteor light,
> The soul bewilders, and unnerves the sight,
> And vice is worshipped, and the very shrine,
> A place impure, and priestly fingers write,
> Precepts unholy, that men deem divine,
> To quench the unborrow'd lights, that in the spirit shine.[64]

The religion of the South is a 'meteor', a local aberration that occludes the spirit's light. But what is perhaps more striking – and here we begin to answer the question about the psychology I just asked – is that depictions of black resistance often include a *double* movement: the dismissing of weather as a local irrelevance, representative of the South's attachment to slavery, but also its return as internal impulse, indeed as a politics. The significance of this movement is that it opens up an internal negotiation between suffering and agency, between a psychology fixated on global trauma and the possibilities of local resistance.

Consider Harriet Beecher Stowe's *Dred: A Tale of the Great, Dismal Swamp*, her more radical revision of *Uncle Tom's Cabin* published in 1856, the same year as *Benito Cereno*. The description of the rebel slave Dred's hidden camp in the Great Swamp has him lying on his back, gazing upwards:

His large, gloomy, dark eyes fixed in revery on the moving tree-tops as they waved in the golden blue. Now his eye followed sailing of islands of white cloud, drifting to and fro above them. There were elements within him which might, under other circumstances, have made him a poet.[65]

On the one hand, there is the mutability of the sky, which a poet might celebrate; on the other, there is Dred's inescapable fate as a rebel rather than a poet, which means that he has little time for responsive reverie: he is driven towards resistance and death. Yet *Dred* also describes rebellion as meteorology, as a Franklin-like tapping of an atmosphere: 'A free colored man in the city of Charleston, named Denmark Vesey, was the one who had the hardihood to seek to use the electric fluid in the cloud [of resistance] thus accumulated. He conceived the hopeless project of imitating the example set by the American race, and achieving independence for the blacks' (204). Describing Dred's burial, Stowe cites Wordsworth's well-known sonnet for Toussaint, the leader of the Haitian slave rebellion, with its use of a metaphor whose assertive brilliance is achieved through paradox, the mutability of weather becoming political memory:

> Thou hast left behind
> Powers that will work for thee; air, earth, and skies;
> There's not a breathing of the common wind
> That will forget thee. (517)

Dred is written into the weather, so that his sublimated inheritance may inspire (in the root meaning of the term: 'breathing life into') rather than haunt. There is also the more utopian suggestion of the final chapter of *Dred*, which describes a visit to the multi-racial orphanage founded in New York by Milly, the freed slave who has found a way 'to get my heart whole' after losing so many children to slavery. Its title: 'Clear Shining After Rain'. This may represent a putting of slavery from memory, an equation of abolition with cure – one object of Morrison's critique in *Beloved* – but at the same time it signals the novels' imagination of the possibilities of change.[66]

A comparable turn away from and return to weather is also apparent in George Boyer Vashon's Pindaric ode 'Vincent Ogé' (1853), surely the most impassioned celebration of black resistance of its period. It begins with a sunset:

> There is, at times, an evening sky –
>   The twilight's gift – of sombre hue,
> All checkered wild and gorgeously
>   With streaks of crimson, gold and blue; –
> A sky that strikes the soul with awe ...[67]

This image stands, however, for a memory of a moment of lost freedom. The Byronic hero of the first Haitian uprising, Ogé, like Dred 'stands unmoved' amidst this beauty, for all that his 'was a mind that joyed / With nature in her every mood' (157). History is a play of meteors, of 'vapours that brilliantly play / Round the glass of the chemist'; and the energies of rebellion are volcanic; 'they wildly pour / Their lava flood of woe and fear' (159). The description of rebellion which follows is meteorological: hope sweeps like 'the simoon's breath' over the scene or is like a 'deluge of rain'; it leads to the 'tempest' of battle with cannon like lightning unleashed by the 'King of the Storm' (162). While these lines edge towards the spasmodic, they nonetheless represent hope as a force opposed to the fixity of slavery, and weather as a break with the 'cold, / Silent solemnity' of the slave owners. Vashon concludes his elegy with the claim 'Upon the slave's o'erclouded sky, / Your gallant actions traced the bow' (164), a prophecy written into the weather. (*The Rainbow* was, incidentally, one of the most famous paintings of Robert S. Duncanson, the first African-American artist to gain an international reputation; in sharp contrast his magnum opus, *The Land of the Lotus Eaters*, has often been read as a political allegory depicting Southern stagnation, like Melville's becalmed ship.)[68]

Vashon's poem reminds us that meteors, in their classical definition, include volcanoes and that the South as a sleeping volcano is a commonplace of abolitionist writing. William Wells Brown repeatedly uses it in *The Black Man, His Antecedents, His Genius, and His Achievements* (1863). Thus 'in every southern household there may be a Nat Turner, in whose soul God has lighted a torch of liberty that cannot be extinguished by the hand of man. The slaveholder should understand that he lives upon a volcano, which may burst forth at any moment, and give freedom to his victim.'[69] Of Vesey he writes, 'Every community the other side of "Dixon's Line" feels that it lives upon a volcano that is liable to burst out at any moment' (142). When he comes to the St. Domingo rebellion, the flames become real:

The splendid villas and rich factories yielded to the furies of the devouring flames; so that the mountains, covered with smoke and burning cinders, borne upwards by the wind, looked like volcanoes; and the atmosphere, as if on fire, resembled a furnace.

Such were the outraged feelings of a people whose ancestors had been ruthlessly torn from their native land, and sold in the shambles of St. Domingo. (96)

It would be easy to multiply examples, some at the level of romantic cliché.[70] Race's status as that which is imposed on the black subject is suggested by 'The Souls of White Folk' chapter of *Darkwater*, in which Du Bois talks of white condescension in terms of a contrast between the trivial contingencies of weather and a permanent marking: 'even the sweeter souls of the dominant world as they discourse to me of weather, weal and woe are continually playing above their actual words an obligato of tune and tone, saying: "My poor, un-white thing!"' But after its powerful condemnation of white racism and imperialism, Du Bois's essay ends with the prophet facing the 'storms' of racism: 'great, ugly whirlwinds of hatred and blood and cruelty'.[71] In these texts, slavery and resistance are meteors: the weather is dismissed but returns as a powerful energizing force, a climate for change. The fixity of slavery, its traumatic imprinting, is replaced by internal and external struggle.

CHARLES CHESNUTT: TRAUMA AND LOCALISM

For a powerful investigation of slavery as weather and climate, we can turn to the conjure stories of the African-America writer Charles Chesnutt, both those published in *The Conjure Woman* (1899) and surrounding tales. What Chesnutt's stories repeatedly offer is a kind of subaltern analysis in which the pragmatics of locality and local power relations enter a dialogue with an allegorical rendition of the painful memories of slavery – in which, in the terms I have used, weather faces trauma.

John, the frame narrator of the conjure stories is (as the genre demands) a Northerner who comes to a South 'somewhat settled' after the war. He hopes to combine profit and necessity: his sick wife has been advised to leave the Great Lakes, and in North Carolina 'the climate was perfect for health; and, in conjunction with the soil, ideal for grape-culture'.[72] He meets and employs the elderly Julius McAdoo, once a slave on his plantation, a useful local informant, able to tell him about soil, crops, water, and weather as well as about folklore. John calls him 'predial' (55), a Latinism referring to a localism which in some states saw the slave defined as real estate rather than chattel (with the rules of debt and inheritance that involved).[73] The Louisiana legal code refers to 'those [rights] which the author of an estate enjoys on a neighboring estate for the benefit of his own estate. They are called *predial or landed servitudes*, because being established for the benefit of an estate, they are rather due to the estate than to the owner personally'.[74] It is this relation to the land, rather than to the landowner, which Julius asserts: he has a right of way established by the history of slavery, and his narratives represent claims on that right.

'The Gophered Grapevine', perhaps Chesnutt's best-known conjure tale, is an example of those claims. But like most of Chestnutt's stories, it also unpicks and allegorizes the assumptions of slavery, asking what it would be like if slaves were indeed purely productive organisms. Julius tells John that a goopher (spell) protected the original master Dugal's grapevines and recounts the tale of the slave Henry, who steals grapes and is forced to rub grape sap on his head as an antidote. The result is that he effectively turns into a vine, withering in winter and blooming in summer. Not only that, but cultivation – the annual pruning – makes him more vigorous than he was before he came to the plantation, growing hair when he was once bald. As a result he can be traded like a seasonal crop: sold in spring health and repurchased, apparently sick and dying, at a discount each winter.[75] As Charles Duncan comments, this 'literalizes the conflation of African Americans and property, in this case transforming a black man into the very land he works'.[76] The story ends when Mars Dugal is gulled by a Yankee trickster into using radical techniques, disturbing the balance of nature, and both the vines and Henry die.

Ostensibly, the frame narrator sees through Julius's stratagems: he posits an economy of narrative and financial returns, implying that Julius tells the story because he wants to protect a line in grape sales; the old man is compensated by being given a job as a coachman. At the same time, as Eric Sundquist and others have shown, he is a more troubling presence, constantly recalling the pain of slavery.[77] In all the stories, there is a residue which cannot be allowed for in this calculation couched in terms of the fortuitous transition from local to national economy. Here Julius 'ain' skeered ter eat de grapes, 'caze I knows de old vines fum de noo ones' (43) – which is to say that he knows where the curse of slavery lies: where its bodies are buried (he offers to show his auditors Henry's grave) and where its pain endures. The fact that it is hinted that he is also a descendant of the slaveholder reinforces this sense of a continuing contradiction.

'The Gophered Grapevine' works through an equation of the person, crop, and season. When Mars Dugal meets the man he has sold Henry to in the spring, he can express the situation as an effect of the weather: 'I 'spec's you wukked him too ha'd dis summer, er e'se de swamps down here don't agree with de san'-hill nigger'. 'Lonesome Ben', perhaps the most fantastic of the tales, extends this equation. In the frame narrative, John thinks of mining a bank of clay for bricks, and as he and Julius watch it a poor-white woman takes some – for eating, Julius disparagingly says. The story he then tells, ostensibly to back up the suggestion that the clay is suitable for brick-making, concerns the runaway slave Ben, who eats the clay to survive, turns yellow, becomes unrecognizable even to his family and master, and ultimately 'turns to clay':

He had hearn 'bout folks turnin' ter clay w'en dey wuz dead, an' he 'lowed maybe he wuz dead an' didn' knowed it, an' dat wuz de reason w'y eve'body run erway f'm 'im an' wouldn' hab nuffin' ter do wid 'im. An' ennyhow, he 'lowed ef he

wa'n't dead, he mought's well be. He wande'ed roun' a day er so mo', an' fin'lly
de lonesomeness, an' de sleepin' out in de woods, 'mongs' de snakes an' sco'pions,
an' not habbin' nuffin' fit ter eat, 'mence ter tell on him, mo' an' mo', an' he kep'
gittin' weakah an' weakah 'til one day, w'en he went down by de crick fer ter git
a drink er water, he foun' his limbs gittin' so stiff hit 'uz all he could do ter crawl
up on de bank an' lay down in de sun. He laid dere 'til he died, an' de sun beat
down on 'im, an' beat down on 'im, an' beat down on 'im, fer th'ee er fo' days, 'til
it baked 'im as ha'd as a brick. (156)

Dirt-eating ('cachexia africana' in slave medicine) was a practice linked
by white commentators to both conjuring and compulsive self-harm in
slaves.[78] The story suggests slavery's deathliness – 'maybe he wuz dead an'
didn' knowed it' – while also literalizing, in a manner characteristic of
Chesnutt, the metaphorical relationship between the slave and the soil.[79]
The motivation for Julius's story from John's impoverished point of view
is not entirely clear, though it later emerges that he has a nephew who
wants work moving the clay. Does he want the clay left there for eating;
or is he truthful when he suggests that the clay reminds him of the degradation of black people and that he would like it removed? What does
seem clear is the status of the clay as a kind of eaten death in a parody of
the Communion – both a potential profit and the bitter taste of the past.
Throughout the stories, as here, there is a tension between the local – the
question of the best clay for bricks, of custom and land use – and the larger issue of slavery. In 'Lonesome Ben' the South's weather and climate are
fatal; they have passed away but left a residue both in the practice of local
people and in Julius's bitter stories.

Even more radically, in 'Dave's Neckliss' (discussed in Chapter 2), as
Sundquist notes, the original scar of slavery – its mythic origin in the sin
of Ham in looking on his naked father Noah – is allegorized in the fate
of Dave, who eventually insists that he *is* ham. Such extreme identifica-
tions with a crop – Henry with the vine, Dave with the ham – signal the
violent marking of the self implicit in slavery and a traumatic inability to
anneal the ensuring wounds. The extreme narrative imbalance of the stories – between, for example, the motivation for 'Dave's Neckliss' implied
by John in his frame narrative (that Julius gets hold of the ham having put
his mistress off) and the horror of the story[80] – suggests again a contrast
between two conflicting accounts of slavery: between the grape-bearing
climatology of the South and Julius as a local spirit, on the one hand,
and a bitter residue, on the other. This is the end of Dave's story: 'There
was a short silence after the old man had finished his story, and then my
wife began to talk to him about the weather, on which subject he was an

authority' (135). 'Just weather', in this text, signals at once inconsequence and the vital instrument of Julius's mastery of his locality and its temporal cycles.

John shows, at times, a flickering awareness of the true status of the stories. They show, he remarks, 'the curious psychological spectacle of a mind enslaved long after the shackles had been struck off from the limbs of its possessor' (124). Nevertheless, 'even the wildest was not without an element of pathos, – the tragedy, it might be, of the story itself; the shadow, never absent, of slavery and of ignorance; the sadness, always, of life as seen by the fading light of an old man's memory' (96). He, too, attempts to resolve this residue by dissolving trauma into the trope of weather, of race tempered by a beneficent climate:

> But in the simple human feeling, and still more in the undertone of sadness, which pervaded his stories, I thought I could see a spark which, fanned by favoring breezes and fed by the memories of the past, might become in his children's children a glowing flame of sensibility, alive to every thrill of human happiness or human woe. (125)

Entrusting history to 'favoring breezes' is, as the example of Delano suggested, a dangerous resort. At the same time, Julius's pragmatism – which goes far beyond the trickster that John thinks he understands – offers a way of understanding the relations between the specifics of locality and the trauma of the past. Julius's stories of weather and woe, or human crops and human bricks, negotiate the past and putting it to work. Julius refuses to speak *just* of weather – he registers trauma – but he uses the weather to do so, and works it towards a notion of restitution.

THE SOUTH'S WEATHER: *THE AMERICAN CLAIMANT*

As I have argued, to eliminate weather would be to threaten the self with a conception of slavery in which it was universalized. I want to turn briefly, in what is admittedly something of a comic aside, to a text which imagines just such a situation, Mark Twain's often disparaged 1892 novel, *The American Claimant*. Its preface is a note on 'The Weather in this Book' which justifies its exclusion because of the 'delays' occasioned by the need to 'fuss up' the weather:

> Of course weather is necessary to a narrative of human experience. That is conceded. But it ought to be put where it will not be in the way; where it will not interrupt the flow of the narrative. . . . The present author can do only a few trifling ordinary kinds of weather, and he cannot do those very good. So it has seemed

wisest to borrow such weather as is necessary for the book from qualified and recognized experts – giving credit, of course. This weather will be found over in the
back part of the book, out of the way. See Appendix. The reader is requested to
turn over and help himself from time to time as he goes along.[81]

The appendix does indeed include a selection of weather in overdone style,
taken from popular writers. Twain's joke is, of course, about just the kind
of cliché we have already edged towards. But I would also relate the lack
of the weather of 'human experience' to another aspect of the text: its preoccupation with zombies. The novel's crackpot schemer, Colonel Sellers,
believes he is about to perfect a technique that would awaken the dead by
a process of 'materialization'; they could then be used as the perfect workforce, needing no feeding and resistant to fatigue and injury.

That this would essentially be a slave workforce is suggested by two
aspects of the text: firstly, by the Colonel's intermittent preoccupation
with the liberation of the very distant population of Siberia ('Russia's
countless multitudes of slaves will rise up and march, march! – eastward,
with that great light transfiguring their faces as they come', 186); and secondly by the linkage of his scheme to the residue of race in the novel.
Sellers discusses with his acolyte 'Senator' Hawkins the 'trouble with old
house servants that were your slaves once' but who now run the household, abruptly adding: 'These two are mighty good and loving and faithful and honest, but hang it, they do just about as they please, they chip
into a conversation whenever they want to, and the plain fact is, they
ought to be killed.' This done, they can be replaced by their own materialized spectres, slaves once again:

'Yes,' he said to himself, 'when I've got the materializing down to a certainty,
I will get Hawkins to kill them, and after that they will be under better control. Without doubt a materialized negro could easily be hypnotized into a state
resembling silence. And this could be made permanent – yes, and also modifiable,
at will – sometimes very silent, sometimes turn on more talk, more action, more
emotion, according to what you want. It's a prime good idea. Make it adjust-
able – with a screw or something.' (82)

In this outrageous allegory, the frictions of Reconstruction are solved by a
literal restoration of the 'social death' and instrumentality of slavery.

There is also a trace of race in the convoluted main plot of the novel,
which concerns Sellers's interaction with Berkeley, the heir to the Earl
of Rossmore – whose title the Colonel claims. Berkeley is caught up in
a hotel fire and reincarnates himself as the cowboy 'Tracy'. Because of a
change of clothes Sellers and Hawkins believe that Tracy is the zombified

dead robber One-Armed Pete – or rather his English ancestor, since they explain his accent by positing that his materialization has been successful only up to an intermediate ancestor. But Sellers balks at enslaving him:

'I need money, but God knows I am not poor enough or shabby enough to be an accessory to the punishing of a man's ancestor for crimes committed by that ancestor's posterity.'

'But Colonel!' implored Hawkins; 'stop and think; don't be rash; you know it's the only chance we've got to get the money; and besides, the Bible itself says posterity to the fourth generation shall be punished for the sins and crimes committed by ancestors four generations back that hadn't anything to do with them; and so it's only fair to turn the rule around and make it work both ways.' (194)

This is slavery as inherited taint, the inversion spelling out the logic as well as the counter-logic of a traumatic Southern inheritance. Is the South to be blamed for its past; is its present violence is to be mapped onto the antebellum notion of a Southern aristocracy? Mesmerism is evoked in Tracy's state when he says to himself, 'I wonder what he's making those passes in the air for, with his hands. I seem to be the object of them. Can he be trying to mesmerize me?' (202). The idea of a mesmerized instrument matches the traces of mesmeric theory present, Malcolm Bull argues, in the master–slave relation as it is described by both Hegel and Du Bois.[82]

Finally, the question of zombification and the status of the enslaved voice is also – though in an indirect way – raised by the appendix into which the book's weather is stuffed (275–77). The most prominent source of lurid meteorology is W. D. O'Connor's story 'The Brazen Android', first published in the *Atlantic Monthly* in 1891 but with its origins much earlier, in 1857, when O'Connor, now mostly remembered as a defender of Whitman, was heavily involved in abolition.[83] The storm which continues throughout O'Connor's tale of Friar Bacon and Friar Bungy is political, signalling the crisis of legitimacy represented by the reign of Henry III. The story – based on Robert Greene's play and the anonymous pamphlet *The Famous Historie of Fryer Bacon* – concerns Roger Bacon's attempt to use a 'brazen android' to create a night-time vision which might frighten Henry into alliance with the reformist Simon de Montfort. The android is a mechanical body which will test the Aristotelian contention that it is the body which slows down the soul and acts as a barrier between the ideal and the real – as its inspirer, the suggestively satanic Doctor Malatesti of Padua says, the pure soul 'cannot tell you till it be shrined in some form which will permit it voice. It cannot tell you in the evil form of flesh.... But in a form of brass it can tell you' (581).

The indirect relation to slavery is suggestive. If the slave tests the possibility that flesh may be conceived as the pure instrument of the soul of another (as in mesmerism), Bacon's android is part of a long history of pneumatic automata in which the animated (slave) machine is imagined as a blowing of air into a body, as *influenza*. The allusion to the 'sounding brass' of 1 Corinthians 13 suggests a moral emptiness: to make the flesh a machine is to debase the soul. The dead-and-alive android with its expression of 'loving and terrific despair' (582), the soul-obsessed Malatesta who wishes to make it the vehicle for higher truths, the reformist Bacon – all these take on the lineaments of allegory in which the external weather (imported into Twain's appendix) signals turmoil. If the body of Twain's story concerns a comic fantasy of re-enslavement, the appendix suggests both the historical violence and the pneumatic fantasy which underlie that fantasy.

WEATHER AND RACE IN THE TWENTIETH CENTURY

In the literature which follows Chesnutt, there continues to be an interplay between a traumatic conception of race and an evocation of the lightness of air. A few examples can stand for a larger body of literature. Du Bois ends *The Souls of Black Folk* with an evocation of the 'whirl and chaos' of things from which God will emerge and render the prisoners of race 'free as the sunshine trickling down the morning into these high windows of mine'. The weary traveller 'sets his face towards the Morning, and goes his way.'[84] This is the very opposite of 'The Passing of the First-Born', his chapter on the death of his son in which the trauma of slavery – as in *Beloved* – can be avoided only by a sacrifice of the innocent. Or, moving on a little further, we could turn to William Stanley Braithwaite's 1912 essay, 'Twilight: An Impression', which reads like a polished Thoreauvian meditation – until one notices that it deals with the immateriality (Brathwaite uses the word) of colour. Even the white sail on the horizon – an allusion perhaps to Fredrick Douglass's famous oration – fades into a 'woven veil of shadows'.[85] This is partly the figure of creative dusk which runs through black writing in the period, a trope discussed by Rachel Blau DuPlessis.[86] But there is more to it than that: in the evocation of the dark 'womb of time', a world of radiant nodes and clusters, the writer discovers a freedom from the ghosts on the road which 'crowded my memory with images and filled my imagination with voices' (223).

The racial politics of weather figure strongly in the blues tradition – for example, in responses to the disastrous Southern floods of 1927 and the

Okeechobee hurricane, both of which involved scandalous treatment of black refugees. Sterling Brown's poem 'Ma Rainey' depicts an audience driven by gusts of emotion:

> Dey comes to hear Ma Rainey from de little river settlements,
> From blackbottom cornrows and from lumber camps;
> Dey stumble in de hall, jes a'laughin' an' a-cacklin',
> Cheerin' lak roarin' water, like wind in river swamps.

Her song, inserted into the text, is 'Backwater Blues', which describes the floods. What Brown depicts throughout the poem is a shifting of moods, a dynamic interaction between audience and singer, a cathartic flood of emotion in which Ma Rainey herself becomes a kind of internal weather: as the 'fellow' the author talks to comments, 'She jes' catch hold of us, somekindaway'.[87] Brown uses the trope elsewhere, for example, in the 'unfriendly sky' of his poem 'Strange Legacies' – the whole climate of America, that is. His 'Memphis Blues' describes history itself as a hurricane or deluge:

> Memphis go
> By Flood or Flame;
> Nigger won't worry
> All de same –
> Memphis go
> Memphis come back,
> Ain' no skin
> Off de nigger's back.
> All dese cities
> Ashes, rust . . .
> De win' sing sperrichals
> Through deir dus'.[88]

Here 'skin' and 'weather' co-exist in uneasy relation, which is resolved only by the wind as black voice – by a lyric substance (to borrow Daniel Tiffany's phrase) which dissolves matter into the body of the air. Brown's earlier sonnet 'After the Storm', published in the *Crisis* in 1927, rather more conventionally signals the conversion of grim endurance to pathos, and the material of its metaphor ('sullen rain clouds pass') into lyric.[89]

The novel in which weather features most catastrophically is, of course, *Their Eyes Were Watching God*, in which the Okeechobee hurricane disperses the utopian community of the muck, indirectly leads to Tea Cake's death, and reintroduces the topic of racism via the forcible co-option of black workers by the authorities. Here harsh weather represents the drawing to an end of a fantasy of black freedom and cultural celebration, and the reintroduction of the quotidian, including race and gender relations in all their fractious actuality. If the text begins with notions of inherited trauma (centred on the rape of Janey's mother and her grandmother's caution), it ends with stormy weather and a calm return to the everyday. And in a similar way, the ending of Richard Wright's *Black Boy* involves a turn from numbness and pain associated with the South, from 'scars, visible and invisible', to growth in another climate: 'In leaving, I was taking a part of the South to transplant in alien soil, to see if it would grow differently, if it could drink of new and cool rains, bend in strange winds, respond to the warmth of other suns, and, perhaps, to bloom.' He adds that the South, too, might 'overcome its fear, its hate, its cowardice, its heritage of blood and guilt, its burden of anxiety and compulsive cruelty.'[90] Here again we have the opposition of trauma and the hope which is embodied in the weather.

A final example is Jean Toomer's later writings, in the long 'postracial' period which followed *Cane*, during which Toomer declared himself a new composite, an 'American', rather than a 'Negro'.[91] Toomer was intensely interested in the series of abstract cloud photographs Alfred Stieglitz made in the period 1922–34, exhibited under various titles but eventually described as 'Equivalents', a term derived from Kandinsky's notion that art can render the shifting states of the soul. Toomer later wrote to Georgia O'Keefe that he saw parallels between the photographs and his own 'Bona and Paul'.[92] A series of letters to Stieglitz comment on Toomer's own observations of clouds and what he sees as a shared sense of the contingent and the specific in the photographs:

This morning, quite contrary to custom, I awoke early. For some reason my eyes were pulled to the window that frames a portion of the Woman's Day Court and the adjoining prison. Usually, the buildings impinge, oppress, and bulk. Usually too the patch of sky between them is grey and laden. But this morning as I looked, the patch was luminous, golden-crimson. And the sombre masses seemed transfigured in this brightness. There came to me a vivid sense of your pure black. Last evening, the sense of it, flushed me, and for one moment I held a beauty as intense and clear as any I've ever known.[93]

One might compare Toomer's poem 'Cloud', in which its shadow is the distracting texture of the everyday:

> I lay on the great shadow
> Wondering
> Who cast this livid cloud
> Between
> Living beings and the salient light.[94]

A striking feature of those writings is the recurrent description of travels and regions, at times with an underlying environmental impulse, but often simply motivated by the desire to be part of the climate of a place: the piece of a novel entitled 'Doylestown' by his editor meditates on the light flooding from the sky, the breeze, the seasons, the pattern of a day; the essay entitled 'New Mexico after India' refracts the differences between two societies through an account of climate and region. A draft on clouds (c. 1947) entitled 'Part of the Universe' is even more abstract:

And the clouds. Over the mountains, over the high ridges the clouds gather, hang, hover. The clouds hold junta over the mountains. There they meet, around the high humped backbones, clouds like pennants, summer-clouds. There they rest, the grey-white caps, the clouds in strata. There they gang, the blue-black [hoods?] [heads?] thunder-bearing. Sometimes, behind and above the highest peaks, will be seen a titanic cumulus piling up, its multiforms rounded like celestial cotton bolls, all of it a dazzling white, the whole creation slowly soaring into the heavens.[95]

This is the culmination of a series of pieces in which human social organizations (e.g., castes in India) are identified as features of a landscape; in which mind is equated with skyscapes, cloudscapes, and storm. Even the allusions to gangs and cotton in the preceding passage can draw readers to a recollection of the harsh racial zones, north and south, of *Cane* – but here all is emptied out into the individual contemplation of the play of light and air in New Mexico. There is a phenomenology of race dissolved into both the specifics of location and the meditative possibilities of air in Toomer. But that, as we have seen, is the function of weather in so many texts: as a way of imaging race without a wounding, as something which is there but might be dispelled through thought and action.

We began with *Beloved*, and we need to revisit it to draw out one further point. As many commentators have noted, once the seasonal cycle associated with Sethe's month of freedom at number 124 is broken, time is arrested, bound into a catastrophic repetition in which, in Beloved's words, 'All of it is now' (210). Morrison's novel is saturated with the contrast between the past which endures and the everyday experience which is the weather – and which is blotted out by traumatic memory. For Sethe, the past can return at any time: 'She might be hurrying across a field, running practically, just to get to the pump quickly and rinse the chamomile sap from her legs. Nothing else would be in her mind.... Nothing. Just the breeze cooling her face as she rushed towards water' (6) – a cat's-paw of breeze replaced by the catastrophic return of the past. It is traumatic memory which, fixating perception, prevents the mind's engagement with the present: 'Every dawn she saw the dawn, but never acknowledged or remarked its color. There was something wrong with that. It was as though one day she saw red baby blood, another day the pink gravestone chips, and that was the last of it' (39). Similarly Denver 'will forgo the most violent of sunsets, stars as fat as dinner plates and all the blood of autumn and settle for the palest yellow if it comes from her Beloved' (121). In contrast Paul D. is the man who follows the blossoms – the seasonal drift of color – to escape slavery, who remains 'astonished by the beauty of this land that was not his' (268). It is Paul D. who 'made fun of the weather and what it was doing to him'; Sethe, on the other hand, won't kiss him 'lest someone passing the alley see them misbehaving in public, in daylight, in the wind' (47, 118).

Beloved, as an unseasonal child, is not part of the weather. In Beloved's soliloquy it is the 'clouds', or even more stochastically the 'noisy clouds', which prevent her, dead, from seeing or fixing on Sethe as her chosen vehicle. 'I would help her but the clouds are in the way' (210). These clouds have been interpreted in various ways: as associated with gunpowder and the plunder of slaves from Africa, for example. But perhaps, more mundanely, they signal the clutter of history itself: in information terms 'noisy' suggests that which interferes with the transmission of the lost *image* which is so central to Beloved ('how can I say things that are pictures', she says) – the image, the *Nacheinander*, or all-at-once which must be replaced by narrative. If the clouds seem to evaporate at the novel's climax – Sethe sees that 'the sky is blue and clear' and remembers the heat of the Clearing; the women who have come to expel Beloved look up at 'the hot, cloudless sky' (261) – it is so Beloved may not be confused with the everyday reality of race in America, which is acknowledged by the women even as they refuse to allow the past to rule their lives. It is the control of noise, the control of weather, which moves a fixation on the past.

I began by pointing out the intangibility of any analysis of a trope like the weather. As I have suggested, weather can signal the local justification of slavery, but also a form of resistance to that localism. It can signal the actuality of race (as in Hurston's novel), but also (as in descriptions of dusk) its dissolving into invisibility. Most generally, in the texts I have been ranging across, there is a struggle to emerge into weather and to formulate a psychology and sometimes a politics which works through weather rather than trauma. From the point of view of the victim of circumstances, it is the externality of weather which offers a possibility of resistance: it signals a refusal to take circumstances inside the self and accord them a permanence. To speak of the weather is to offer a cure in a particular sense, since 'to weather' can mean to harden a skin, to make it less permeable to wounding. If one account of trauma represents it as a violent rupture, Freud also, famously, provided the model of the 'protective shield' (*Reizschutz*) which samples and regulates the flow of stimuli into the self – a model which seems to relate to the everyday rather than the trans-historical, to the questions of living in time, defending the self, and adjusting to circumstances.

One objection to this argument would run something like this: 'Haven't you just repackaged the old distinction between biological and cultural definitions of race; between "blood" or genetic inheritance, on the one hand, and locality and ethnicity, on the other'? To be sure, those terms are implicit in some of what I have argued. But the centring of race on trauma, on the wound, is not essentialist in that sense, or it is so only to the extent that it renders race itself as an historical inheritance, in which what is described as deep and ineradicable truth. Race can be created only by a violent inscription and the history it engenders. Similarly, to speak of race as weather is more than to dissolve it into culture, since climate has a relation both to the way we collectively describe and experience the world and to the way we conceive the material of the self.

The opposition here is something like that which energizes the recent work of the controversial German philosopher Peter Sloterdijk – mentioned briefly in Chapter 3 – between a critique fixated on restitution and the 'real' (or trauma, in the terms used here) and a re-imagination of resistance in terms of the irreducible complexity of being-in-the-world: the vagaries of ocean currents and the airy substance of the self. In Sloterdijk's thinking, our obsession with foundations and unconscious determinants is passing, and with it 'our dark, pathos-laden memories' are abating – his term is *entlastet*, which is intended to suggest the lifting of a burden, though it is sometimes translated more problematically as 'exoneration' in recent texts.[96] While one would not want to extrapolate that way of thinking into a blithe indifference to the past (or an avoidance of historical culpability on the part of slaving nations), it captures one element of the dialectic we have explored. The underlying spirit is that of Nietzsche's self-origination and Franz Fanon's ringing declaration that '[t]he body of history does not determine a single one of my actions. I am my own foundations' – that is to say, a determination that the subject shall not be *finally* defined by memory or the collective experience from which it emerges.[97]

If slavery has bequeathed to us a version of the self in which it is burdened by an inheritance of loss, by a traumatic fixity, it has in its figures also offered us a resource for hope. Thinking about the weather, for the African-American writer, involves a movement from materiality to lyric; from the wound to the impulse; from a 'stuck' temporality to the politics of the quotidian; and often from placelessness to location. In the coda to *Beloved*, her memory is locked away, weathering with the seasons: 'a latch latched and lichen attached its apple-green bloom to the metal' (275). The 'claim' that Sethe has imposed on herself ('more important than what Sethe had done was what she claimed', 164) is relinquished in favour of an open acknowledgement which does not pretend to an impossible reciprocity; which leaves the dead where they are. 'Although she has claim, she is not claimed.' The fact that 'the rest is weather' does not imply an end to race, but rather its passing into everyday experience.

Any final dissolving of race into weather represents an avowedly utopian impulse; and it is interesting, in Morrison's case, that she moved on, in *Paradise*, to describe a group of women one of whom is said to be white, though we never discover who she is. Such writing deals with the immaterial materiality of race, its existence as an image, as a set of relations, as something which exists in time. Delano's 'yon bright sun has forgotten it all' seems to receive an answer in the downtrodden white girl Amy Denver's declaration, in *Beloved*, 'Sleeping with the sun in your face is the best old feeling' (80) – sleeping, that is, when you should be working, paying your debts. This is also, perhaps, to imagine stolen time, and a state in which race might just become a waking dream. Amy says she has slept in the sun just twice; *Paradise* ends with two women, one white and one black, lying in the sun. The fact that they are dead and seemingly do not haunt anyone seems to suggest that the experience of race too might become stormy weather, something which comes, has always come, but which on some days might just pass away.

Notes

NOTES TO INTRODUCTION

1 Malcolm Bull, *Seeing Things Hidden: Apocalypse, Vision and Totality* (London: Verso, 1999).

2 Toni Morrison, *Playing in the Dark: Whiteness and the Literary Imagination* (Cambridge, MA: Harvard University Press, 1992), p. 63.

3 Recent debates on race from a literary-cultural perspective are too extensive to footnote easily, but take in the work of Antony Appiah and Amy Gutmann, Henry Louis Gates, Toni Morrison, Paul Gilroy, and Walter Benn Michaels, among many others.

4 Ross Posnock, *Color and Culture: Black Writers and the Making of the Modern Intellectual* (Cambridge, MA: Harvard University Press, 1998), ch. 4.

5 For a critique of Du Bois which draws out the instability of his position, see Paul C. Taylor, 'Appiah's Uncompleted Argument: W. E. B. Du Bois and the Reality of Race', *Social Theory and Practice* 26:1 (2000), 103–28.

6 Peter Munz's discussion of typology in *The Shapes of Time: A New Look at the Philosophy of History* (Middletown, CT: Wesleyan University Press, 1977) is useful in that he argues for a philosophy of history which 'accomplishes its task of relating the various subjectivities [of different periods] to each other by confining itself to the typology that is inherent in the subjectivities themselves'. This explains why the process of understanding is, Munz suggests, an 'asymmetrical' one, predicated on a later act of recovery on the part of the later observer and requiring a series of interpretive links across a temporal divide. See also his *When the Golden Bough Breaks: Structuralism or Typology?* (London: Routledge & Kegan Paul, 1973).

7 W. E. B. Du Bois, 'The Concept of Race', in *The Oxford W. E. B. Du Bois Reader*, ed. Eric J. Sundquist (New York: Oxford University Press, 1996), p. 87.

8 Eric J. Sundquist, *To Wake the Nations: Race in the Making of American Literature* (Cambridge, MA: Harvard University Press, 1993), p. 18.

9 Saidiya V. Hartman, *Scenes of Subjection: Terror, Slavery, and Self-making in Nineteenth-Century America* (New York: Oxford University Press, 1997); Stephen Best, *The Fugitive's Properties: Law and the Poetics of Possession* (Chicago: University of Chicago Press, 2004).

10 Marcus Wood, *Blind Memory: Visual Representations of Slavery in England and America, 1780–1865* (Manchester: Manchester University Press, 2000).
11 For an account of the continuities, see Bull, *Seeing Things Hidden*, ch. 6.
12 These are expounded carefully in Peter Garnsey, *Ideas of Slavery from Aristotle to Augustine* (Cambridge: Cambridge University Press, 1996), pp. 119–24.
13 Elizabeth Young, *Black Frankenstein: The Making of an American Metaphor* (New York: New York University Press, 2008), p. 79.
14 The persistent Western association, from Quintilian on, of inflated or over-copious language with the threatening feminine body – make-up, dilation – suggests the persistence of this disciplinary regime. See, e.g., Patricia Parker, *Literary Fat Ladies: Rhetoric, Gender, Property* (New York: Routledge, 1987).
15 Georges Canguilhem, *A Vital Rationalist: Selected Writings from Georges Canguilhem*, ed. Francois Delaporte, trans. Arthur Goldhammer, intro. Paul Rabinow (New York: Zone, 2000), p. 304; subsequently cited in text as *VR*.
16 Georges Canguilhem, 'Machine and Organism', in *Incorporations* [*Zone 6*], ed. Jonathan Crary and Stanford Kwinter (New York: Urzone, 1992), pp. 44–69 (p. 60 cited). The citation is from *Kant's Critique of Judgement*, trans. J. H. Bernard (1892; rev. ed. London: Macmillan, 1914), §§43, pp. 183–84.
17 Bernard Stiegler, *Technics and Time 1: The Fault of Epimetheus*, trans. Richard Beardsworth and George Collins (Stanford, CA: Stanford University Press, 1998), pp. 141–42.
18 G. W. F. Hegel, *Hegel's Phenomenology of Spirit*, selections trans. and anno-tated Howard P. Kainz (University Park: Pennsylvania State University Press, 1994), p. 3.
19 Aristotle, *The Politics*, trans. T. A. Sinclair, rev. Trevor J. Saunders (London: Penguin, 1992); subsequent citations in text by standard (Bekker) reference and page number.
20 Pliny the Elder, *Natural History* 29.8; for consistency I have used the trans-lation supplied by Hanns Sachs in *The Creative Unconscious: Studies in the Psychoanalysis of Art* (Cambridge: Sci-Art, 1942), p. 113, discussed in Chapter 3. Pliny's complaint is often cited as applying to slavery; in fact, its immediate context is a longer tirade against Greek doctors – though the sense of giving the body up to others remains strong, as is the sense of a dangerous enemy within (poisoning, adultery, intrigue). For commentary, see Thomas Wiedemann, *Greek and Roman Slavery* (London: Croom Helm, 1981), pp. 68–69.
21 Bull, *Seeing Things Hidden*, p. 221; Paul Gilroy, *The Black Atlantic: Modernity and Double Consciousness* (London: Verso, 1993), ch. 4.
22 W. E. B. Du Bois, *The Souls of Black Folk*, ed. Henry Louis Gates, Jr., and Teri Hume Oliver (1903; New York: Norton, 1999), p. 127.

NOTES TO CHAPTER I

1 On the background here, see Michael T. Martin and Marilyn Yaquinto, eds., *Redress for Historical Injustices in the United States: On Reparations for Slavery, Jim Crow and Their Legacies* (Durham, NC: Duke University Press, 2007); on

the specific issues, see in the same volume Martha Biondi, 'The Rise of the Reparations Movement', pp. 255–69, and the California Insurance Policy Bill, pp. 522–23.

2 See Todd L. Savitt, 'Slave Life Insurance in Virginia and North Carolina', *Journal of Southern History* 43 (1977), 583–600; Robert S. Starobin, *Industrial Slavery in the Old South* (New York: Oxford University Press, 1970); Sharon Ann Murphy, 'Slavery, Life Insurance and Industrialization in the Upper South', *Journal of the Early Republic* 25 (2003), 615–52.

3 Vivian A. Rotman Zelizer, *Morals and Markets: The Development of Life Insurance in the United States* (New York: Columbia University Press, 1979).

4 This question is asked, but not clearly answered, by Michael Sean Quinn, 'Examining Slave Insurance in a World 150 Years Removed', *Insurance Journal* (24 July 2000).

5 On the evolution of these terms, see Victor Dover, *A Handbook to Marine Insurance*, 8th ed. (London: Witherby, 1987).

6 John Weskett, *A Complete Digest of the Theory, Laws and Practice of Insurance* (London: Frys, Couchman and Collier, 1781), 252. Unless otherwise indicated, emphasis in quotes is in the original.

7 Wilhelm Benecke [of Lloyds], *A Treatise on the Principles of Indemnity in Marine Insurance, Bottomry and Respondentia* (London: Baldwin, Cradock & Joy, 1824), p. 169.

8 Geoffrey Clark, *Betting on Lives: The Culture of Life Insurance in England, 1695–1775* (Manchester: Manchester University Press, 1999), p. 19.

9 Ibid., p. 22; Zelizer, *Morals and Markets*, pp. 68–72.

10 *The Marine Insurance Code of France, 1681*, trans. Douglas Barlow (The author, 1989), pp. 22–23. Barlow notes that Article 9 was largely copied from the *Guidon de la Mer*, a collection of precedents from the 1500s.

11 Weskett, *A Complete Digest*, p. 72; emphasis added.

12 Clarke, *Betting on Lives*, p. 16.

13 The issue of ransom and property in persons was bound up with that of family law and property rights. According to the French *Code Civil*'s laws on forced heirship (i.e., on children receiving a minimum portion of the estate), the right could be lost because of serious offences, such as violence against the parent. The seventh of ten offences was '[i]f the child refused to ransom them, detained in captivity'. See James O. Fuqua, comp., *Civil Code of the State of Louisiana, with Statutory Amendments from 1825 to 1866 Inclusive* (New Orleans: B. Bloomfield, 1867), p. 225. The extension of such relations beyond the family again is significant as a step towards a general capitalization of human relations.

14 Zelizer, *Morals and Markets*, p. 71.

15 To some extent this history is also written into the history of the term 'person', which originally refers to a mask or persona, someone who acts a part, but later also refers to the body of a person (as opposed to the soul), and then to 'the actual self or being of a man or woman' (*Oxford English Dictionary*, 5), often used reflexively ('his own person'). The person is thus part of a

history in which the self emerges as personal property; it achieves identity with it-self.

16 Theodor W. Adorno and Max Horkheimer, *Dialectic of Enlightenment*, trans. John Cumming (London: Verso, 1997), p. 57.

17 See Michael Lobban, 'Slavery, Insurance and the Law', *Journal of Legal History*, 28:2 (2007), 319–28; special issue: 'The *Zong*: Legal, Social and Historical Dimensions'. As James Oldham shows in the same issue, the law in this area was far from coherent and bound by traditional practice as much as statute or, indeed, the wording of its own contracts: 'Insurance Litigation Involving the *Zong* and Other British Slave Ships, 1780–1807', 299–318.

18 See *Tatham v. Hodgson* (1796), Charles Durnford and Edward Hyde East, *Term Reports in the Court of King's Bench*, 4th ed. (London: J. Butterworth, 1794–1802), 6: 656, in which it is reported that slaves starved to death after a voyage was extended from six to nine weeks to more than six months. The judges ruled that it would undermine the recent act if the claim was allowed, since it meant that 'every person going on this [or any] voyage should find his interest combined with his duty' (Lord Kenyon, p. 658); 'natural death' thus must include starvation. Judge Lawrence stressed that 'I do not know that it was ever decided that a loss arising from a mistake of the Captain was a loss within the perils of the sea', citing the *Zong* case (p. 659) – implying that a captain is to blame even in such an extreme case. Cf. Laurence R. Baily, *Perils of the Sea, and Their Effects on Policies of Insurance* (London: Effingham Wilson, 1860), pp. 197–98.

19 Herbert Klein, *The Middle Passage: Comparative Studies in the Atlantic Slave Trade* (Princeton, NJ: Princeton University Press, 1978), p. 153.

20 See, e.g., *Hunter, Murphy, and Talbot v. General Mutual Insurance Company of New York* (1856), discussed in Judith Kelleher Schafer, *Slavery, the Civil Law, and the Supreme Court of Louisiana* (Baton Rouge: Louisiana State University Press, 1994), esp. pp. 164–65.

21 Weskett, *A Complete Digest*, pp. 525, 11.

22 *Jones v. Schmoll*, Guildhall Tr. Vac. 1785, Durnford and East, *Term Reports*, I 130n; James Allan Park, *A System of the Law of Marine Insurances*, 2d ed. (London: T. Whieldon, 1790), p. 56.

23 On the rebellion, see Howard Jones, 'The Peculiar Institution and National Honor: The Case of the *Creole* Slave Revolt', *Civil War History* 21 (1975), 28–50; Maggie Montesinos Sale, *The Slumbering Volcano: American Slave Ship Revolts and the Production of Rebellious Masculinity* (Durham, NC: Duke University Press, 1997), chs. 3 and (on Douglass) 5; also John Cullen Guesser, 'Taking Liberties: Pauline Hopkins's Recasting of the *Creole* Rebellion', in *The Unruly Voice: Rediscovering Pauline Elizabeth Hopkins*, ed. John Cullen Gruesser (Urbana: University of Illinois Press, 1996), pp. 98–118. Douglass's 'The Heroic Slave' has received extensive commentary.

24 Benjamin was at later moments both a slave owner and defender of slavery. See Robert D. Meade, *Judah P. Benjamin: Confederate Statesman* (New York: Oxford University Press, 1943), esp. pp. 40–42.

25 *Supreme Court. Edward Lockett versus the Merchants' Insurance Company*. Brief of
     Slidell, Benjamin and Conrad, for Defendants (New Orleans, 1842), pp. 26–27.
26 Boulay Paty, cited in ibid., p. 33.
27 *Thomas McCargo v. Merchant's Insurance Company* (New Orleans, 1842).
28 The Exchequer case is described by Oldham, 'Insurance Litigation Involving
     the *Zong*', and in Andrew Lewis's summary in the *Journal of Legal History*,
     28:2 (2007), 357–70. As this book goes to press, James Walvin's *The Zong: A
     Massacre, the Law and the End of Slavery* (New Haven, CT: Yale University
     Press, 2011) has appeared, offering a comprehensive overview of the case.
29 The appeal hearing took place on 22 May 1783; there is no record of a second
     case, and it is usually presumed that the owners withdrew their case for com-
     pensation. See James Allan Park, *A System of the Law of Marine Insurances*,
     2d ed. (London: T. Whieldon, 1790), p. 62; Sylvester Douglas, *Reports of
     Cases Argued and Determined in the Court of King's Bench*, vol. 3, compiled
     by Henry Roscoe (London: S. Sweet, A. Maxwell & Stevens and Sons, 1831),
     pp. 233–35; Robert Weisbord, 'The Case of the Slave-Ship *Zong*, 1783', *History
     Today* 19 (1969), 561–67. Statutes subsequently passing included 30 G. 3, c.33,
     *f.*8; and 34 G. 3, c.80, *f.*10, prohibiting any losses due to throwing overboard,
     ill-treatment, or natural death.
30 The account here draws on the bound set of manuscript records of the case
     Granville Sharp had made from shorthand transcripts, 'In the King's Bench,
     Wednesday May 21 1783' and other materials, *Documents Relating to the Ship
     Zong*, National Maritime Museum, London, REC/19 (subsequently cited in
     text as *Sharp Transcript*). These are the 'vouchers' which Sharp attached to his
     protest to the Admiralty; see Prince Hoare, *Memoirs of Granville Sharp, Esq.*
     (London: Henry Colburn, 1820), pp. 242–44, app. 8; abbreviated forms have
     been spelled out.
31 Ian Baucom, *Specters of the Atlantic: Finance Capital, Slavery, and the
     Philosophy of History* (Durham, NC: Duke University Press, 2005).
32 Anita Rupprecht, ' "A Very Uncommon Case": Representations of the *Zong*
     and the British Campaign to Abolish the Slave Trade', *Journal of Legal History*,
     28:2 (2007), 329–46; special issue: 'The *Zong*: Legal, Social and Historical
     Dimensions'.
33 One useful aspect of the Freudian framework here is its notion of 'working-
     through' as 'becoming more conversant with resistance' – as a repetition-with-
     interpretation which enables the past to be mastered, including (as Laplanche
     and Pontalis put it) 'the repetitive insistence characteristic of unconscious
     formulations'. However, the relation of working-through to trauma itself
     often seems less than clear. See J. Laplanche and J.-B. Pontalis, *The Language
     of Psychoanalysis*, trans. Donald Nicholson-Smith (London: Karnac, 1988),
     pp. 488–89.
34 P. J. Bishop, *A Short History of the Royal Humane Society* (London: The Society,
     1974). The organizer and guiding spirit was the unstoppable Dr. William
     Hawes, whose energies seem to have displaced his co-founder, Dr. Thomas
     Cogan, from the histories.

35 Hans Blumenberg, *Shipwreck with Spectator: Paradigm of a Metaphor for Existence*, trans. Steven Rendell (Cambridge, MA: MIT Press, 1997).

36 See Christopher Baugh, *Garrick and Loutherbourg* (Cambridge: Chadwick-Healey, 1990), pp. 79–80; Iain McCalman, 'Magic, Spectacle and the Art of de Loutherbourg's Eidophusikon', in *Sensation and Sensibility: Viewing Gainsborough's Cottage Door*, ed. Ann Bermingham (New Haven, CT: Yale University Press, 2005), pp. 180–97.

37 E. Thomas [astronomer], *The Shipwreck of the Halsewell East-Indiaman: A Poem* (Shrewsbury: T. Wood, c. 1786), p. 18.

38 Archibald Duncan, *The Mariner's Chronicle; or, Authentic and Complete History of Popular Shipwrecks*, 6 vols. (London: J. & J. Cundee, 1810), I: iii.

39 Henry Greathead, inventor of the first modern lifeboat, was one of the 'thousands' who witnessed the stranding and loss of the crew of the *Adventure* in 1789 off Tynemouth. George Manby, inventor of the lifeline-carrying mortar, saw the loss of the naval brig *Snipe* off Yarmouth in the storm of February 1807, in which sixty-seven died within 60 yards of shore. John Bell, who developed a similar device, had been present at the wreck of the *Royal George*. Henry Trengrouse, one of the developers of the rocket-line, witnessed the wreck of the *Anson* and the loss of more than a hundred in Cornwall. Sir William Hillary, founder of the National Shipwreck Institute (later RNLI), saw the wreck of the *Vigilance* and other ships off the Isle of Man in 1822 (all details from *Oxford Dictionary of National Biography*).

40 Mary Robinson, 'The Negro Girl', *Lyrical Tales* (London: T. N. Longman and O. Rees, 1800), p. 112.

41 *The Slave Trade: A Poem. Written in the Year 1788* (London: J. Desmond, 1793), pp. 12–13. The poem was later attributed to Morland's friend William Collins, Sr. (c. 1740–1812). On the paintings and their context, see Marcus Wood, *Blind Memory: Visual Representations of Slavery in England and America, 1780–1865* (Manchester: Manchester University Press, 2000), pp. 36–37.

42 The original of Moreland's *African Hospitality* (1791) is in the Museum Africa, Newtown, Johannesburg – though it should be said that the painting does not have a close relationship to contemporary accounts of the wreck. A matching story entitled 'Negro Devotion' – about a black servant who sacrificed himself to save his two young charges from shipwreck – is told in Reuben and Shotlo Percy, eds., *The Percy Anecdotes* (London: T. Boys, 1823), pp. 63–64.

43 The story is told in a narrative by a 12-year-old passenger, J. B. Romaigne, in George Francis Dow, *Slave Ships and Slaving* (Salem, MA: Marine Research Society, 1927), pp. xxviii–xxxv (p. xxxiii cited). Ophthalmia sufferers would often recover after a period.

44 Samuel Webber, *The Slave Ship: A Ballad* (Cambridge: Hilliard and Metcalf, 1821).

45 Benecke, *A Treatise on the Principles of Indemnity in Marine Insurance*, p. 168.

46 Voucher 1, Plea to the Court of Exchequer, Hilary Term 23 Geo. 3, in *Sharp Transcript*, p. 132.

47 Robert Dover, *A Handbook to Marine Insurance*, 8th ed. (London: Whiterby, 1987), p. 628.

48 See Captain [J. N.] Inglefield's *Narrative, Concerning the Loss of His Majesty's Ship the Centaur, of Seventy-Four Guns ... A New Edition* (London: J. Murray, 1783).

49 Hoare, *Memoirs of Granville Sharp*, app. 8.

50 Peter Fryer, *Staying Power: The History of Black People in Britain* (London: Pluto Press, 1984), p. 125; Edmund Heward, *Lord Mansfield* (Chichester: Barry Rose, 1979), p. 146.

51 A. W. Brian Simpson, *Cannibalism and the Common Law* (1984; London: Hambledon Press, 1994), pp. 251–52.

52 The case of the *William Brown* (*U.S. v. Holmes*), described by Simpson, ibid., p. 162.

53 Simpson, *Cannibalism*, p. 249.

54 *Mr James Janeway's Legacy to his Friends, Containing Twenty Seven Famous Instances of God's Providences in and about Sea Dangers and Deliverances, with the Names of Several that were Eye-Witnesses to many of them. Wereto is Added a Sermon on the same Subject* (London: Dorman Newman, 1674), pp. 3–6, 15.

55 See, e.g., *Melancholy Shipwreck, and Remarkable Instance of the Interposition of Divine Providence* (1834), related by Mrs. Mathews, a missionary's wife bound for India from Portsmouth. After sixteen days in an open boat, lots are proposed. She then gets the others to defer a day and prays. They prepare lots, she gets another hour for prayer, and a sail appears.

56 Edward Smedley, *Jonah: A Poem* (London: John Murray, 1815), p. 6; James William Bellamy, *Jonah* (London: Taylor & Hessey, 1815). Neither is the issue of lots raised in Jacob Durché's 1781 Humane Society sermon, on Jonah 2:5–6, which simply offers a moralization of straying.

57 George Abbot, D.D., *An Exposition upon the Prophet Jonah*, 2 vols. (1600; London: Hamilton, Adams, 1845), 1: 90; cf. Thomas Harding, *Expository Lectures on the Book of Jonah* (London: A Heylin, 1856), p. 45.

58 Rev. W. K. Tweedie, *Man by Nature and by Grace: or, Lessons from the Book of Jonah* (Edinburgh: Johnstone & Hunter, 1850), pp. 72–73.

59 René Girard, *The Scapegoat* (London: Athlone Press, 1986), p. 113.

60 Neil Hanson, *The Custom of the Sea* (London: Doubleday, 1997), p. 138.

61 George Fitzhugh, *Cannibals All, or, Slaves without Masters* (Richmond, VA: A. Morris, 1857).

62 David Harrison, *The Melancholy Narrative of the Distressful Voyage and Miraculous Deliverance of Captain David Harrison of the Sloop Peggy* (London: James Harrison, 1766), p. 23; subsequent references in text. The case is discussed in Peter Thompson, 'No Chance in Nature: Cannibalism as a Solution to Maritime Famine c. 1750–1800', in *American Bodies: Cultural Histories of the Physique*, ed. Tim Armstrong (New York: New York University Press, 1996), pp. 32–44.

63 Edgar Allan Poe, *The Narrative of Arthur Gordon Pym of Nantucket*, ed. Harold Beaver (London: Penguin, 1975), pp. 141, 144–45.

64 *An Account of the Loss of the Luxborough Galley, by fire, on her voyage from Jamaica to London: with the sufferings of her crew, in the year 1727, by William Boys, Second Mate* (London: J. Johnson, 1787), p. 9. Boys was later Lieutenant-Governor of the Royal Hospital at Greenwich and seems to have commissioned Cleveley's painting; this account was published by his son William, Jr., who testified that his father fasted every year for twelve days on the anniversary (p. iv).

65 *Gentleman's Magazine*, 89 (July 1737), 449–50.

66 Other examples include the *Francis Spaight* (1846), where the sailors bled and ate their way through four crew members, beginning with a ballot, probably rigged, amongst the cabin boys; the *Exuine* and *Cospatrick*; and the *Sallie M. Stedman* off Cape Hateras in 1878, where a black sailor went mad and was killed and eaten. For others, see Simpson, *Cannibalism*, 128–33, 139; Hanson, *The Custom of the Sea*; Alan Rice, *Radical Narratives of the Black Atlantic* (London: Continuum, 2003), ch. 5.

67 On the text's status, see the introduction to Robin F. A. Fabel, trans. and ed., *Shipwreck and Adventures of Monsieur Pierre Viaud* (Pensecola: West Florida University Press, 1990).

68 It is usually described as Breton in origin; French and Portuguese versions were noted as early as the sixteenth century. An American version is 'Sept ans sur mer', recorded in Louisiana in 1934, *A Treasury of Library of Congress Field Recordings*, Rounder CD 1500.

69 Simpson, *Cannibalism*, p. 141.

70 Steve Beil, *Down with the Old Canoe: A Cultural History of the Titanic Disaster* (New York: Norton, 1996), pp. 107–108, 114–17.

71 *A Narrative of the Shipwreck of the Nottingham Galley*, &c, revised and reprinted with additions in 1726 (London, n.d.), p. 20. On the case generally, see R. H. Warner, 'Captain John Deane and the Wreck of the *Nottingham Galley*: A Study of History and Bibliography', *New England Quarterly* 68 (1995), 106–17.

72 *A Narrative of the Sufferings, Preservation and Deliverance of Capt. John Jean and Company* (London: R. Tookey, n.d. [1711]).

73 *A True Account of the Voyage of the Nottingham-Galley of London, John Dean Commander, from the River Thames to New-England* (London: S Popping, n.d.[1711]; subsequent references in text. A pirated version of Deane's account, condensing it and converting the first-person narration to third, appeared as *A Sad and Deplorable, but True Account of the Dreadful Hardships, and Sufferings of Capt. John Dean, and his Company, on Board the Nottingham Galley* (London: J Dutton, 1711).

74 *Narrative of the Shipwreck and Suffering of Miss Ann Saunders* (Providence, RI: Z. S. Crossman, 1827). Various editions of this narrative appeared, as did accounts in the press. One could compare this marital communion to that described in the wreck of the *George*, 1822: 'Her wretched husband was compel'd / Her precious blood to taste' (Simpson, *Cannibalism and the Common Law*, p. 117).

75 *Shipwreck and Suffering*, pp. 19–20. A letter from the Lieutenant [later Rear Admiral], R. F. Gambier, describing the rescue, is in the National Maritime Museum, London, ms. 73/073.

76 On visual representations, and Turner in particular, see Wood, *Blind Memory*, pp. 59–68.

77 Susan L. Mizruchi, *The Science of Sacrifice: American Literature and Modern Social Theory* (Princeton, NJ: Princeton University Press, 1998), pp. 256, 303–307.

NOTES TO CHAPTER 2

1 Saidiya V. Hartman, *Scenes of Subjection: Terror, Slavery, and Self-Making in Nineteenth-Century America* (New York: Oxford University Press, 1997); Stephen Best, *The Fugitive's Properties: Law and the Poetics of Possession* (Chicago: University of Chicago Press, 2004).

2 Best, *The Fugitive's Properties*, p. 81.

3 *State v. Mann* (1829), cited by Thomas D. Morris, *Southern Slavery and the Law, 1619–1860* (Chapel Hill: University of North Carolina Press, 1996), p. 431.

4 See J. Laplanche and J. B. Pontalis, *The Language of Psychoanalysis*, trans. Donald Nicholson-Smith (London: Karnac Books, 1988), pp. 166–69; Jacques Lacan, 'On a Question Prior to any Possible Treatment of Psychosis', *Écrits: A Selection*, trans. Alan Sheridan (London: Tavistock, 1977).

5 Gavin Wright, *Slavery and American Economic Development* (Baton Rouge: Louisiana State University Press, 2006), pp. 6–7; also Jacob M. Price, 'Credit in the Slave Trade and Plantation Economies', in *Slavery and the Rise of the Atlantic* System, ed. Barbara L. Solow (New York: Cambridge University Press, 1991), pp. 293–339.

6 T. R. R. Cobb, *An Inquiry into the Law of Negro Slavery in the United States* (Philadelphia: T. & J. W. Johnson, 1858), pp. 3–4; cf. Ariela J. Gross, *Double Character: Slavery and Mastery in the Antebellum Southern Courtroom* (Princeton, NJ: Princeton University Press, 2000).

7 Alan Watson, *Slave Law in the Americas* (Athens: University of Georgia University Press, 1989), pp. 66, 133.

8 See Mark V. Tushnet, *The American Law of Slavery, 1810–1860: Considerations of Humanity and Interest* (Princeton, NJ: Princeton University Press, 1981).

9 James O. Fuqua, comp., *Civil Code of the State of Louisiana, with Statutory Amendments from 1825 to 1866 Inclusive* (New Orleans: B. Bloomfield, 1867), pp. 30, 33. Louisiana's slave code was ultimately derived from the *Code noir* of Louis XIV, the more liberal Spanish provisions tempered by the harsher French code: see Judith Kelleher Schafer, *Slavery, the Civil Law, and the Supreme Court of Louisiana* (Baton Rouge: Louisiana State University Press, 1994), pp. 2–9 and *Becoming Free, Remaining Free: Manumission and Enslavement in New Orleans, 1846–1862* (Baton Rouge: Louisiana State University Press, 2003).

10 Charles S. Davis, *The Cotton Kingdom in Alabama* (1939; Philadelphia, Porcupine Press, 1974), pp. 104, 111–12.

11 Morris, *Southern Slavery and the Law*, chs. 18, 19.

12 Tushnet, *The American Law of Slavery*, p. 6.

13 Schafer, *Slavery, the Civil Law*, pp. 115–16.

14 Cf. Hartman, *Scenes of Subjection*, p. 69.

15 Henry Banner, in *The American Slave: A Composite Autobiography*, ed. George
    P. Rawick (Westport, CT: Greenwood Press, 1972–79), vol. 8: *Arkansas
    Narratives*, pts. 1 and 2, p. 105. Also available from *The Project Gutenberg
    EBook of Slave Narratives: A Folk History of Slavery in the United States from
    Interviews with Former Slaves, by Work Projects Administration*, vol. 2: *Arkansas
    Narratives*, http://www.gutenberg.org/files/11255/11255-h/11255-h.htm.

16 W. J. T. Mitchell, 'Narrative, Memory and Slavery', in *Cultural Artifacts and
    the Production of Meaning: The Page, the Image, and the Body*, ed. Margaret
    J. M. Ezell and Katherine O'Brien O'Keeffe (Ann Arbor: University of
    Michigan Press, 1994), pp. 199–222.

17 Charles Chesnutt, 'A Solution for the Race Problem', *Essays and Speeches
    of Charles Chesnutt*, ed. Joseph McElrath, Jr., Robert C. Leitz, and Jesse S.
    Crisler (Stanford, CA: Stanford University Press, 1999), p. 391. On *coartación*,
    see Watson, *Slave Law*, pp. 50–62.

18 Ira Berlin, *Generations of Captivity: A History of African-American Slaves*
    (Cambridge, MA: Belknap Press, 2003), p. 89. See also Kimberly S. Hanger,
    *Bounded Lives, Bounded Places: Free Black Society in Colonial New Orleans,
    1769–1803* (Durham, NC: Duke University Press, 1997).

19 Berlin, *Generations of Captivity*, p. 142.

20 See Shawn Cole, 'Capitalism and Freedom: Manumissions and the Slave
    Market in Louisiana, 1725–1820,' *Journal of Economic History* 65:4 (2005),
    1008–27.

21 Schafer, *Slavery, the Civil Law*, pp. 220–21.

22 On the fear of cities, see John Ashworth, *Slavery, Capitalism and Politics
    in the Antebellum Republic*, vol. 1: *Commerce and Compromise, 1820–1850*
    (Cambridge: Cambridge University Press, 1995), pp. 99–101.

23 Sharon Ann Murphy, 'Slavery, Life Insurance and Industrialization in the
    Upper South', *Journal of the Early Republic* 25 (2003), 615–52 (616 cited).

24 Jonathan D. Martin, *Divided Mastery: Slave Hiring in the American South*
    (Cambridge, MA: Harvard University Press, 2004), pp. 192, 77, 80–81.

25 Murphy, 'Slavery', pp. 620, 652.

26 Todd L. Savitt, 'Slave Life Insurance in Virginia and North Carolina', *Journal
    of Southern History* 43 (1977), 583–600 (585 cited).

27 See Gross, *Double Character*, p. 104 (on hire cases, pp. 320–33, 102–104).

28 Schafer, *Slavery, the Civil Law*, ch. 4 (esp. pp. 109–10, 121).

29 Morris, *Southern Slavery and the Law*, pp. 380–85 (p. 383 cited).

30 Ibid., pp. 31–36, 373, 406–407.

31 George Fitzhugh, *Sociology for the South, or the Failure of Free Society*
    (Richmond, VA: A. Morris, 1854), pp. 259–91. Edicts against freedmen cli-
    maxed in the Arkansas Free Negro Expulsion Act of 1859.

32 Murphy, 'Slavery', pp. 619–20, 626–27 (p. 619 cited).

33 See Gross, *Double Character*, p. 154.

34 *A Narrative of the Life of Rev. Noah Davis, A Colored Man. Written by Himself, at the Age of Fifty-Four* (Baltimore: John F. Weishampel, Jr., 1859), pp. 42, 56, 59; subsequent references in text.

35 Douglass in the *North Star*, 13 July 1849; see Margaret M. R. Kellow, 'Conflicting Imperatives: Black and White Abolitionists Debate Slave Redemption', in *Buying Freedom: The Ethics and Economics of Slave Redemption*, ed. Kwame Anthony Appiah and Martin Bunzel (Princeton, NJ: Princeton University Press, 1997), pp. 200–12 (p. 205 cited).

36 John Stauffer, 'Frederick Douglass and the Politics of Slave Redemption', in *Buying Freedom*, ed. Appiah and Bunzel, p. 220.

37 Lunsford Lane, *The Narrative of Lunsford Lane, formerly of Raleigh, N.C., embracing an account of his early life, the purchase of himself and his family from slavery, and his banishment from the place of his birth for the crime of wearing a colored skin*, 2d ed. (Boston: The author, 1842), pp. 8–9.

38 Frederick Douglass, *A Narrative of the Life of Frederick Douglass, an American Slave, Written by Himself*, ed. Robert B. Stepto (Cambridge, CA: Belknap Press, 2009), p. 78.

39 William Hayden, *Narrative of William Hayden, containing a faithful account of his travels for a number of years, whilst a slave, in the South* (Cincinnati: The author, 1846), p. 23; subsequent references in text.

40 Solomon Northup, *Twelve Years a Slave: Narrative of Solomon Northup, a Citizen of New-York, Kidnapped in Washington City in 1841, and Rescued in 1853* (Auburn, NY: Derby & Miller, 1853), pp. 291, 311, 233–36.

41 Olaudah Equiano, *The Interesting Narrative of the Life of Olaudah Equiano*, ed. Angelo Costanzo (Peterborough, ON: Broadview Press, 2001), pp. 156–57; subsequent references in text.

42 Georges Bataille, *The Accursed Share: An Essay on General Economy*, vol. 1: *Consumption*, trans. Robert Hurley (New York: Zone, 1991).

43 Norman R. Yetman (ed.), *Voices from Slavery: 100 Authentic Slave Narratives* (Mineola, NY: Dover, 2000), p. 333.

44 See Douglas A. Blackmon, *Slavery by Another Name: The Re-enslavement of Black Americans from the Civil War to World War II* (New York: Doubleday, 2008).

45 See Jay Mandle, *Not Slave, Not Free* (Durham, NC: Duke University Press, 1992), ch. 3.

46 Charles Chesnutt, 'The Race Problem', *Essays and Speeches*, p. 117.

47 Hartman, *Scenes of Subjection*, ch. 5 (p. 131 cited).

48 Orlando Patterson, *Slavery and Social Death: A Comparative Study* (Cambridge, MA: Harvard University Press, 1982), p. 5.

49 Civil Code of the State of Louisiana, p. 34. Louisiana's Civil Code was a unique legacy of its Roman law inheritance, but the Code of the State of Georgia (1861) was similarly amended and ratified in 1867.

50 See Daniel A. Novak, *The Wheel of Servitude: Black Forced Labor after Slavery* (Lexington: University Press of Kentucky, 1978), pp. 34, 39.

51 Ibid., pp. 56–60.
52 W. E. B. Du Bois, *The Souls of Black Folk*, ed. Henry Louis Gates, Jr., and Teri Hume Oliver (1903; New York: Norton, 1999), p. 90.
53 Ibid., p. 10.
54 Ibid., p. 134. On Du Bois and sacrifice, see Susan L. Mizruchi, *The Science of Sacrifice: American Literature and Modern Social Theory* (Princeton, NJ: Princeton University Press, 1998), ch. 4.
55 Zora Neale Hurston, *Their Eyes Were Watching God*, intro. Holly Eley (1937; London: Virago, 1987), p. 286. As Hurston's protagonist's harvest of memory includes the rabies-infected lover she has had to kill, the doom-ridden black (male) body continues to haunt even this text.
56 Orlando Patterson, *Rituals of Blood: Consequences of Slavery in Two American Centuries* (New York: Basic Books, 1998), p. 210.
57 It is, however, reprinted in Charles W. Chesnutt, *The Conjure Woman and Other Conjure Tales*, ed. Richard H. Brodhead (Durham, NC: Duke University Press, 1993), pp. 123–35.
58 Eric J. Sundquist, *To Wake the Nations: Race in the Making of American Literature* (Cambridge, MA: Harvard University Press, 1993), pp. 377–84.
59 Zora Heale Hurston, 'What White Publishers Won't Print' (1950), in *Within the Circle: An Anthology of African American Literary Criticism from the Harlem Renaissance to the Present*, ed. Angelyn Mitchell (Durham, NC: Duke University Press, 1994), p. 120.
60 James Baldwin, 'A Fly in Buttermilk', *Nobody Knows My Name* (London: Michael Joseph, 1964), p. 86.
61 Richard Wright, *Native Son*, the restored text, intro. Arnold Rampersad (1940; New York: HarperPerennial, 1998), p. 455; subsequent references in text.
62 See Edward Said, *Beginnings: Intention and Method* (New York: Basic Books, 1975).
63 Photography is understood more positively in *12 Million Black Voices* (1941), which Wright published with Farm Security Administration photographer Edwin Rosskam.
64 On Marx's comments in *The German Ideology*, see W. J. T. Mitchell, *Iconology: Image, Text, Ideology* (Chicago: University of Chicago Press, 1986), ch. 6.
65 See Miriam Hansen, 'Mass Culture as Hieroglyptic Writing', and Anson Rabinbach, '"Why Were the Jews Sacrificed?"' in *Adorno: A Critical Reader*, ed. Nigel Gibson and Andrew Rubin (Oxford: Blackwell, 2002), pp. 57–85, 123–49; Roger Caillois, 'Mimicry and Legendary Psychasthenia', in *The Edge of Surrealism: A Roger Caillois Reader*, ed. Claudine Frank (Durham, NC: Duke University Press, 2003), pp. 89–103.
66 Sharon Patricia Holland discusses the 'always already "dead" position of African-Americans' in *Raising the Dead: Reading Death and (Black) Subjectivity* (Durham, NC: Duke University Press, 2000), p. 6.
67 My argument at this point touches on Best's consideration of voice and image rights in the context of slavery, *The Fugitive's Properties*, pp. 14–16.

68 Chester Himes, *If He Hollers Let Him Go* (1945; London: Pluto Press, 1986), pp. 149–50; subsequent references in text.

69 Ralph Ellison, *Invisible Man* (1952; London: Penguin, 1987), pp. 56, 59; subsequent references in text.

70 Jean-Paul Sartre, On '*The Sound and the Fury*', *Literary and Philosophical Essays*, trans. Annette Michelson (London: Rider, 1955), p. 81.

71 William Faulkner, *Light in August* (1932; London: Penguin, 1964), p. 249; subsequent references in text.

72 Henri Bergson, *Creative Evolution*, trans. Arthur Mitchell (1911; Mineola, NY: Dover, 1998), pp. 250–51.

73 Grace Elizabeth Hale and Robert Jackson, ' "We're Trying Hard as Hell to Free Ourselves": Southern History and Race in the Making of William Faulkner's Literary Terrain', in *A Companion to William Faulkner*, ed. Richard C. Moreland (Oxford: Blackwell, 2006), p. 37.

74 William Faulkner, *Intruder in the Dust* (1948; London: Vintage, 1996), p. 7; subsequent references in text. The tale has narrative links with Faulkner's other fiction, in particular *Go Down, Moses* and Lucas's thematic linking there to inherited money and its refusal. For an account of Faulkner's tendency to multiply or resurrect characters who enact the traumas of the South, see Richard Godden, *Fictions of Labor* (Cambridge: Cambridge University Press, 1997), p. 193.

75 Margaret Walker, 'Faulkner and Race', *How I Wrote Jubilee and Other Essays on Life and Literature*, ed. Maryemma Graham (New York: Feminist Press, 1990), p. 148.

76 Remembering Chick's meal at Beauchamps's house, we might note that 'annealed' is connected to food in chapter 10, where Chick's uncle suggests that we eat the substance of the world 'to be annealed' (p. 207), to become one with it and vanquish ego.

77 The comparison between Faulkner and Twain has been made by Irving Howe, Michael Millgate, and others; see also Philip J. Skerry, '*The Adventures of Huckleberry Finn* and *Intruder in the Dust*: Two Conflicting Myths of the American Experience', *Ball State University Forum*, 13:1 (1972), 4–13.

78 Patterson, *Rituals of Blood*, pp. 229–31.

79 The most comprehensive gathering of this material is Michael T. Martin and Marilyn Yaquinto, eds., *Redress for Historical Injustices in the United States: On Reparations for Slavery, Jim Crow and Their Legacies* (Durham, NC: Duke University Press, 2007).

80 Ibid., p. 672.

81 For discussion of the 'turn to history', see Paul Gilroy, *The Black Atlantic: Modernity and Double Consciousness* (London: Verso, 1993), ch. 6.

82 David Bradley, *The Chaneysville Incident* (1981; London: Serpent's Tail, 1986); subsequent references in text. There is something of a tradition of referring to the novel as 'neglected'. Among the few extended recent discussions of the text is Edward Michael Pavlić, *Crossroads Modernism: Descent and Emergence in African-American Literary Culture* (Minneapolis: University of Minnesota Press, 2002), pp. 266–86.

83 Octavia E. Butler, *Xenogenesis* (*Dawn, Adulthood Rites, Imago*). The trilogy was subsequently renamed and published in one volume as *Lilith's Brood* (New York: Warner, 1999). Its relation to slavery has been the occasion of much debate, especially between those who see the Oankali as offering something close to slavery in their 'trading' of bodies and those who stress the more deconstructive approach to identity in the text; see, e.g. Jenny Wolmark, *Aliens and Others: Science Fiction, Feminism and Postmodernism* (New York: Harvester Wheatsheaf, 1993), vs. Amanda Boulter, 'Polymorphous Futures: Octavia E. Butler's *Xenogenesis* Trilogy', in *American Bodies: Cultural Histories of the Physique*, ed. Tim Armstrong (New York: New York University Press, 1996), pp. 170–85.

84 Butler, *Dawn*, pt. 1 of *Lilith's Brood*, p. 248.

85 'Xenophilic' is Butler's term; see "A Conversation with Octavia Butler," wab. org,http://www.wab.org/events/allofrochester/2003/interview.shtml.

86 Octavia E. Butler, *Fledgling* (New York: Warner, 2005), pp. 226–310; subsequent reference in text.

87 For an analysis of 1970s sociobiology in the text, see Oliver Belas, 'Race and Culture in African American Crime and Science Fiction', PhD dissertation, University of London, 2008, ch. 4.

NOTES TO CHAPTER 3

1 Harriet Beecher Stowe, *Uncle Tom's Cabin*, ed. Jean Fagan Yellin (1852; Oxford: Oxford University Press, 1998), p. 18.

2 Georges Canguilhem, *A Vital Rationalist: Selected Writings from Georges Canguilhem*, ed. Francois Delaporte, trans. Arthur Goldhammer, intro. Paul Rabinow (New York: Zone, 2000), pp. 291–96.

3 Hanns Sachs, 'The Delay of the Machine Age', trans. Margaret J. Powers, *Psychoanalytic Quarterly* 2 (1933), 404–24. The essay was first published in German as 'Die Verspätung des Maschinenzeitalters', *Imago* 20:1 (1934). It is reprinted in Hanns Sachs, *The Creative Unconscious: Studies in the Psychoanalysis of Art* (Cambridge: Sci-Art, 1942), and in *Arion* 4:3 (1965), 496–511. Subsequent references in text are to first English printing.

4 Marc Chapiro, 'Liberty and the Machine', trans. Hans Kaal, *Diogenes* (1962), 43–60 (51 cited). For a judgment on other factors influencing the growth of technology in antiquity contemporary with Sachs, see Abbott Payson Usher, *A History of Mechanical Inventions* (1929; rev. ed. Cambridge, MA: Harvard University Press, 1954), esp. pp. 100–101, 155–60.

5 Gerald Piel, 'Ideas of Technology: Commentary', *Technology and Culture* 3:4 (Autumn 1962), 463–65 (465 cited).

6 M. I. Finley, ed., *Slavery in Classical Antiquity* (Cambridge: W. Heffer, 1960), p. 234. Supporting studies include F. W. Walbank, *The Decline of the Roman Empire and the West* (London, 1946); Benjamin Farrington, *Head and Hand in Ancient Greece* (London: Watts, 1947); and R. J. Forbes, *Studies in Ancient Technology*, vol. 2 (Leiden: Brill, 1955).

7 Seymour Dresher, *The Mighty Experiment: Free Labour versus Slavery in British Emancipation* (New York: Oxford University Press, 2002), p. 20.

8 Lucio Russo, *The Forgotten Revolution: How Science Was Born in 300 BC and Why It Had to Be Reborn*, trans. Silvio Levy (Berlin: Springer, 2004).

9 M. I. Finley, *Economy and Society in Ancient Greece*, ed. and intro. Brent D. Shaw and Richard P. Saller (London: Chatton & Windus, 1981), pp. 176–95 (p. 194 cited).

10 Aldo Schiavone, *The End of the Past: Ancient Rome and the Modern West*, trans. Margery J. Schneider (Cambridge, MA: Harvard University Press, 2000), p. 136.

11 M. I. Finley, *Ancient Slavery and Modern Ideology* (London: Chatto & Windus, 1980), pp. 137–38.

12 Lewis Mumford, *Technics and Civilization* (London: George Routledge, 1934), p. 41.

13 Pliny, *Natural History* 29.8 (Sachs's translation in *The Creative Unconscious*, p. 113).

14 Aristotle, *The Politics*, trans. T. A. Sinclair, rev. Trevor J. Saunders (London: Penguin, 1992), p. 73; subsequent citations in text by standard (Bekker) reference and page number.

15 Jack Lindsay, *Blast Power and Ballistics: Concepts of Force and Energy in the Ancient World* (London: Frederick Muller, 1974); subsequent references in text.

16 See Ryan Bishop and John Phillips, *Modernist Avant-Garde Aesthetics and Contemporary Military Technology: Technicities of Perception* (Edinburgh: Edinburgh University Press, 2010).

17 For a comparison with the ancient world on this score, see Schiavone, *The End of the Past*, ch. 9.

18 Charles B. Dew, *Ironmaker to the Confederacy: Joseph R. Anderson and the Tredegar Iron Works* (New Haven, CT: Yale University Press, 1966), esp. ch. 2. See also Stephen B. Hodin, 'The Mechanisms of Monticello: Saving Labor in Jefferson's America,' *Journal of the Early Republic* 26:3 (2006), 377–418; Norris W. Preyer, 'Why Did Industrialization Lag in the Old South?' *Georgia Historical Quarterly* 55:3 (1971), 378–96; Rodney D. Green, 'Black Tobacco Factory Workers and Social Conflict in Antebellum Richmond: Were Slavery and Urban Industry Really Compatible?' *Slavery & Abolition* 8:2 (1987), 183–203. Other historians have rejected the thesis that slavery and industry were incompatible, seeing issues such as the relative profitability of agriculture as the real inhibitors; see, e.g., R. Keith Aufhauser, 'Slavery and Technological Change', *Journal of Economic History* 34: 1 (1974), 36–50 (cf. response by Heywood Fleisig in same issue, 79–83); Carl N. Degler, *Place over Time: The Continuity of Southern Distinctiveness* (Athens: University of Georgia Press, 1997), esp. pp. 52–54.

19 Gavin Wright, *Slavery and American Economic Development* (Baton Rouge: Louisiana State University Press, 2006), p. 121.

20 John Ashworth, *Slavery, Capitalism and Politics in the Antebellum Republic*, vol. 1: *Commerce and Compromise, 1820–1850* (Cambridge: Cambridge University Press, 1995), pp. 99–101.

21 Elizabeth Fox-Genovese and Eugene D. Genovese, *The Mind of the Master Class: History and Faith in the Southern Slaveholders' Worldview* (New York: Cambridge University Press, 2005), p. 285.

22 On one strand of progressivism within slavery, see John Patrick Daly, *When Slavery Was Called Freedom: Evangelicalism, Proslavery, and the Causes of the Civil War* (Lexington: University Press of Kentucky, 2002).

23 See, e.g., Arnold Whitridge, 'Eli Whitney: Nemesis of the South', *American Heritage* 6:3 (1955), 4–11. It has often been believed that Whitney's saw gin (for separating cotton fibre and seeds) perpetuated slavery by replacing a primitive 'finger ginning' associated with Africa, giving new strength to a (supposedly) dying Southern economy. This is a myth: as Angela Lakwete demonstrates, a variety of roller gins predated Whitney's invention; see her *Inventing the Cotton Gin: Machine and Myth in Antebellum America* (Baltimore: Johns Hopkins University Press, 2003), pp. chs. 7–8.

24 See Richard Follett, *The Sugar Masters: Planters and Slaves in Louisiana's Cane World, 1820–1860* (Baton Rouge: Louisiana State University Press, 2005), pp. 102–16. Cf. Mark M. Smith, 'Time, Slavery and Plantation Capitalism in the Ante-Bellum American South', *Past & Present* 150 (1996), 142–68.

25 Follet, *The Sugar Masters*, p. 122.

26 Eugene D. Genovese, *Roll, Jordan, Roll: The World the Slaves Made* (1974; New York, Vintage, 1976), p. 390. For examples see Judith Carney, 'Landscapes of Technology Transfer: Rice Cultivation and African Continuities', and Portia James, 'Invention and Innovation, 1619–1930', in *Technology and the African-American Experience*, ed. Bruce Sinclair (Cambridge, MA: MIT Press, 2004), pp. 19–48, 49–70, respectively.

27 Genovese, *Roll, Jordan, Roll*, p. 295.

28 Nicholas K. Bromell, *By the Sweat of the Brow: Literature and Labour in Antebellum America* (Chicago: University of Chicago Press, 1993), p. 181.

29 George Fitzhugh, *Sociology for the South* (1854), rpt. as vol. 1 of *The Early Sociology of Race and Ethnicity*, ed. Kenneth Thompson (London: Routledge, 2005), p. 151.

30 David Brion Davis, *The Problem of Slavery in Western Culture* (1966; Oxford: Oxford University Press, 1988), p. 70.

31 Georges Canguilhem, 'Machine and Organism', *Incorporations* [*Zone* 6], ed. Jonathan Crary and Stanford Kwinter (New York: Urzone, 1992), pp. 44–69 (50).

32 Horst O. Hardenberg, *The Middle Ages of the Internal-Combustion Engine, 1794–1886* (Warrendale, PA: Society of Automotive Engineers, 1999), p. 17. Earlier engines were proposed using gunpowder.

33 John Dumbell, *The Commercial Aqueduct* (London: The Author, 1799), pp. 18–22.

34 There is also an implicit argument here for industrial investment generally, since the period from 1790 to the abolition of the British slave trade in 1807 was associated with exceptionally high profits for the plantations – money which did not easily make its way to industry. See Robin Blackburn, *The Making of New World Slavery: From the Baroque to the Modern, 1492–1800* (London: Verso, 1997), pp. 543–54.

35 Edward Everett, *Orations and Speeches on Various Occasions*, 6th ed. (1860), 2: 244–45, cited in David Brion Davis, *Slavery and Human Progress* (New York: Oxford University Press, 1984), pp. 232–33.

36 Jay Mandle, *Not Slave, Not Free* (Durham, NC: Duke University Press, 1992), 51–52, 90–92; Richard Godden, *Fictions of Labor: William Faulkner and the South's Long Revolution* (Cambridge: Cambridge University Press, 1997), p. 121.

37 Clarence Cason, *90° in the Shade*, intro. Wayne Flint (1935; University: University of Alabama Press, 1983), ch. 8.

38 See e.g. Gillian Brown, *Domestic Individualism: Imagining Self in Nineteenth-Century America* (Berkeley: University of California Press, 1990), ch. 1.

39 This is an area in which work has been sparse, but a useful bibliography is provided in Sinclair ed., *Technology and the African-American Experience*.

40 Ron Eglash, 'Broken Metaphor: The Master–Slave Analogy in Technical Literature', *Technology and Culture* 48:2 (2007), 360–69.

41 See Louis R. Harlan, *Booker T. Washington: The Wizard of Tuskegee, 1901–1915* (New York: Oxford University Press,1983), pp. 227–29.

42 Booker T. Washington, *Working with the Hands* (New York: Doubleday, 1904; London: Alexander Moring, n.d.), pp. 16–17; subsequently cited in the text as *WH*.

43 Extracts from an Address Delivered at Fisk University, 1895, *Selected Speeches of Booker T. Washington*, ed. E. Davidson Washington (Garden City, NY: Doubleday, Doran, 1932), p. 40.

44 Booker T. Washington, *Up from Slavery: An Autobiography* (1901; Oxford: Oxford University Press, 1945); subsequently cited in text as *US*.

45 On 'dovetailing' and resistance to it, see Louis R. Harlan, *Booker T. Washington: The Making of a Black Leader, 1856–1901* (New York: Oxford University Press, 1972), pp. 149–52; Harlan, *The Wizard of Tuskegee, 1901–1915* (New York: Oxford University Press, 1983), pp. 226–27.

46 Booker T. Washington, *My Larger Education* (Garden City, NY: Doubleday, Page, 1911), p. 9.

47 Booker T. Washington, 'Industrial Education for the Negro', in *The Negro Problem: A Series of Articles by Representative American Negroes of Today* (New York: James Pott, 1903), pp. 7–31 (pp. 18–19 cited).

48 Washington, *My Larger Education*, p. 285.

49 Charles Chesnutt, 'On the Future of the People' (1900), *Essays and Speeches of Charles Chesnutt*, ed. Joseph McElrath, Jr., Robert C. Leitz, and Jesse S. Crisler (Stanford, CA: Stanford University Press, 1999), p. 117.

50 See, e.g., Du Bois's 'The Training of Negroes for Social Power' (1903), in *The Oxford W. E. B. Du Bois Reader*, ed. Eric J. Sundquist (New York: Oxford University Press, 1996), pp. 354–62.

51 Booker T. Washington, *Up From Slavery*, intro. Ishmael Reed (New York: Signet, 2000), xviii. Amiri Baraka has adopted similar positions in relation to the 'careerist Negro'.

52 'Careers Open to College-Bred Negroes', *W. E. B. Du Bois Speaks: Speeches and Addresses, 1890–1919*, ed. Philip S. Foner (New York: Pathfinder, 1970), p. 109.

53 Ibid., p. 167. The conclusion was reiterated in the Atlanta University study *The Negro Artisan* (1912); in Du Bois's review of W. W. Crossland's *Industrial Conditions among Negros in St. Louis* in *Crisis* 9 (1914), 45; and elsewhere.

54 Cited in Robert S. Starobin, *Industrial Slavery in the Old South* (New York: Oxford University Press, 1970), p. 179.

55 *Congressional Record*, 53:6 (64th Congress, 1st session, 1916), p. 5571.

56 Karl Marx, *Capital*, vol. 1, intro. Ernest Mandel, trans. Ben Fowkes (Harmondsworth: Penguin, 1976), pp. 303–304.

57 W. E. B. Du Bois, 'Industrial Education – Will It Solve the Negro Problem?' *Colored American Magazine*, 7 (May 1904); rpt. in *A Hammer in Their Hands: A Documentary History of Technology and the African-American Experience*, ed. Carroll Pursell (Cambridge, MA: MIT Press, 2005), p. 125.

58 W. E. B. Du Bois, 'The Superior Race', *The Oxford W. E. B. Du Bois Reader*, p. 65.

59 W. E. B. Du Bois, *The Gift of Black Folk: The Negroes in the Making of America* (Boston: Stratford, 1924), pp. 53–54, 70.

60 See Nina Lerman, 'New South, New North: Region, Ideology and Access in Industrial Education', in *Technology and the African-American Experience*, ed. Sinclair, p. 99.

61 W. E. B. Du Bois, *Darkwater: Voices from Within the Veil* (1920; Mineola, NY: Dover, 1999), pp. 63–92 (p. 70 cited); subsequent references in text.

62 Alan Hyde, *Bodies of Law* (Princeton, NJ: Princeton University Press, 1997), chs. 1, 2.

63 Ralph Ellison, *Invisible Man* (1952; London: Penguin, 1987), p. 177; subsequent references in text.

64 Edward Kempf, *Psychopathology* (St. Louis: C. V. Mosby, 1921), pp. 423–35.

65 David Nye, *Electrifying America: Social Meanings of a New Technology, 1880–1940* (Cambridge, MA: MIT Press, 1990), p. 271; Mary King Sherman, 'Housewives Must Come Up from Slavery', National Electric Light Association, *Proceedings of the Forthy-Ninth Convention*, 1926.

66 Stuart Chase, *Men and Machines* (London: Jonathan Cape, 1929), pp. 12–13.

67 Silas Bent, *Machine Made Man* (New York: Farrar & Rinehart, 1930); Bent, *Slaves by the Billion: The Story of Mechanical Progress in the Home*, intro. Katherine Fisher (New York: Longman, Green, 1938). Subsequently cited in text as *MMM* and *SB*, respectively.

68 The history here is muddled, but most commentators suggest that Watt and Boulton made an honest estimate using a pony then scaled upwards for a horse, with an added margin of (commercial) error to ensure that their machines reliably out-performed any horses they replaced.

69 This is somewhat aside from – but obviously has some links to – the metaphorical relations between man and mule which exist in and around black culture.

70 Peter Garnsey, *Ideas of Slavery from Aristotle to Augustine* (Cambridge: Cambridge University Press, 1996), p. 111.

71 Harriet Ritvo, *The Animal Estate: The English and Other Creatures in the Victorian Age* (Cambridge, MA: Harvard University Press, 1987), p. 20.

72 See Peter Stoneley, 'Sentimental Emasculations: *Uncle Tom's Cabin* and *Black Beauty*', *Nineteenth-Century Literature*, 54:1 (1999), 53–72.

73 Thomas Carlyle, 'The Present Time', *Latter-Day Pamphlets, Collected Works of Thomas Carlyle*, vol. 13 (London: Chapman & Hall, 1858), p. 48.

74 David M. Levy, *How the Dismal Science Got Its Name: Classical Economics and the Ur-Text of Racial Politics* (Ann Arbor: University of Michigan Press, 2001), p. 97.

75 See Philip D. Morgan, 'Work and Culture: The Task System and the World of Low Country Blacks, 1700 to 1880', *William & Mary Quarterley*, 3d ser., 39:4 (1982), 563–99.

76 He made a parallel claim in a follow-up book, *De la marine antique à la marine moderne. La révolution du gouvernail, contribution à l'histoire de l'esclavage* (1935), that modern shipping developed only after slavery.

77 R. F. Lefebvre de Noëttes, *La force motrice animale à travers les âges* (Paris, 1924); rpt. as *L'attelege. Le cheval de selle à travers les âges*, 2 vols. (Paris: Picard, 1931), pp. 185–86 cited.

78 Noëttes is rebutted in J. Spruyette, *Early Harness Systems*, trans. Mary Littauer (London: J. A. Allen, 1983). His findings were reproduced in books such as V. G. Childe's *What Happened in History* (London: Penguin, 1942).

79 Carroll Roop Daughterty, 'The Development of Horse-Power Equipment in the United States', PhD dissertation, University of Pennsylvania, 1927; rpt. as Water-Supply Paper 579, U.S. Geological Survey, Washington, DC, pp. 30–33.

80 The main exception was coal mining: UK pit ponies peaked at 70,000 in 1913, and a large number remained in harness into the 1950s.

81 Daniel Bell, 'Veblen and the Technocrats: On *The Engineers and the Price System*,' in his *The Winding Passage: Sociological Essays and Journeys* (New Brunswick, NJ: Transaction, 1991), pp. 69–90.

82 See Henry Elsner, *The Technocrats: Prophets of Automation* (Syracuse, NY: Syracuse University Press, 1967); Edwin T. Layton, *The Revolt of the Engineers: Social Responsibility and the American Engineering Profession* (Cleveland: Case-Western University Press, 1971); Peter J. Kuznick, *Beyond the Laboratory: Scientists as Political Activists in 1930s America* (Chicago: University of Chicago Press, 1987); William E. Akin, *Technocracy and the American Dream: The Technocrat Movement, 1900–1941* (Berkeley: University of California Press, 1977).

83 Howard Smith et al., *Introduction to Technocracy* (New York: John Day, 1933), pp. 20–21; subsequent references cited in text. This section of the volume is attributed to Frederick Ackerman.

84 'Why Technocracy?' Information Brief No. 28, 1955 (available at Technocracy website, http://www.technocracy.org).

85 Ibid.

86 Peter Sloterdijk, 'What Happened to the Twentieth Century?', *Cultural Politics*, Peter Sloterdijk Special Issue, 3:3 (2007), 327–56 (342 cited); subsequent references in text.

87 See, e.g., Daniel M. Fox, *The Discovery of Abundance: Simon N. Patten and the Transformation of Social Theory* (Ithaca, NY: University of Cornell Press,

1967); Lawrence Birkin, *Consuming Desire: Sexual Science and the Emergence of a Culture of Abundance, 1871–1914* (Ithaca, NY: Cornell University Press, 1988); William Leach, *Land of Desire: Merchants, Power, and the Rise of a New American Culture* (New York: Vintage, 1994).

88 Andrew Ross, *Strange Weather: Culture, Science and Technology in the Age of Limits* (London: Verso, 1991), p. 120.

89 Hannah Arendt, *The Human Condition*, 2d ed. (Chicago: University of Chicago Press, 1999), p. 122; subsequent references in text.

90 This distinction is critiqued by Derrida in *Given Time I: Counterfeit Money*, trans. Peggy Kamuf (Chicago: University of Chicago Press, 1992).

91 Timothy Clark, 'Deconstruction and Technology', in *Deconstructions: A User's Guide*, ed. Nicholas Royle (Basingstoke: Palgrave, 2000), pp. 239–40. Clark borrows the term from Richard Beardsworth.

NOTES TO CHAPTER 4

1 Kirk Savage, *Standing Soldiers, Kneeling Slaves: Race, War and Monument in Nineteenth-Century America* (Princeton, NJ: Princeton University Press, 1997), p. 28.

2 See, e.g., Jean Fagin Yellin, *Women and Sisters: The Antislavery Feminists in American Culture* (New Haven, CT: Yale University Press, 1989); Joy Kasson, *Marble Queens and Captives: Women in Nineteenth-Century American Sculpture* (New Haven, CT: Yale University Press, 1990); T. Walter Herbert, 'The Erotics of Purity: The Marble Faun and the Victorian Construction of Sexuality', *Representations* 36 (1991), 114–32; Wendy Jean Katz, *Regionalism and Reform: Art and Class Formation in Antebellum Cincinnati* (Colombia: Ohio State University Press, 2002), ch. 4.

3 Elizabeth Barrett Browning, 'Hiram Powers' Greek Slave', *Selected Poems*, ed. Margaret Forster (Baltimore: Johns Hopkins University Press, 1988), p. 211.

4 Nathaniel Hawthorne, *The French and Italian Notebooks*, ed. Thomas Woodson (Columbus: Ohio State University Press, 1980), p. 492. The speaker is Joseph Mozier.

5 On the creation of series and commercial versions of sculpture, see Jean L. Wasserman, ed., *Metamorphoses in Nineteenth-Century Sculpture* (Cambridge, MA: Fogg Art Museum / Harvard University Press, 1975); the examples used are mainly French. On the general issues, see also *Sculpture and Its Reproductions*, ed. Anthony Hughes and Erich Ranfft (London: Reaktion, 1997).

6 Unpublished letter, 7 August 1853, cited in Donald M. Reynolds, 'The "Unveiled Soul": Hiram Powers's Embodiment of the Ideal', *Art Bulletin* 59:3 (1977), 394–414 (394 cited).

7 Charlotte A. [Waldie] Eaton, *Rome in the Nineteenth Century*, 5th ed. (London: Bohn, 1852), 2: 302.

8 Reynolds, 'The "Unveiled Soul"', 403.

9 *Aristotle's Theory of Poetry and Fine Art*, trans. and with critical notes by S. H. Butcher (1894; New York: Dover, 1951), p. 206.

10 'Life of Pericles', *Plutarch's Lives*, trans. John Dryden, rev. Arthur Hugh Clough (London: J. M. Dent, 1910), pp. 226–27.

11 Aristotle, *The Politics*, trans. T. A. Sinclair, rev. Trevor J. Saunders (London: Penguin, 1992), 1341a5, p. 469; subsequent citations in text by standard reference (Bekker) and page number. For a summary of other sources, see Aldo Schiavone, *The End of the Past: Ancient Rome and the Modern West* (Cambridge, MA: Harvard University Press, 2000), pp. 136–42.

12 Hannah Arendt, *The Human Condition*, 2d ed. (Chicago: University of Chicago Press, 1999), p. 82 n7.

13 'Statuary', *North American Review* 32:70 (January 1831), 5.

14 Aristotle, *Metaphysics*, bk. 7, pt, 3, in *The Basic Works of Aristotle*, ed. Richard McKeon (New York: Random House, 1941), p. 785.

15 William James, *The Principles of Psychology* (1890; New York: Dover, 1950), pp. 288–89.

16 Arendt, *The Human Condition*, p. 161.

17 Immanuel Kant, *The Critique of Judgement*, in *Continental Aesthetics: Romanticism to Postmodernism – An Anthology*, ed. Richard Kearney and David Rasmussen (Oxford: Blackwell, 2001), §§ 43, 47, pp. 33, 36.

18 See Benedict B. Read, *Victorian Sculpture* (New Haven, CT: Paul Mellon Center, 1982), pp. 52–65. See also Fouad Sayed Mahmoud El-Sewaify, 'Preparation and Finish in Nineteenth Century European Sculpture', PhD dissertation, University of Reading, 1981.

19 See Umberto Baldini, *The Complete Sculpture of Michelangelo* (London: Thames & Hudson, 1982), pp. 11–14. In this context the recent suggestion that the Laocoön may have been faked by Michelangelo himself is intriguing, to say the least.

20 Hawthorne, *The French and Italian Notebooks*, p. 74.

21 'Various Items', citing a 'Mr Weed', *Pittsfield Sun* 52:2690 (April 1852), 3. Other accounts suggest Powers took a more active role.

22 Marjorie Trusted, *The Return of the Gods: Neoclassical Sculpture in Britain* (London: Tate, 2008), p. 7.

23 Cited in Joseph Voght, *Ancient Slavery and the Idea of Man*, trans. Thomas Wiedemann (Oxford: Basil Blackwell, 1974), p. 171. On his opposition to modern slavery, however, see his *Essai politique sur l'île de Cuba* (Paris, 1826), ch. 7 (the chapter was removed in the English translation) and the useful overview (including unpublished material from letters) in Hartmut Keil's paper 'Race and Ethnicity: Slavery and the German Radical Tradition', http://mki.wisc.edu/Resources/Online_Papers/keil.html.

24 Page duBois, *Slaves and Other Objects* (Chicago: University of Chicago Press, 2008), p. 21.

25 Frances E. Willard, 'How Statues Are Made', *Young Folks*, 16 December 1882.

26 G. H. Calvert, 'The Process of Sculpture', *Literary World*, 18 September 1847, http://utc.iath.virginia.edu/sentimnt/snar22at.html.

27 Kasson, *Marble Queens*, p. 10.

28 *Glasgow Herald*, 29 December 1882.

29 The original article was written by a barrister employed by *Vanity Fair*, 20 August 1881, working from a deposition by Lawes. Lawes then wrote to the Lord Mayor of London, who was considering Belt for a public commission, drawing his attention to the piece.

30 Joseph Dean, *Hatred, Ridicule or Contempt: A Book of Libel Cases* (London: Constable, 1953), pp. 235–59; subsequently cited in text as *H*. See also Montague Williams, *Leaves of a Life* (London: Macmillan, 1890), 2: 220–33; and *Times* law reports 22 June 1882 to 18 March 1884.

31 *Times*, 29 December 1882, 7.

32 Supplement to *Society*, 24 February 1883; *Vanity Fair*, 12 May 1883.

33 *Times*, 24 June 1884, 6; partially cited in Dean, *Hatred*, p. 242.

34 Brock was a sculptor in his own right.

35 See UK Public Monument and Sculpture Association National Recording Project, http://pmsa.cch.kcl.ac.uk/CL/CLCOL215.htm.

36 See, e.g., Dalya Alberge, 'Damien Hirst Faces Eight New Claims of Plagiarism', *Guardian*, 3 September 2010, 13, among many other articles.

37 James Jackson Jarves, *Art Thoughts: The Experiences and Observations of an American Amateur in Europe* (Cambridge, MA: Riverside, 1869), pp. 3–4.

38 'Mr Storey and His Critics', *Western Mail*, 18 April 1874.

39 William Wetmore Storey, *Conversations in a Studio*, 2. vols. (Edinburgh: Blackwood, 1890), 1: 161.

40 Cited in Charmian A. Nelson, *The Color of Stone: Sculpting the Black Female Subject in Nineteenth-Century America* (Minneapolis: University of Minnesota Press, 2007), p. 43. As Nelson points out, there may have been reasons for Lewis's difficulty with sitters, given her origins. On originality, one could compare Thomas Jefferson's comment about Wheatley in *Notes on the State of Virginia* and many suggestions that slave narratives were written by white sponsors.

41 Nelson, *The Color of Stone*, p. 39. Storey reported in the *Athenaeum* watching her make the statue.

42 Hannah F. Lee, *Familiar Sketches of Sculpture and Sculptors* (Boston: Crosby, Nichols, 1854), 2: 222 (citing 'A New Star in the Arts' from the *Tribune*).

43 Harriet Hosmer, 'The Process of Sculpture', *Atlantic Monthly* 14: 86 (1864), 734–47; subsequent citations in text. For context see Nelson, *The Color of Stone*.

44 Reynolds, 'The "Unveiled Soul"', 409.

45 Powers to Sidney Brooks, 5 August 1852; cited in Reynolds, 'The "Unveiled Soul"', 407; emphasis added.

46 Hawthorne, *The French and Italian Notebooks*, p. 314.

47 Simon Richter, *Laocoon's Body and the Aesthetics of Pain: Winckelmann, Lessing, Herder, Moritz, Goethe* (Detroit: Wayne State University Press, 1992), pp. 11, 129–30.

48 Richter, *Laocoon's Body*, pp. 33, 94.

49 Elaine Scarry, *The Body in Pain: The Making and Unmaking of the World* (New York: Oxford University Press, 1985), p. 170.

50 Arendt, *The Human Condition*, p. 129.

51 Ibid., p. 130.

52 *The Collected Works of Phillis Wheatley*, ed. John C. Shields (New York: Oxford University Press, 1988), pp. 101–13. Shields questions the suggestion that she may have seen Wilson's Niobe paintings in England in 1773 and argues that it is more likely she knew them from engravings.

53 Jennifer Thorn, "'All Beautiful in Woe': Gender, Nation, and Phillis Wheatley's "Niobe"', *Studies in Eighteenth Century Culture* 37 (2008), 233–58 (245 cited).

54 'Phillis's Reply to the Answer', in Wheatley, *Collected Works*, p. 144.

55 The Sandys and Garth texts are most easily compared at the University of Virginia Ovid collection, http://etext.lib.virginia.edu/latin/ovid/index.html.

56 Thorn, "'All Beautiful in Woe"', 251.

57 Joan R. Sherman, ed., *African-American Poetry of the Nineteenth Century* (Champaign: University of Illinois Press, 1992), p. 115.

58 See Saidya V. Hartman, *Scenes of Subjection: Terror, Slavery and Self-Making in Nineteenth-Century America* (New York: Oxford University Press, 1997).

59 Sue V. Beeson, 'The Gospel of Pain', *Journal of Speculative Philosophy* 16:4 (1882), 426–30 (430 cited). The contents page lists the title as 'Domenichino's St. Jerome, or the Gospel of Pain'.

60 'Winckelmann's Remarks on the Laökoön', trans. E. S. Morgan, *Journal of Speculative Philosophy* 2:4 (1869), 215. In contrast, Thomas Davidson writes on the Niobe Group, following one of the classical sources in suggesting that Zeus turned Niobe to stone out of pity – though that, as have seen, is an interpretation which denies her agency in grief. Thomas Davidson, 'The Niobe Group', *Journal of Speculative Philosophy* 9:2 (1875), 142–71.

61 On the work generally see Marilyn Richardson, 'Edmonia Lewis's "The Death of Cleopatra"', *International Review of African American Art*, 12:2 (1995), 36–52; Rinna Evelyn Wolfe, *Edmonia Lewis: Wildfire in Marble* (Parsippany, NJ: Dillon Press, 1998).

62 William J. Clark, *Great American Sculptors* (Philadelphia: Gebbie & Barrie, 1878), p. 141; cited in Romare Bearden and Harry Henderson, *A History of African-American Artists from 1792 to the Present* (New York: Pantheon, 1993), p. 74.

63 Harriet Beecher Stowe, 'Sojourner Truth, The Libyan Sibyl', *Atlantic Monthly* 11:66 (1863), 473–81. Charles Cumberworth's paired statues, based on *Paul et Virginie*, are in the Louvre.

64 For further discussion of this connection, see Yellin, *Women and Sisters*, pp. 81–87. Yellin suggests that both Storey and Powers's statues encode passivity, a reading which seems right in terms of iconography but which neglects their hypnotic power over viewers.

65 Sylvia E. Crane, *White Silence: Greenough, Powers, and Crawford, American Sculptors in Nineteenth-Century Italy* (Coral Gables, FL: University of Miami Press, 1972).

66 Freeman Henry Morris Murray, *Emancipation and the Freed in American Sculpture: A Study in Interpretation* (1916; Freeport, NY: Books for Libraries

Press, 1972), p. 2. Murray co-founded *Horizon*, the precursor to the *Crisis*, with Du Bois in 1907.

67 Nathaniel Hawthorne, *The Marble Faun, or, The Romance of Monte Beni*, in *Novels* (New York: Library of America, 1983), pp. 948–49; subsequent references in text.

68 James Jackson Jarves, *Art-Hints: Architecture, Sculpture and Painting* (New York: Harper, 1855), p. 167.

69 This is based on Hawthorne's own experiences of being present at the excavation of the St. Petersburg Venus; see *The French and Italian Notebooks*, pp. 516–18.

70 Winckelmann quoted in Hugh Honor, *Neo-Classicism* (1968; London: Penguin, 1991), p. 101.

71 Ibid., p. 107.

72 See Ellen Perry, *The Aesthetics of Emulation in the Visual Arts of Ancient Rome* (Cambridge: Cambridge University Press, 2005); Miranda Marvin, 'Roman Sculpture Reproductions or Polykleitos: The Sequence', in *Sculpture and Its Reproductions*, ed. Hughes and Ranfft, pp. 7–28.

73 Seymour Howard, *Antiquity Restored: Essays on the Afterlife of the Antique* (Vienna: IRSA, 1990), p. 25.

74 Robin Blackburn, *The Making of New World Slavery: From the Baroque to the Modern, 1492–1800* (London: Verso, 1997), p. 551; John Lord, *Capital and Steam Power, 1750–1800* (London: King, 1923), p. 113.

75 James Patrick Muirhead, *The Life of James Watt* (London: John Murray, 1858), pp. 268–78. See also H. W. Dickinson, *James Watt: Craftsman & Engineer* (Cambridge: Babock & Wilcox, 1835).

76 For example, Cheverton, Sauvage, Collas, and Meynier: on the last three see Jacques de Caso, 'Serial Sculpture in Nineteenth-Century France', *Metamorphoses*, ed. Wasserman, pp. 1–28.

77 Henry Howe, *Memoirs of the Most Eminent American Mechanics* (New York: Alexander V. Blake, 1844), p. 457.

78 Ibid., p. 457.

79 Rebecca Harding Davis, *Life in the Iron Mills*, ed. Cecelia Tichi (1861; Boston: Bedford / St. Martin's, 1998), p. 52; subsequent references in text.

80 The sculptor usually associated with the unfinished roughness of the korl statue is William Rimmer, who produced figures in this style in the period. Later the unfinished, handcrafted style became, in the shadow of Rodin, the basis of a 'craft modernism' – for example, in the work of the Paris-based American Paul Bartlett, who severed his links with his French foundry in 1892 and began to cast his own small figures influenced by the craft style of Palissy pottery and Japanese glazing techniques. Thomas P. Soma, 'Sculpture vs. Craft: Two French Torsos by Paul Waylaw Bartlett', in *Perspectives on American Sculpture before 1925*, ed. Thayer Tolles (New York: Metropolitan Museum of Art, 2003), pp. 82–93.

81 A partial exception is Maribel W. Molyneaux, 'Sculpture in the Iron Mills: Rebecca Harding Davis's Korl Woman', *Women's Studies* 17 (1990), 157–77.

On the body see Mark Seltzer, *Bodies and Machines* (New York: Routledge, 1992); on class see, e.g., Jean Pfaelzer, 'Rebecca Harding Davis: Domesticity, Social Order, and the Industrial Novel', *International Journal of Women's Studies* 4 (1981), 234–44, and (with a very useful analysis of 'wage slavery') Amy Schrager Lang, *The Syntax of Class: Writing Inequality in Nineteenth-Century America* (Ann Arbor: University of Michigan Press, 2006), ch. 3.

82 Savage, *Standing Soldiers, Kneeling Slaves*, p. 8.

83 See, e.g., the reproduction of Powers's *Greek Slave* as exemplary of the female form in C. W. Gleason, *Seven Lectures on the Philosophy of Life, and the Art of Preserving Health* (Columbus, OH: Scott & Bascom, 1852), p. 137.

84 See Michael Anton Budd, *The Sculpture Machine: Physical Culture and Body Politics in the Age of Empire* (Basingstoke: Macmillan, 1997); on bodybuilding and whiteness see Richard Dyer, *White* (London: Routledge, 1997), ch. 4.

85 David Chapman, *Sandow the Magnificent: Eugen Sandow and the Beginnings of Bodybuilding* (Champaign: University of Illinois Press, 1994), pp. 132–33.

86 'The Superior Race' (1923), in *The Oxford W. E. B. Du Bois Reader*, ed. Eric J. Sundquist (New York: Oxford University Press, 1996), p. 61. The famous photographs of the naked Paul Robeson in classical poses are also surely a response to this tradition.

87 Savage, *Standing Soldiers*, p. 11.

88 Sherman, ed., *African-American Poetry*, p. 147.

89 See David Batchelor, *Chromophobia* (London: Reaktion, 2000).

90 'Sculpture', *New England Magazine* 5:6 (December 1833), 481.

91 See the 'Colour' issue of *Sculpture Review* 52:3 (2003), esp. E. Adina Gordon, 'Color in Sculpture: Scandal and Revival', 34–39.

92 The aesthetic consequences of this tension between an ideal totality and the fragment have been examined by Alex Potts, who argues that in Winckelmann's thought there is an inherent conflict between the aesthetics of self-enclosed totality and power, struggle, and incompletion:

> There is, then, an unacknowledged splitting in the ideal subjectivity embodied in the Greek ideal as Winckelmann projects it. On one hand he gives us the images of a youthful narcissistic self, existing in a state of undisturbed self-absorption and sensual plenitude, in effect isolated from any confrontation with the external world. On the other he portrays an active manly self, heroic or divinely powerful, existing in violent confrontation with or domination over what surrounds it, engaging in actions which theoretically speaking can only disturb its beauty.

> Potts sees this as an expression of Greek culture in general; but it also provides a map of the Aristotelian understanding of slavery in terms of natural superiority, and in terms of the exercise of power (tyranny) and the need to direct, delegate, and employ instruments. See Alex Potts, *Flesh and the Idea: Winckelmann and the Origins of Art History* (New Haven, CT: Yale University Press, 1994), pp. 171–79 (173 cited).

93 Richard Spuler, *'Germanistik' in America: The Reception of German Classicism, 1870–1905* (Stuttgart: Heinz, 1982), p. 44.

94 See Elizabeth Fox-Genovese and Eugene D. Genovese, *The Mind of the Master Class: History and Faith in the Southern Slaveholders' Worldview* (New York: Cambridge University Press, 2005), ch. 8.

95 Shamoon Zamir, *Dark Voices: W. E. B. Du Bois and American Thought, 1888–1903* (Chicago, University of Chicago Press, 1995), pp. 119–25.

96 See James A. Good, 'A "World-Historical Idea": The St. Louis Hegelians and the Civil War', *Journal of American Studies* 34 (2000), 447–64; Dorothy G. Rogers, *American's First Women Philosophers: Transplanting Hegel, 1860–1925* (New York: Continuum, 2005), p. 18. On the group generally, see William H. Goetzmann, ed., *The American Hegelians: An Intellectual Episode in the History of Western America* (New York: Alfred A. Knopf, 1973).

97 William T. Harris, *Hegel's Logic: A Book on the Genesis of the Categories of the Mind* (Chicago: S. C. Griggs, 1890), pp. 87–89; Joshia Royce, *The Spirit of Modern Philosophy* (Boston: Houghton & Mifflin, 1892).

98 James A. Good, 'The Value of Thomas Davidson', *Transactions of the Charles S. Peirce Society*, 40:2 (2004), 289–318.

99 William James, in *Memorials of Thomas Davidson*, ed. William Knight (Boston: Ginn, 1907), p. 109.

100 Thomas Davidson, *The Evolution of Sculpture*, Evolution Series 13, Lectures and Discussions before the Brooklyn Ethical Association (New York: D. Appleton, 1891), pp. 343–59 (p. 353 cited).

101 Thomas Davidson, *The Parthenon Frieze and Other Essays* (London: Kegan Paul, Trench, 1882), p. 127.

102 'Winckelmann's Description of the Torso of the Hercules of Belvedere in Rome', trans. Thomas Davidson, *Journal of Speculative Philosophy*, 2:3 (1868), 187–89 (188 cited).

103 Robert Visher's influential *On the Optical Sense of Form: A Contribution to Aesthetics* (1873), for example, dwells on the way in which the body-ego projects itself into and inhabits external objects as a part of an empathetic aesthetic response. It contains the following reflection on the 'vital foundation' which may conjure a whole from a fragment:

> The lax relationship of the parts must be made more stringent; the independence of this undisciplined and incomplete existence must be forced back into a bodily centre; everything superfluous that swirls out beyond the natural limits must be tempered and eradicated. There is a 'quiet pathos of being', a silent mysticism of the simple, breathing body and life that can lead the true artist to the highest ecstasy. One need only consider the studies of Raphael or Dürer; many of them speak simply through this organic purity and through its astonishing effect (the torso of Hercules, the charm of a fragmentary limb, an arm or leg).

> *Empathy, Form, and Space: Problems in German Aesthetics, 1873–1893*, intro. and trans. Harry Francis Mallgrave and Eleftherios Ikonomou (Santa Monica, CA: Getty Centre, 1994), p. 119.

104 Javes, *Art Thoughts*, p. 309.

105 Charles Taylor, *Hegel* (Cambridge: Cambridge University Press, 1975), p. 156.

106 Hermann Grimm, 'The Venus of Milo,' trans. A. S. Millard, *Journal of Speculative Philosophy* 5:1 (1871), 78–83 (82 cited).

107 Herman Grimm, 'Raphael and Michael Angelo', trans. Ida M. Eliot, *Journal of Speculative Philosophy* 13:3 (1879), 289–309 (298–99, 308 cited).

108 Adolf Hildebrand, 'The Problem of Form in the Fine Arts' (1893), in *Empathy, Form and Space*, pp. 227–79; subsequent citations in text.

109 *The Crayon: A Journal Devoted to the Graphic Arts* 1:9 (28 February 1855), 149.

110 Bruno Latour, 'On Technical Mediation – Philosophy, Sociology, Genealogy', *Common Knowledge* 3:2 (1994), 29–64 (64 cited).

NOTES TO CHAPTER 5

1 See Yuval Taylor and Hugh Barker, *Faking It: The Quest for Authenticity in Popular Music* (New York: Norton, 2007); Marybeth Hamilton, *In Search of the Blues: Black Voices, White Visions* (London: Cape, 2007); Benjamin Filene, *Romancing the Folk: Public Memory & American Roots Music* (Chapel Hill: University of North Carolina Press, 2000).

2 In this respect, the chapter offers a complement to Marcus Wood's account of pain in visual images in *Blind Memory: Visual Representations of Slavery in England and America, 1780–1865* (Manchester: Manchester University Press, 2000), ch. 5.

3 Charles Babbage, *Ninth Bridgewater Treatise: A Fragment*, 2d ed. (London: John Murray, 1838), p. 114; subsequent references in text. The reference to the slave ship did not appear in the first edition.

4 Recent work on Schopenhauer and music includes Mark Asquith, *Thomas Hardy, Metaphysics and Music* (London: Palgrave, 2005); Dale Jacquette, ed., *Schopenhauer, Philosophy and the Arts* (Cambridge: Cambridge University Press, 1996); Andrew Bowie, *Music, Philosophy, and Modernity* (Cambridge: Cambridge University Press, 2007).

5 Wood, *Blind Memory*, pp. 306–307; Caryl Phillips, *The Atlantic Sound* (London: Faber & Faber, 2000).

6 Norman R. Yetman, ed., *Voices from Slavery: 100 Authentic Slave Narratives* (1970; Mineola, NY: Dover, 2000), pp. 167, 229 (see also p. 335). For other examples see W. B. Allen's narrative in *Remembering Slavery*, ed. Ira Berlin et al. (New York: New Press, 1996), p. 56; George Rawick, *From Sundown to Sunup: The Making of a Black Community* (Westport, CT: Greenwood Press, 1972), p. 37; Dena J. Epstein, *Sinful Tunes and Spirituals: Black Folk Music to the Civil War* (Urbana: University of Illinois Press, 1977), p. 237; Genovese, *Roll, Jordan, Roll: The World the Slaves Made* (New York: Random House, 1988), pp. 236–37.

7 Édith Lecourt, 'The Musical Envelope', in *Psychic Envelopes*, ed. Didier Anzieu, trans. Daphne Briggs (London: Karnak Books, 1990), pp. 211–35 (p. 213 cited).

8 Ibid., pp. 218, 225.

9 Eric J. Sundquist, *To Wake the Nations: Race in the Making of American Literature* (Cambridge, MA: Harvard University Press, 1993), 384.

10 James Weldon Johnson, *God's Trombones: Seven Negro Sermons in Verse* (1927; New York: Penguin, 1976), pp. 42–43.

11 Ibid., p. 11.

12 William Francis Allen, Lucy McKim Garrison, and Charles Pickard Ware, eds., *Slave Songs of the United States* (New York: A. Simpson, 1887), p. 24. Subsequent references in text.

13 *National Anti-Slavery Standard*, 28 (11 December 1867), cited in Epstein, *Sinful Tunes*, pp. 338–39.

14 James Monroe Trotter, *Music and Some Highly Musical People* (Boston: Lee & Shepard, 1878), p. 324. See also Robert Stevenson, 'America's First Black Music Historian,' *Journal of the American Musicological Society* 26:3 (1973), 383–404.

15 W. E. B. Du Bois, *The Souls of Black Folk*, ed. Henry Louis Gates, Jr., and Terri Hume Oliver (1903; New York: Norton, 1999), 155.

16 Sundquist, *To Wake the Nations*, ch. 5.

17 Address by J. Miller McKim, Philadelphia, 9 July 1862, in Allen et al., eds., *Slave Songs of the United States*, xviii.

18 J. B. I. Marsh, ed., *The Story of the Jubilee Singers with Their Songs* (London: Hodder & Stoughton, 1875), 85, 87.

19 Epstein, *Sinful Tunes*, p. 225.

20 Allen et al., eds., *Slave Songs of the United States*, p. 327.

21 Thomas Wentworth Higginson, 'Negro Spirituals', *Atlantic Monthly* (June 1867), 685–94.

22 Jon Cruz, *Culture on the Margins: The Black Spiritual and the Rise of American Cultural Interpretation* (Princeton, NJ: Princeton University Press, 1999), p. 5.

23 Paul Allen Anderson, *Deep River: Music and Memory in Harlem Renaissance Thought* (Durham, NC: Duke University Press, 2001), pp. 79–80.

24 Lawrence W. Levine, *Black Culture and Black Consciousness* (Oxford: Oxford University Press, 1977), pp. 165–69.

25 Frederick Douglass, *A Narrative of the Life of Frederick Douglass, an American Slave, Written by Himself*, ed. Robert B. Stepto (1845; Cambridge, MA: Belknap Press, 2009), pp. 25–26.

26 Frederick Douglass, *My Bondage and My Freedom*, ed. John Stauffer (1855; New York: Modern Library, 2003), p. 44.

27 Sundquist, *To Wake the Nations*, 92.

28 *Musical Gazette* 1 (July 1846); see Epstein, *Sinful Tunes*, pp. 219–28.

29 Genovese, *Roll, Jordan, Roll*, p. 249.

30 Du Bois, *The Souls of Black Folk*, pp. 154–55.

31 John Wesley Work, *Folk Song of the American Negro* (Nashville: Fisk University Press, 1915), pp. 39–42.

32 Work, *Folk Song*, p. 22.

33 Ronald Radano, 'Denoting Difference: The Writing of the Slave Spirituals', *Critical Inquiry* 22:3 (1996), 525–26.

34 Marion Alexander Haskell, 'Negro "Sprituals", *The Century: A Popular Quarterly*, 58:4 (August 1899), 576–81 (577, 579 cited).

35 Dorothy Scarborough, *On the Trail of Negro Folk-Songs* (Cambridge, CA: Harvard University Press, 1925), pp. 281–82.

36 See Tim Brooks, *Lost Sounds: Blacks and the Birth of the Recording Industry, 1890–1919* (Urbana: University of Illinois Press, 2004).

37 'Canning Negro Melodies', *Literary Digest* 52:22 (27 May 1916), 1556–59 (1556 cited) (unsigned), referring to a piece in the *Musical Courier*. Miller later wrote scores based on black songs.

38 Brooks, *Lost Sounds*, p. 425.

39 Cited in ibid., p. 169.

40 The latter, utopian view of racial dissolution in Du Bois is explored by Ross Posnock in *Color and Culture: Black Writers and the Making of the Modern Intellectual* (Cambridge, MA: Harvard University Press, 1998), ch. 4, esp. pp. 89–98.

41 James Weldon Johnson, *The Autobiography of an Ex-Colored Man*, ed. William L. Andrews (1912; New York: Penguin, 1990); subsequent references in text.

42 See Neil Leonard, 'Reactions to Ragtime', in *Ragtime: Its History, Composers and Music*, ed. John Edward Hasse (New York: Schirmer, 1985), pp. 102–13.

43 Walter Benn Michaels, '*Autobiography of an Ex-Colored Man*: Why Race is Not a Social Construct', *Transition* 73 (1997), 122–43.

44 James Weldon Johnson, ed., *The Book of American Negro Poetry* (New York: Harcourt, Brace, 1922), pp. 105–106.

45 Ibid., p. 40.

46 Charles Chesnutt, *Essays and Speeches of Charles Chesnutt*, ed. Joseph McElrath, Jr., Robert C. Leitz, and Jesse S. Crisler (Stanford, CA: Stanford University Press, 1999), p. 160.

47 Henry Louis Gates, *The Signifying Monkey: A Theory of African-American Literary Criticism* (New York: Oxford University Press, 1988), ch. 4. The Rabelais episode is *Gargantua and Pantagruel*, ch. 56.

48 Mark Twain, 'A True Story, Repeated Word for Word as I Heard It', *Atlantic Monthly* 34: 205 (November 1874), 591–94. Its status and sources are discussed by Shelley Fisher Fishkin, 'Race and the Politics of Memory: Mark Twain and Paul Laurence Dunbar', *Journal of American Studies* 40:2 (2006), 283–310.

49 Letter to W. D. Howells, 2 September 1874, *Mark Twain–Howells Letters: The Correspondence of Samuel L. Clements and William Dean Howells, 1872–1910*, 2 vols., ed. Henry Nash Smith and William M. Ginson (Cambridge, CA: Belknap Press, 1960), 1: 22. In a follow-up letter, he wrote to Howells, 'I amend dialect stuff by talking & *talking* it till it sounds right'.

50 The inevitable comparison is with Twain's reworking of 'Sociable Jimmy' as described by Shelly Fisher Fishkin in *Was Huck Black? Mark Twain and African-American Voices* (New York: Oxford University Press, 1994).

51 Anderson, *Deep River*, pp. 66–77.

52 Jean Toomer, *Cane*, ed. Darwin T. Turner (1923; New York: Norton, 1988), p. 14; subsequent references in text.

53 For an interpretation stressing Toomer's agon in the face of race, see Paul Stasi, 'A "Synchronous but More Subtle Migration": Passing and Primitivism in Toomer's *Cane*', *Twentieth-Century Literature* 55:2 (2009), 145–74.
54 *The Letters of Jean Toomer, 1919–1924*, ed. Mark Whalan (Knoxville: University of Tennessee Press, 2006), pp. 7–8.
55 Janet M. Whyde, 'Mediating Forms: Narrating the Body in Jean Toomer's *Cane*', *Southern Literary Journal*, 26:1 (1993), 42–53 (43 cited).
56 Charles Scruggs and Lee VanDemarr, *Jean Toomer and the Terrors of American History* (Philadelphia: University of Pennsylvania Press, 1998), p. 150. As they point out, 'Fern' seems to respond strongly to Waldo Frank's *Our America* in mapping Jewish and African-American experience.
57 George P. Rawick, ed., *The American Slave: A Composite Autobiography* (Westport, CT: Greenwood Press, 1972–79), vols. 18, 19; John B. Cade, 'Out of the Mouths of Ex-Slaves', *Journal of Negro History* 20 (1935), 294–337. For further context, see Bernard W. Bell, *The Contemporary African American Novel: Its Folk Roots and Modern Literary Branches* (Amherst: University of Massachusetts Press, 2004), xix–xx; and the foreword to Berlin et al., eds., *Remembering Slavery: African Americans Talk About Their Personal Experiences of Slavery and Emancipation* (New York: New Press, 1996).
58 Laura Doyle, *Bordering on the Body: The Racial Matrix of Modern Fiction and Culture* (New York: Oxford University Press, 1994), ch. 4.
59 Ralph Ellison, *Invisible Man* (1952; London: Penguin, 1987), p. 221.
60 One possible source of the trope is the 'Why I Am So Wise' section of Nietzsche's *Ecce Homo*, where he speaks of 'that psychology of "looking around the corner"' as an art of nuance and as part of a shift from a 'morbid' perspective to 'rich life' and a 'revaluation of all values'. *'On the Genealogy of Morals' and 'Ecce Homo'*, trans. Walter Kaufmann and R. J. Hollingdale (New York: Vintage, 1969), p. 223.
61 Ralph Ellison, *Shadow and Act* (New York: Vintage, 1964), p. 195. For a more complete discussion of Ellison and sonic reproduction, see Sam Halliday, *Sonic Modernism* (Edinburgh: Edinburgh University Press, forthcoming).
62 Jean Laplanche and J.-B. Pontalis, 'Fantasy and the Origins of Sexuality', *International Journal of Psychoanalysis* 49:1 (1968), 1–18 (11 cited). I was directed to this passage by David Musselwhite.
63 Reed Smith, ed., *South Carolina Ballads, with a Study of the Traditional Ballad To-day* (Cambridge, MA: Harvard University Press, 1928).
64 Arthur Palmer Hudson, ed., *Specimens of Mississippi Folk Lore*, published under the auspices of the Mississippi Folk-Lore Society (Ann Arbor, MI: Edwards Brothers, 1928), v.
65 Barre Toelken, 'Context and Meaning in the Anglo-American Ballad', in *The Ballad and the Scholars: Approaches to Ballad Study*, ed. D. K. Wilgus and Barre Toelken (Los Angeles: William Andrew Clark Memorial Library, 1986), pp. 29–53 (32 cited).
66 See Filene, *Romancing the Folk*, pp. 34–39.

67 See Deborah Kodish, *Good Friends and Bad Enemies: Robert Winslow Gordon and the Study of American Folksong* (Urbana: University of Illinois Press, 1986), pp. 65–71.

68 Nolan Peterfield, *Last Cavalier: The Life and Times of John A. Lomax, 1867–1948* (Urbana: University of Illinois Press, 1996), p. 114; subsequently cited in text as *LC*. Kittredge's ballad course did not run that year. On Lomax generally, see also Filene, *Romancing the Folk*, ch. 2; Hamilton, *In Search of the Blues*, ch. 4.

69 John A. Lomax, *Adventures of a Ballad Hunter* (New York: Macmillan, 1947), p. 171; subsequently cited in text as *A*.

70 Okeah's 'field expedition' to Atlanta in June 1923 is said to have involved the first use of modern equipment capable of producing wax masters in the field.

71 See, e.g., Michael Taussig, *Mimesis and Alterity: A Particular History of the Senses* (New York: Routledge, 1993).

72 The same story is repeated in Alan Lomax, *Selected Writings, 1934–1997*, ed. Ronald D. Cohen (New York: Routledge, 2003), p. 51; subsequently cited in text as *SW*.

73 Peterfield, *Last Cavalier*, p. 111.

74 Hamilton, *In Search of the Blues*, p. 192; Elijah Wald, *Essaying the Delta: Robert Johnson and the Invention of the Blues* (New York: HarperCollins, 2004), pp. 86–89.

75 William Ferris, *Blues from the Delta* (New York: Da Capo, 1984), p. v.

76 Aristotle, *The Politics*, trans. T. A. Sinclair, rev. Trevor J. Saunders (London: Penguin, 1992), 1341a5, 1341a26, pp. 469–71.

77 Ernst Bloch, 'Magic Rattle and Human Harp', *Literary Essays*, trans. Andrew Joron et al. (Stanford, CA: Stanford University Press, 1998), p. 291.

78 William D. Snow, 'Extract from an Unpublished Poem on Freedom', *Autographs for Freedom*, ed. Julia Griffiths (Auburn: Alden, Beardsley, 1854), p. 261 n13.

79 Alexander S. Weheliye, ' "Feenin": Posthuman Voices in Contemporary Black Popular Music', *Social Text* 20:2 (2002), 21–47 (25–26 cited).

80 These ideas were expounded in Tim Armstrong, *Modernism, Technology and the Body* (Cambridge: Cambridge University Press, 1998), pp. 224–26, and explored in greater depth in Alice Maurice, '"Cinema at Its Source": Synchronizing Race and Sound in the Early Talkies', *Camera Obscura* 17:1 (2002), 31–71.

81 Stephen Best, *The Fugitive's Properties: Law and the Poetics of Possession* (Chicago: University of Chicago Press, 2004), pp. 54–59. Recent studies of Tom include Deirdre O'Connell, *The Ballad of Blind Tom, Slave Pianist* (New York: Overlook Press, 2009), and Geneva Handy Southall, *Blind Tom, the Black Pianist-Composer (1849–1908), Continually Enslaved* (Lanham, MD: Scarecrow Press, 2002).

82 Herriman depicted just one obviously black figure, Musical Moses, before developing the Krazy Kat cartoons for which he was justly famous. Moses

'impussinates' people of other nationalities, including a Scotsman with a bag-pipe. See Patrick McDonnell, *Krazy Kat: The Comic Art of George Herriman* (New York: Abrams, 2004).

83 See, e.g., *John Davis Plays Blind Tom*, Newport Classic 1999, NDP 85660, liner notes.

84 These are the words of John Law, Scotland, 1866, cited in *The Marvelous Musical Prodigy, Blind Tom, the Negro Boy Pianist. Whose performances at the Great St. James and Egyptian Halls, London, and Salle Herz, Paris, have created such a profound sensation. Anecdotes, Songs, Sketches of the Life, Testimonials of Musicians and Savans [sic], and opinions of the American and English Press of 'Blind Tom'* (New York: French & Wheat, n.d. [c. 1880?], apparently used as the London programme pamphlet), p. 12.

85 *The Marvelous Musical Prodigy*, back cover.

86 Willa Cather, *The World and the Parish: Willa Cather's Articles and Reviews, 1893–1902*, ed. William M. Curtin (Lincoln: University of Nebraska Press, 1970), 1: 166.

87 Willa Cather, *My Ántonia*, ed. Charles Mignon et al. (1918; Lincoln: University of Nebraska Press, 1994), pp. 181–82.

88 'Letter from Mark Twain', San Francisco *Alta California*, 1 August 1869; http://www.twainquotes.com/18690801.html.

89 The Author of 'Margret Howth' [Rebecca Harding Davis], 'Blind Tom', *Atlantic Monthly*, 10: 61 (November 1862), 580–85; rpt. in *A Rebecca Harding Davis Reader*, ed. Jean Pfaelzer (Pittsburgh: University of Pittsburgh Press, 1995), pp. 104–11.

90 Cather, *My Ántonia*, pp. 179, 183.

91 *The Marvelous Musical Prodigy*, p. 5.

92 Best, *The Fugitive's Properties*, pp. 37–38, 53, 59.

93 Elaine Scarry, *The Body in Pain: The Making and Unmaking of the World* (New York: Oxford University Press, 1985), p. 62.

94 Ibid., p. 172.

NOTES TO CHAPTER 6

1 For a study including Asian-American perspectives, see Anne Anlin Cheng, *The Melancholy of Race: Psychoanalysis, Assimilation, and Hidden Grief* (New York: Oxford University Press, 2001); J. Brooks Bouson, *Quiet as It's Kept: Shame, Trauma, and Race in the Novels of Toni Morrison* (Albany: State University of New York Press, 2000); Laurie Vickroy, *Trauma and Survival in Contemporary Fiction* (Charlottesville: University of Virginia Press, 2002); Michael Rossington and Anne Whitehead, eds., *Theories of Memory: A Reader* (Edinburgh: Edinburgh University Press, 2007).

2 Toni Morrison, *Beloved* (1987; London: Picador, 1988), pp. 274–75.

3 Herman Melville, *Benito Cereno*, in *Billy Budd, Sailor and Other Stories*, ed. Harold Beaver (London: Penguin, 1985), p. 217; subsequent references in text.

4 On Melville and slavery generally, see Michael Paul Rogin, *Subversive Genealogy: The Politics and Art of Herman Melville* (New York: Knopf, 1983); John Stauffer, 'Melville, Slavery, and the American Dilemma', in *A Companion to Herman Melville*, ed. Wyn Kelly (Oxford: Blackwell, 2006), ch. 14. On *Benito Cereno* in its historical context see Eric Sundquist, *To Wake the Nations: Race in the Making of American Literature* (Cambridge, MA: Belknap Press, 1993), ch. 2; also Gavin Jones, 'Dusky Comments of Silence: Language, Race and Herman Melville's "Benito Cereno"', *Studies in Short Fiction* 32:1 (1995), 39–50.

5 Readings attentive to the dialogue of past and present in any reading of the text's ambiguities include Maurice S. Lee, 'Melville's Subversive Political Philosophy: "Benito Cereno" and the Fate of Speech', *American Literature* 72:3 (2000), 495–519; Dana Luciano, 'Melville's Untimely History: "Benito Cereno" as Counter-Monumental Narrative', *Arizona Quarterly* 60 (2004), 33–60.

6 *Appendix to the Congressional Globe, 31st Congress, 1st Session* (1850), p. 127 (5–6 February 1850).

7 Cited in Don E. Fehrenbacher, *The Slaveholding Republic: An Account of the United States Government's Relations to Slavery* (New York: Oxford University Press, 2001), p. 317.

8 See Mark Seltzer, *Serial Killers: Life and Death in America's Wound Culture* (New York: Routledge, 1998). On trauma, see Cathy Caruth, ed., *Trauma: Experience and Memory* (Baltimore: Johns Hopkins University Press, 1995); Caruth, *Unclaimed Experience: Trauma, Narrative and History* (Baltimore: John Hopkins University Press, 1996); Roger Luckhurst, *The Trauma Question* (London: Routledge, 2008).

9 This homeostatic understanding of systems is developed in the work of Niklas Luhmann; see, e.g., *Social Systems*, trans. John Bednarz (Standford, CA: Stanford University Press, 1995).

10 See, e.g., Lawrence Langer, *Preempting the Holocaust* (New Haven, CT: Yale University Press, 1998); Robert Eaglestone, *The Holocaust and the Postmodern* (Oxford: Oxford University Press, 2005), pp. 31–33.

11 On the history of trauma, see, e.g., Henri Ellenberger, *The Discovery of the Unconscious* (New York: Basic Books, 1970); Eric Michael Kaplan, 'Trains, Brains and Sprains: Railway Spine and the Origins of Psychoneuroses', *Bulletin of the History of Medicine* 69 (1995), 387–419.

12 Anita Rupprecht, '"A Very Uncommon Case": Representations of the *Zong* and the British Campaign to Abolish the Slave Trade', *Journal of Legal History*, special issue on the *Zong* case, 28:3 (2007), 329–46.

13 See Kathleen Collins, 'The Scourged Back', *History of Photography* 9 (January 1985), 43–45.

14 Sigmund Freud, 'A Child Is Being Beaten' [1919], *Penguin Freud Library*, vol. 10: *On Psychopathology*, ed. Angela Richards (London: Penguin, 1993), p. 164. On the erotics of such moments, see Marianne Noble, 'The Ecstasies

of Sentimental Wounding in *Uncle Tom's Cabin*', *Yale Journal of Criticism* 10:2 (1997), 295–320.

15 Ron Eyerman, *Cultural Trauma: Slavery and the Formation of African-American Identity* (Cambridge: Cambridge University Press, 2001), p. 2.

16 See ibid, p. 33, for additional useful comments on these issues.

17 W. E. B. Du Bois, *The Souls of Black Folk*, ed. Henry Louis Gates, Jr., and Terri Hume Oliver (1903; New York: Norton, 1999), pp. 11.

18 Richard Wright, *Native Son*, the restored text, into. Arnold Rampersad (1940; New York: HarperPerennial, 1998), p. 42.

19 Franz Fanon, *The Wretched of the Earth*, trans. Constance Farrington (Harmondsworth: Penguin, 1967), pp. 12, 45, 112.

20 Du Bois, *The Souls of Black Folk*, p. 11; Franz Fanon, *Black Skin, White Masks*, trans. Charles Lam Markmann (New York: Grove Weidenfeld, 1967), pp. 111–12.

21 James Weldon Johnson, *The Autobiography of an Ex-Colored Man*, ed. William L. Andrews (1912; New York: Penguin, 1990), p. 11. Similar moments are included in *Their Eyes Were Watching God* and other texts.

22 Morrison, *Beloved*, pp. 18, 79, 61.

23 Du Bois, *The Souls of Black Folk*, 127.

24 See Peter Nicholls, 'The Belated Postmodern: History, Phantoms and Toni Morrison', in *Psychoanalytic Criticism: A Reader*, ed. Sue Vice (Cambridge: Polity, 1995), pp. 50–74.

25 For a more fine tuned attempt to quantify historical suffering, see John Baugh, 'It Ain't about Race: Some Lingering (Linguistic) Consequences of the African Slave Trade and Their Relevance to Your Personal Historical Hardship Index', *Du Bois Review* 3:1 (2006), 145–69.

26 W. J. T. Mitchell, 'Narrative, Memory and Slavery', in *Cultural Artefacts and the Production of Meaning: The Page, the Image and the Body*, ed. Margaret J. M. Ezell and K. O. O'Keefe (Ann Arbor: University of Michigan Press, 1994), p. 215.

27 Caruth, *Unclaimed Experience*, p. 18.

28 Nicholas Abraham and Maria Torok, *The Shell and the Kernel*, vol. 1, ed. and trans. Nicholas Rand (Chicago: University of Chicago Press, 1994), p. 171.

29 Barnor Hesse, 'Forgotten Like a Bad Dream: Atlantic Slavery and the Ethics of Postcolonial Memory', in *Relocating Postcolonialism*, ed. David Goldberg and Ato Quayson (Oxford: Blackwell, 2002), pp. 143–73 (p. 162 cited).

30 David Hume, *Dialogues Concerning Natural Religion*, 2d ed. (London, 1779), pt. IV, 93. Cf. *A Treatise on Human Nature*: 'There is a general course of nature in human actions, as well as in the operations of the sun and the climate. There are also characters peculiar to different nations and particular persons, as well as common to mankind. The knowledge of these characters is founded on the observation of an uniformity in the actions, that flow from them; and this uniformity forms the very essence of necessity.' Hume, *On Human Nature and the Understanding*, ed. Antony Flew (New York: Collier, 1962), p. 272.

31 See Jan Golinski, *British Weather and the Climate of Enlightenment* (Chicago: Chicago University Press, 2007), pp. 140–50; James Rodger Fleming, *Meteorology in America, 1800–1870* (Baltimore: Johns Hopkins University Press, 1990). Works reflecting the Hippocratic revival include John Arbuthnot's *An Essay Concerning the Effects of Air on Human Bodies* (1733) and William Falconer's *Remarks on the Influence of Climate* (1781); and in the American context, Lionel Chalmers's *An Account of the Weather and Diseases of South Carolina* (1776) and Noah Webster's *A Brief History of Epidemic and Pestilential Diseases with the Principal Phenomena of the Physical Worlds, Which Precede and Accompany Them*, 2 vols. (1799).

32 Arden Reed, *Romantic Weather: The Climates of Coleridge and Baudelaire* (Hanover, NH: University Press of New England, 1983), p. 241.

33 Gilles Deleuze and Félix Guattari, *A Thousand Plateaus: Capitalism and Schizophrenia*, trans. Brian Massumi (London: Athlone Press, 1988), p. 261.

34 Ibid., p. 262. This is, to be sure, only one of the states of the self described in *A Thousand Plateaus*; and Deleuze does explore, in his own earlier work, the notion of the 'phantasm' as an imprinting or inheritance. See David Musslewhite, *Social Transformation in Hardy's Tragic Novels: Megamachines and Phantasms* (Basingstoke: Palgrave Macmillan, 2003), pp. 108–11.

35 Michel Serres, *Genesis*, trans. Geneviève James and James Nielson (Ann Arbor: University of Michigan Press, 1995), pp. 87, 101.

36 *Violets and Other Tales* (1895), rpt. in *The Works of Alice Dunbar-Nelson*, vol. 1, ed. Gloria T. Hull (New York: Oxford University Press, 1988), p. 63.

37 Vladimir Janković, *Reading the Skies: A Cultural History of English Weather, 1650–1820* (Manchester: Manchester University Press, 2000).

38 See the debate started by the *Du Bois Review* 3:1 (2006), special issue on Katrina.

39 Jean-Jacques Rousseau, *Social Contract, Discourse on the Virtue Most Necessary for a Hero, Political Fragments, and Geneva Manuscript*, trans. Judith R. Bush et al. (Hanover, NH: Dartmouth College Press, 1994), p. 181.

40 See Karen Kupperman, 'Fear of Hot Climates in the Anglo-American Colonial Experience', *William and Mary Quarterly* 41 (1984), 213–39; Gary Puckrein, 'Climate, Health and Black Labour in the English Americas', *Journal of American Studies* 13 (1979), 179–93; Natalie J. Ring, 'Inventing the Tropical South: Race, Region, and the Colonial Model', *Mississippi Quarterly* 56 (2003), 619–31; Mart A. Stewart, ' "Let Us Begin with the Weather": Climate, race and Cultural Distinctiveness in the American South', in *Nature and Society in Historical Context*, ed. Miklaus Teich et al. (Cambridge: Cambridge University Press, 1997), 240–56; Edgar T. Thompson, 'The Climactic Theory of the Plantation', *Agricultural History* 15:1 (1941), 49–60.

41 On Montesquieu see David Brion Davis, *The Problem of Slavery in the Age of Revolution, 1770–1823* (New York: Oxford University Press, 1999), 493. On the United States see, e.g., Larry E. Tise, *Proslavery: A History of the Defense of Slavery on America, 1701–1840* (Athens: University of Georgia Press, 1987).

42 Notions of Southern productivity buttressed by the claim that 'given certain special conditions slavery could at least equal, and perhaps even outperform, free labour. Among those conditions by far that most important were those relating to climate'. John Ashworth, *Slavery, Capitalism and Politics in the Antebellum Republic*, vol. 1: *Commerce and Compromise, 1820–1850* (Cambridge: Cambridge University Press, 1995), p. 251 (including Hammond citation).

43 See also Conevery Bolton Valencius, *The Health of the Country: How American Setters Understood Themselves and Their Land* (New York: Basic Books, 2002), ch. 5.

44 Josiah C. Nott, *Two Lectures* (1844), in *The Ideology of Slavery: Proslavery Thought in the Antebellum South*, ed. Drew Gilpin Faust (Baton Rouge: Louisiana State University Press, 1981), p. 221; see also Nott's later 'Thoughts on Acclimation and Adaptation of Races to Climates', *American Journal of Medical Science* 32 (1856), 320–34.

45 Thomas Roderick Dew, 'The Abolition of Negro Slavery' (1932), in *The Ideology of Slavery*, pp. 73–74.

46 Henry Morley and Charles Dickens, 'North American Slavery', *Household Words* 6 (18 September 1852), 1–6 (5 cited); George Frederickson, *The Black Image in the White Mind: The Debate on Afro-American Character and Destiny, 1817–1914* (New York: Harper & Row, 1971), ch. 5.

47 *Groves v. Slaughter* (1841), 15 Peters 508, http://supreme.justia.com/us/40/449/case.html. There were dissenters from their position – e.g., William Harper, who asserted that slavery was a natural state that could be abolished only by 'positive legislation'. 'Memoir on Slavery' (1838), in *The Ideology of Slavery*, p. 96.

48 See, e.g., Sally Hadden, 'Judging Slavery: Thomas Ruffin and *State v. Mann*', in *Local Matters: Race, Crime, and Justice in the Nineteenth-Century South*, ed. Christopher Waldrep and Donald G. Nieman (Athens: University of Georgia Press, 2001), pp. 1–28.

49 This happened even as the rising prevalence of 'hiring out' eroded the plantation-based economy; see Bertram Wyatt-Brown, 'Modernizing Southern Slavery: The Proslavery Argument Reinterpreted,' in *Religion, Race and Reconstruction: Essays in Honor of C. Vann Woodward*, ed. J. Morgan Kousser and James M. McPherson (New York: Oxford University Press, 1982), 27–50.

50 See Christine MacDonald, 'Judging Jurisdictions: Geography and Race in 1830s Slave Law and Literature', *American Literature* 71:4 (1999), 625–55. Theoretical and historical perspectives on the legal issues are provided by Alan Hyde, *Bodies of Law* (Princeton, NJ: Princeton University Press, 1997), and Davis *The Problem of Slavery*, ch. 10.

51 Valencius, *The Health of the Country*, pp. 182–83; on race see ch. 8.

52 *Hippocrates on Airs, Waters and Places* (London: Wyman and Sons, 1881), bk 5, sec. 86 (p. 71); Aristotle, *Politics*, 1327b23–33, pp. 409–10.

53 George W. Williams, *History of the Negro Race in America*, vol. 1 (New York: G. P. Putnam's Sons, 1883), p. 59.

54 The historical *locus classicus* is Ulrich Bonnell Phillips's *Life and Labour in the Old South* (Boston: Little, Brown, 1929), which opens: 'Let us begin by discussing the weather.'

55 The idea of national forecasting was associated, in the nineteenth century, with manifest destiny – e.g., in the doctrine of Janes Pollard Espy, 'The Storm King', that 'rain follows the plough', that burn-off and the resulting thermals near the frontier create climate change. See Andrew Ross, *Strange Weather: Culture, Science and Technology in the Age of Limits* (London: Verso, 1991), pp. 215, 224; Fleming, *Meteorology in America*. One correlative was the tradition which Lawrence Buell labels 'literary bioregionalism', including Susan Fenimore Cooper's *Rural Hours* (1850), Celia Thaxter's *Among the Isles of Shoals* (1873), and Sarah Orme Jewett's *The Country of the Pointed Firs*. Lawrence Buell, *The Environmental Imagination* (Cambridge, MA: Belknap Press, 1995), pp. 405–406; also Robert L. Dorman, *Revolt of the Provinces: The Regionalist Movement in America, 1920–1945* (Chapel Hill: University of North Carolina Press, 1993).

56 On the origins of this image, see David W. Hughes, 'The World's Most Famous Meteor Shower Picture', *Earth, Moon, and Planets* 68:1–3 (1995), 311–22.

57 See Jerry A Herndon, 'Faulkner: Meteor, Earthquake, and Sword', in *Faulkner: The Unappeased Imagination*, ed. Glenn O. Carey (Troy, NY: Whiston, 1980), pp. 175–93 (esp. 186–87).

58 Carl Carmer, *Stars Fell on Alabama* (1934; rpt. University: University of Alabama Press, 1985), p. xx.

59 Clarence Cason, *90° in the Shade*, intro. Wayne Flint (1935; University: University of Alabama Press, 1983), p. 8.

60 Ibid., p. 110.

61 William O. Blake, ed., *The History of Slavery and the Slave Trade, Ancient and Modern* (Columbus, OH: H. Miller, 1861), p. 599.

62 *The Autobiography of the Rev. Josiah Henson ('Uncle Tom') from 1789 to 1883*, preface Mrs. Harriet Beecher Stowe, ed. John Lobb (London: Christian Age, 1890), p. 109.

63 George Bataille, *The Accursed Share: An Essay on General Economy*, vol. 1, trans Robert Hurley (New York: Zone, 1991), pp. 56–57.

64 *Narrative of William Hayden, Containing a Faithful Account of His Travels for a Number of Years, Whilst a Slave, in the South. Written by Himself* (Cincinnati, OH, 1846), p. 143; *Zodiac* 1:2 (1835), 32. The poem, 'India – A Poem', begins in the previous issue of this Albany journal and is attributed to the Rev. Grey, 'who died a short time since in India'.

65 Harriet Beecher Stowe, *Dred: A Tale of the Great Dismal Swamp* (1856; New York: Penguin, 2000), p. 446; subsequent references in text.

66 On abolition and cure, see Stephen M. Best, *The Fugitive's Properties: Law and the Poetics of Possession* (Chicago: University of Chicago Press, 2004), p. 2. In *Dred* the Christianity of the slaves is also described in terms of racial and

climatological categories when the narrator comments that 'when this orien-
tal seed, an exotic among us [Anglo-Saxons], is planted back in the fiery soil
of a tropical heart, it bursts forth with an incalculable ardor of growth' (211).

67 Joan R. Sherman, ed., *African-American Poetry of the Nineteenth Century: An
Anthology* (Urbana: University of Illinois Press, 1992), p. 155.

68 See Joseph D. Ketner, *The Emergence of the African-American Artist: Robert S.
Duncanson, 1821–1872* (Columbia: University of Mississippi Press, 1993), pp.
90–93.

69 William Wells Brown, *The Black Man, His Antecedents, His Genius, and His
Achievements* (New York: Thomas Hamilton, 1863), p. 73.

70 Adah Menken's 'My Heritage' plays melodramatically on the same trope, for
example:

> But turning the fevered cheek to meet the soft kiss of the winds, my eyes look
>   to the sky, where I send up my soul in thanks. The sky is clouded – no
>   stars – no music – the heavens are hushed.
> My poor soul comes back to me, weary and disappointed.
> The very breath of heaven, that comes to all, comes not to me.
> Bound in iron gyves of unremitting toil, my vital air is wretchedness.

Menken's ostensible focus is 'life', and she routinely obscured her New
Orleans Creole origins, but the word 'heritage' is an open sign (hinted at also
in 'gyves', shackles). Hope is a 'pale, / Blue mist', 'A little child talking to the
gay clouds'; the escape from heritage, being a 'slave of time', is an escape into
a realm of free action, unanchored to the earth. Adah Isaacs Menken, *Infelicia*
(Philadelphia: J. B. Lippincott, 1868), pp. 17–19.

71 W. E. B. Du Bois, *Darkwater: Voices from within the Veil* (1920; Mineola, NY:
Dover, 1999), pp. 18, 29.

72 Charles W. Chesnutt, *The Conjure Woman and Other Conjure Tales*, ed.
Richard H. Brodhead (Durham, NC: Duke University Press, 1993), p. 31;
subsequent references in text.

73 See Thomas D. Morris, *Southern Slavery and the Law, 1619–1860* (Chapel Hill:
University of North Carolina Press, 1996), ch. 3.

74 James O. Fuqua, ed., *The Civil Code of the State of Louisiana* (New Orleans:
Bloomfield, 1867), art. 642, p. 95.

75 A cynical reply to Chesnutt's gently provocative tale is provided by Jorge
Luis Borges's 'The Dread Redeemer Lazarus Morell', in *A Universal History
of Infamy*, trans. Norman Thomas di Giovanni (Harmondsworth: Penguin,
1975), pp. 19–30. The story, based on an account provided by Mark Twain,
describes the semi-legendary John Murrell, a bandit who allegedly encouraged slaves to escape and be resold repeatedly in order to create a capital base
for their escape; they would (so the story goes) eventually be killed to prevent
their exposing the scheme.

76 Charles Duncan, *The Absent Man: The Narrative Craft of Charles W. Chesnutt*
(Athens: Ohio University Press, 1998), p. 109. See also Ben Slote, 'Listening
to "The Goophered Grapevine" and Hearing Raisins Sing', *American Literary
History*, 6:4 (1994), 684–94.

77 Sundquist, *To Wake the Nations*, ch. 4.

78 Eugene D. Genovese, *Roll, Jordan, Roll: The World the Slaves Made* (1973; New York: Vintage, 1976), p. 217.

79 The reference to brick might bring to mind a well-known object in the African-American creative tradition: the brick which Ignatz Mouse hurls again and again and again at Krazy Kat in George Herriman's cartoon strips between 1913 and 1944 and which Krazy perversely interprets as a love token: a marker of one person's pleasurable object being another's expression of anger and pain. 'George Herriman, Afro-American' is one of those to whom Ishmael Reed's comic novel *Mumbo Jumbo* (1972) is dedicated, though accounts of Herriman often play down his New Orleans Creole origins and eschew investigation of the African-American origins of his trickster figure.

80 As Eugene Terry comments, '[T]he sufferings of his people become the script with which he [Julius] makes his meagre purchases of honey and suits and grapes'. 'The Shadow of Slavery in *Charles Chesnutt's* The Conjure Woman', *Ethnic Groups*, 4 (1982), 115.

81 Mark Twain, *The American Claimant*, intro. Bobbie Anne Mason, afterword Peter Messent (New York: Oxford University Press, 1996), p. ix; subsequent references in text.

82 Malcolm Bull, *Seeing Things Hidden: Apocalypse, Vision and Totality* (London: Verso, 1999), ch. 6.

83 William Douglas O'Connor, 'The Brazen Android', *Atlantic Monthly* 67: 402–404 (1881), 402–403, 433–54, 577–600.

84 Du Bois, *The Souls of Black Folk*, pp. 163–64.

85 William Stanley Braithwaite, 'Twilight: An Impression', *The Crisis Reader*, ed. Sondra Kathryn Wilson (New York: Modern Library, 1999), pp. 221–23 (p. 222 cited). Originally in *Crisis*, April 1912.

86 Rachel Blau DuPlessis, *Genders, Races and Religious Cultures in Modern American Poetry, 1908–1934* (Cambridge: Cambridge University Press, 2001), ch. 5.

87 Sterling A. Brown, *The Collected Poems of Sterling A. Brown*, ed. Michael D. Harper (Evanston, IL: Northwestern University Press, 1980), pp. 62–63.

88 Ibid., 97, 61.

89 Sterling Brown, 'After the Storm', *Crisis*, April 1927 (one of a number of uncollected early poems).

90 Richard Wright, *Black Boy* (London: Vintage, 2000), 262.

91 See, e.g., George Hutchinson, 'Jean Toomer and American Racial Discourse', *Texas Studies in Literature and Language* 35:2 (1993), 226–50.

92 See Werner Sollers, 'Ethnic Modernism', in *The Cambridge History of American Literature: Prose Writing, 1910–1950*, ed. Sacvan Bercovitch (Cambridge: Cambridge University Press, 2002), p. 449.

93 Toomer to Stieglitz, 10 January 1924, in *The Letters of Jean Toomer, 1919–1924*, ed. Mark Whalan (Knoxville: University of Tennessee Press, 2006), p. 189.

94 Jean Toomer, *The Collected Poems of Jean Toomer*, ed. Robert B. Jones and Margery Toomer Latimer (Chapel Hill: University of North Carolina Press, 1998), p. 95.

244   *Notes to Pages 201–203*

95 Jean Toomer, *A Jean Toomer Reader: Selected Unpublished Writings*, ed. Frederik L. Rusch (New York: Oxford University Press, 1993), p. 255.
96 See Sjoerd van Tuinen, 'Critique Beyond Resentment: An Introduction to Peter Sloterdijk's Jovial Modernity', *Cultural Politics*, special issue on Peter Sloterdijk, 3:3 (2007), 275–306, esp. 294–98; and Sloterdijk's own 'What Happened to the Twentieth Century?' ibid., 327–56 (329 cited). The debt to Bataille's notion of 'restricted' and 'general' economy is clear.
97 Fanon, *Black Skin, White Masks*, p. 231.

Index